T0305064

International Marketing and the Country of Origin Effect

International Marketing and the Country of Origin Effect

The Global Impact of 'Made in Italy'

Edited by

Giuseppe Bertoli

Full Professor of Marketing at University of Brescia, Italy

Riccardo Resciniti

Full Professor of International Marketing at University of Sannio, Italy

Edward Elgar

Cheltenham, UK • Northampton, MA, USA

Published by
Edward Elgar Publishing Limited
The Lypiatts
15 Lansdown Road
Cheltenham
Glos GL50 2JA
UK

Edward Elgar Publishing, Inc.
William Pratt House
9 Dewey Court
Northampton
Massachusetts 01060
USA

A catalogue record for this book
is available from the British Library

Library of Congress Control Number: 2012947120

ISBN 978 1 78195 560 4

Typeset by Servis Filmsetting Ltd, Stockport, Cheshire
Printed and bound by MPG Books Group, UK

Contents

Contributors

Bernardo Balboni, University of Modena and Reggio Emilia (Italy)

Loretta Battaglia, Catholic University of Milan (Italy)

Guido Bortoluzzi, University of Trieste (Italy)

Tiziano Bursi, University of Modena and Reggio Emilia (Italy)

Elena Cedrola, University of Macerata (Italy)

Alessandra De Chiara, University 'L'Orientale', Napoli (Italy)

Patrizia de Luca, University of Trieste (Italy)

Alessandro De Nisco, University of Sannio (Italy)

Barbara Francioni, University of Urbino (Italy)

Silvia Grappi, University of Modena and Reggio Emilia (Italy)

Giada Mainolfi, University of Salerno (Italy)

Vittoria Marino, University of Salerno (Italy)

Elisa Martinelli, University of Modena and Reggio Emilia (Italy)

Michela Matarazzo, University Guglielmo Marconi in Rome (Italy)

Fabio Musso, University of Urbino (Italy)

Maria Rosaria Napolitano, University of Sannio (Italy)

Alessandro Pagano, University of Urbino (Italy)

Tommaso Pucci, University of Siena (Italy)

Christian Simoni, University of Florence (Italy)

Donata Vianelli, University of Trieste (Italy)

Marina Vignola, University of Modena and Reggio Emilia (Italy)

Lorenzo Zanni, University of Siena (Italy)

Foreword: 'Italy' and 'made-in research': a marriage made in heaven?

> 'You've got pretty good taste', she said.
> 'I like Italian suits,' he replied.
> 'I've had a couple of British suits, and they were okay,
> but they felt . . . constructed. Like I was wearing a building.
> But the Italians – they know how to make a suit.'
> (Sandford 1999, p. 222)

We can leave it to the character in Sandford's novel to explain how a British suit can feel like 'wearing a building' – but much of the world is certainly aware that the Italians 'know how to make a suit', and that is why gentlemen like Armani, Brioni, Zegna, Canali, and many others have become symbols of Italian excellence in design and fine workmanship. The brief passage above, and countless others like it in literature, movies, music, advertising, or virtually any other human expression one may think of, is just one indication of how deeply embedded in our culture is the notion that some peoples can do some things better than others can. This 'ability differential' is, of course, the marketing manifestation of what our economist friends know of as Ricardo's comparative advantage – the underlying theory that explains trade and many other kinds of human activity.

Ricardo, of course, did not invent comparative advantage. In putting forth his theory he was articulating a concept that has been with us since time immemorial – the notion of 'place', including the people associated with it and the kinds of things they produce or invent, which has always been central to human life. 'All the best things come from Syracuse!', exclaims a merchant in a novel about ancient Rome (Saylor 2007, p. 185); in more contemporary times, 'all the best things are made in Japan!' according to a character in the movie *Back to the Future*; and, in a more realistic spirit that acknowledges that a place cannot be 'best' at everything (and so, unwittingly, echoes Ricardo), Steve Tyrell sings, in his song *New York is Where I Live*: 'L.A. where I see the stars / Germany where I buy my cars . . . Italy where I buy my shoes / New Orleans where I sing the blues . . . Alaska where I skate on ice / Vegas where I roll the dice . . .'.

In this context, there are three main reasons that make this book so important and unique. First, it deals with an issue that is itself important; the idea of 'place' is ubiquitous in our culture, and the book deals with the nature and role of the images of places as product origins. Second, by virtue of its focus and contributing authors the book is firmly embedded in the Italian experience – and what could be better as a base for discussing made-in than a country which is famous for making some of the finest things in life, from fashion to wines and from cheese to cars? And third, it features the work of outstanding scholars who are known to do good research that leads to insightful and useful conclusions.

To briefly speak, first, about 'place', one must note that, considering its centrality, it is not surprising that it has been studied in many disciplines ranging from geography to environmental psychology and from anthropology to international marketing. The traditional and narrow view of place as simply a 'location' has given way in our times to considering it as a socially constructed experience. Kearney and Bradley (2009, p. 79) rightly stress that 'place . . . cannot be separated from people'. That is to say, a place is not just a spot on a map – it is a complex construct that, among many other characteristics, can evoke strong 'us versus them' feelings ranging from attachment to what we call 'home' to admiration, animosity, or indifference toward the places of others.

Attachment to 'home' is as strong an emotion as can be, and the mere thought of it brings forth a flood of images: 'Africa . . . wisdom, understanding, good things to eat . . . the smell of sweet cattle breath . . . the white sky across the endless, endless bush . . .; O Botswana, my country, my place' (McCall Smith 2002, p. 234). Horace was among the first to encapsulate such emotions eloquently into the notion of patriotism, in his 'Dulce et decorum est pro patria mori' ('It is sweet and fitting to die for your country'; Odes III.2.13), and he has been followed by many. 'I love my country because it is mine,' the 14th century Armenian poet Stephan Orbelian wrote, for example, summarizing in a simple phrase the powerful notion of 'home' (Gelven 1994, p. 163). Needless to say, such strong feelings find their way to the marketplace – in, among others, the construct of consumer ethnocentrism, which is studied in this book.

While most people love 'home', views about other places and what they stand for often diverge. For example, many admire German engineering, French fashion, or Japanese electronics, while others can be quite vitriolic in discussing various places. A character in one novel notes that 'Vienna was not a big city and never has been: it is a little provincial town where narrow-minded peasants go to the opera, instead of the pig market, to exchange spiteful gossip' (Deighton 1989, p. 92). In another example, a comparison between Sweden and Tuscany does not speak well of the former and pays a compliment to the latter: 'The Swedish are a humourless, sterile race . . . For them, there are no lazy hours in the bar, no strolling down the street with an easy gait and a Mediterranean nonchalance' (Booth 2004, p. 205). Do such views matter? Of course they do – they contextualize human experience, give it depth, and help to explain why some things are the way they are. Why, in a nutshell, Brioni makes good suits. Let us borrow one last reference from popular culture to emphasize this point, because it is important – this one from the movie *The Third Man*, with words spoken by Orson Welles: 'In Italy, for thirty years under the Borgias, they had warfare, terror, murder, and bloodshed, but they produced Michaelangelo, Leonardo da Vinci and the Renaissance. In Switzerland, they had brotherly love, they had five hundred years of democracy and peace – and what did they produce? The cuckoo clock.'

So, 'place' is everywhere. The term can be used in reference to anything from a glade in the forest to a room, a building, a neighbourhood or a city, a country, a region within a country or one that encompasses many countries (e.g., the EU), or the world at large. As a result, we experience place in a multitude of ways, from living in it to buying products from it, hearing about it on the news, reading about it in a novel, going to it for a holiday, and so on. Cognitive psychology tells us that the information we collect over time about a place is stored in the brain in the form of mental schemata. These are complex networks of associations that include generalizations, objects, events, or feelings, which are hierarchically structured and linked in ways that help us understand our environment.

Mental schemata can be activated by either intrinsic or extrinsic information, such as, respectively, a detailed examination of a car's engine versus the same car's brand name. Since 'objective' technical information is often hard to get, time consuming, and many times beyond the average consumer's level of understanding, and since our lives are rather busy these days and many of us suffer to one degree or other from cognitive overload, we often rely on extrinsic cues (in this example, the brand name) that conveniently 'bundle' many technical characteristics into one easy-to-get piece of external information ('I know a Ferrari is better than a Mazda Miata, I don't need to research it'). It is these types of extrinsic cues, which activate strong mental associative networks that we often call 'stereotypes' (much like those in the popular culture examples cited above) that guide much of our marketplace behaviour. And country of origin, or a place's made-in image, is one of the most powerful extrinsic cues in existence.

The relative importance of the images of places in international marketing is reflected in the attention paid to the subject in both research and practice. On the academic side, a number of scholars have called country of origin 'the most researched' field in international marketing – and a comprehensive database I maintain shows that research in this area is indeed voluminous: as of the end of 2011 the database includes more than 1600 works, of which well over 800 are refereed journal articles (the remainder are books, book chapters and conference papers). This database includes works on nation branding but not those on TDI, or tourism destination image, which comprise at least another 200 journal articles. With regards to practice, in a recent study we used the 'content analysis' technique to identify and catalogue in detail the place cues appearing in over 6000 business and consumer magazine advertisements from five countries – and what we found exceeded even our highest predictions. In summary, more than 80 per cent of all the ads contained at least one place cue; the average number of place cues per ad was about 6.5; and place-based approaches were the seventh most-used out of 27 types of advertising executions found in these ads, outscoring such common approaches as testimonials and problem-solution ads. The evidence, in other words, shows that both academics and marketing managers agree on the importance of place in buyer behaviour.

Turning to the second main strength of this book, the fact that it carries an Italian pedigree, one does not need to say much – the importance of made-in to Italy, and of Italy to made-in, is self-evident and reasonably well understood both in Italy itself and elsewhere. Three examples can help to make the point. The first concerns the Chinese workers who started coming to Prato province some 20 years ago and have since set up over 3000 companies specializing in low-end fashions (Donadio 2010), or *pronto moda*, as they prefer to call it. Concerns in the region were not just limited to immigration, or the potential cultural effects of some 10 000 expatriates plonked in the middle of Tuscany – they also extended to a thorny issue that lies at the heart of made-in: to what extent might 'cheap fashions made in Italy by Chinese companies and workers' undermine the prestige of 'Made in Italy' in traditional high-end markets?

The second example refers to two cases (Owen 2008) that help to portray not only some contemporary Italian problems related to made-in but also the broader complexity of the issue. One arose when Paris Hilton promoted a drink called Rich Prosecco, which comes in a can and includes wine with fruit juice. Italian concern in this case was not just over the copyright of the name 'prosecco'; it also expressed the fear that, as a local representative of Italian prosecco producers in Treviso emphasized, Ms Hilton is helping to shape consumer opinion in the wrong direction that prosecco is 'an alcoholic fruit drink'. The other case arose from the 2007 European Court of Justice decision which assigned the term 'Tocai' exclusively to the 'Tokaji' wine-producing region in Hungary. Producers of 'Tocai Friulano' in Italy's Friuli region saw this development as more than just the loss of a name which they had been using for centuries; reminiscent of the statements above about 'home', by Horace on *patria*, McCall Smith on Botswana, and Stephan Orbelian the poet on Armenia, a local wine-maker stressed that Italy must defend its wines 'as part of its identity and tradition'. Indeed. These two cases buttress the statement made above, that mental schemata are complex representations of the world around us: in the world of marketing what others do in relation to our product may greatly affect its standing in the marketplace – and 'product'-related issues may go much beyond product-only considerations and end up involving the entire identity of a people.

To put it differently, 'where a product is made' is much more than 'where a product is made' – it involves everything from how images about foreign products are created in consumers' minds to how brands and products are intertwined with everything from manufacturing to social identity. Perhaps nowhere can this be seen more clearly than in two international kerfuffles some ten years ago, concerning the meaning of 'Italian food'. In 2002, Italy's then-minister of agriculture Giovanni Alemanno announced plans about a 'seal of approval' for Italian restaurants worldwide if (and only if) they were prepared to submit to certification verifying their use of authentic Italian ingredients. This was followed in 2004 by a similar plan about what is a 'real' pizza. The ideas were benign and reflected both pride and pragmatism: if a restaurant in, say, Toronto, New York or Melbourne flies the Italian flag and claims to serve 'Italian' food, it had better use true Italian ingredients. But . . .

But, perhaps predictably, the world media greeted the announcements with hoots of laughter, as indicated by this sampling of newspaper head-lines: 'Spaghetti justice' (*Ottawa Citizen*); 'Italian taste police coming to a restaurant near you' (*The Guardian*); 'Italy's pizza police will leave no tomato unturned' (*Chicago Sun-Times*); 'Italians take aim at world's pasta pirates' (*Toronto Star/Reuters*). But behind all this merriment were some very real issues. For example, a country's name is its brand, and its flag is its logo – and if, as it is often said, the brand name and logo of a Coca-Cola or a McDonald's is worth billions, how many trillions are Italy's name and flag worth in the food business? And given this, why should Italy not protect its market assets the same way that Coke and McDonald's protect theirs? On the other hand, such thinking can lead to a potentially slippery slope; as those following the EU's 'protected origin' legislation, which so far includes several hundred placenames, know well, the issue isn't just one country or place. As an article under one of the headlines cited above asked, 'what's next'? If China takes an interest in how 'Peking duck' is cooked in a Parisian restaurant, Greece in how 'Greek yoghourt' is made in the US, and so on, then many places and foods – indeed, the entire food sector as well as many other sectors – are in for a long battle over what 'made in' really means and who has the right to fly which flag under what circumstances.

As can be seen, the issues surrounding the made-in construct, both generally and specifically in the case of Italy, are many and complex – which leads to the last, but certainly not least, strength of this book: the substance and quality of the book itself, and its ability to deal effectively with very complex subject matter. This is not just a random anthology of articles that simply happen to be related by virtue of a shared theme (made-in) and provenance (Italy). Having read all the chapters, I believe, instead, that this volume reflects a well-coordinated effort with a much tighter focus than one finds in collections of this kind. Part of this focus is due to the steady hand of the two co-editors, Dr Giuseppe Bertoli and Dr Riccardo Resciniti, who are well-qualified to lead this type of work. Both are very well published: Professor Bertoli mainly on globalization and a range of branding issues, from co-branding and brand value to made-in effects; and Professor Resciniti on fields ranging from logistics to small and medium-sized enterprises, competitiveness, and various topics in international marketing.

Another reason for the book's successful approach to its theme is, of course, the individual chapter contributions, which come from authors who know the area well and have carefully chosen which issues to address. The chapters refer to a wide range of issues, including made-in effects in relation to ethnocentrism and to corporate social responsibility in small and medium-sized enterprises, the interactions and synergistic effects between product-related made-in images and the images of places as tourism destinations, distribution channel issues, made-in topics in relation to emerging markets and, of course, a review of the relevant literature on country of origin effects. The approach of the chapters that comprise this volume is academically rigorous and at the same time managerially relevant, which is why I believe the book helps to push the made-in research agenda forward at the same time as it provides practitioners with new ideas they can apply to their brands. I should note that notwithstanding the Italian emphasis, the chapters individually and the book as a whole cover a lot of territory within the made-in domain, and so they have much to offer to the broader audience of researchers and practitioners in other countries.

To conclude, then, what more can one ask for than a book that offers a high-quality discussion on an important issue, from the perspective of researchers who understand its focal theme, 'Made in Italy', better than anybody else? In short, through their solid scholarship these chapters give us answers to many questions and tools for practical applications, but also more of what we can never have enough of: new questions and much food for thought.

Dr Nicolas Papadopoulos
Chancellor's Professor
Eric Sprott School of Business
Carleton University
Ottawa, Canada

REFERENCES

Booth, Martin (2004), *The American*, New York, NY: St. Martin's Press.

Deighton, Len (1989), *Spy Line*, Grafton Books.

Donadio, Rachel (2010), 'Chinese Remake the "Made in Italy" Fashion Label', *The New York Times*, September 13, A1.

Gelven, Michael (1994), *War and Existence: A Philosophical Inquiry*, University Park, PA: Penn State Press.

Kearney, A. and J.J. Bradley (2009), '"Too strong to ever not be there": place names and emotional geographies', *Social & Cultural Geography*, 10(1), 77–94.

McCall Smith, Alexander (2002), *The No. 1 Ladies' Detective Agency*, Toronto, ON: Random House Canada, p. 234.

Owen, Richard (2008), 'Winemakers in northern Italy insulted by celeb's promotion of canned wine drink', *The London Times*, January 5.

Sandford, John (1999), *Secret Prey*, Berkley Books.

Saylor, Steven (2007), *Roma*, St. Martin's Griffin.

Introduction

Giuseppe Bertoli and Riccardo Resciniti

---

1. THE NEED FOR INTERNATIONALIZATION

We can almost say that there are no companies that are not carrying out or planning a strategy of international growth, and those few are nevertheless obliged to suffer foreign competition in their home markets.

The main reasons for the growing importance of internationalization are well known: economic globalization; the saturation of western markets; the rise of the new economic powers (first China and India, but also Brazil, Russia, the Arab countries, and South Africa); the progress of technologies in transportations and communications; and the increasing international articulation of value chains.

The extent of this phenomenon has not been demonstrated in statistical data, because it is not only related to import/export and foreign direct investment flows, but also to all the corporate capabilities (from operations to marketing, from finance to research and development (R&D), from human resources (HR) to logistics and supply chain management). Moreover, the qualitative aspect of the phenomenon – the strategic relevance of foreign operations, the organizational articulation of foreign activities, the quality of knowledge acquired abroad, the importance of international relationships (even the ones not formalized by agreements) – evades statistics. Generally, statistics cannot capture the change of perspective in business choices, because of the priority gained by the international scenario.

The macroeconomic approach – mainly based on quantitative models and data – is limited in understanding the real logics of internationalization and the development paths of businesses. As a consequence, it is also of little effectiveness in proposing proper lines of action to businesses and policy makers. One rather needs firm-oriented approaches, able to identify and analyse the business strategies with their own decision and managerial problems on the one hand, and their impact on customers' perceptions and behaviors in the various markets on the other. Within this scope, marketing takes on great importance in analysing the demand, selecting the markets to enter, defining the entry strategies and modes, and choosing the market position and the product offer.

This reasoning applies in general, but gains particular importance in the case of Italian companies working in the typical 'Made in Italy' industries. Although they are suffering from the world crisis, they still boast a competitive advantage based on a consolidated image of the quality and creativity of their products, particularly in the fashion, specialized mechanics, and furniture industries, with a strong design content, and the food and wine industries.

Italy has felt the effects of this crisis more than other countries (Draghi, 2011, p. 5), because the economic downturn has been violent[1] and the recovery is turning out to be uncertain and very slow, which is the reason economists now talk of recession. Businesses need strategic models that take the new competitive world scenario into account, because they have to 'think international'. That means they do not have to limit their perspective of action to their home markets, but rather look towards other nations – particularly towards countries with high growth in terms of GDP, savings, and consumption – not only for commercial and productive purposes, but also to discover, evaluate, and explore any entrepreneurial opportunities, if applicable (Eckhardt and Shane, 2003).

2. EMERGING MARKETS

Since the 'big contraction', the recovery has slowly begun. Global growth is over 4 percent, even though it differs greatly from one country to another, and from one industry to another. Indeed, the emerging economies are growing even more than the industrialized ones; in this way sustaining a great part of the world recovery, including through the growth of internal demand. The different trends are evident from the data related to GDP (gross domestic product), international trade, and FDI (foreign direct investment).[2]

UNCTAD data (*Handbook of Statistics*, 2011) concerning GDP points out that, in the period 2007–2010, a new order of international economy has emerged, characterized by wide fluctuations in economic activity and by the fact that the emerging countries, unlike the advanced ones, seem to have better absorbed the crisis. Considering the values of GDP in the 2005–2010 period, the world economy on the whole has grown 27.48 percent (+22.83 per capita), the developed economies have registered +14.36 percent (+11.84 percent per capita), the developing economies +62.21 percent (+55.7 percent per capita), and the transition economies +49.65 percent (+49.05 percent per capita).

With reference to the last two years (Table 0.1), between 2010 and 2011 the European Union countries (EU) and the United States still represent,

Table 0.1 *World economies in terms of GDP*

	Gross Domestic Product (var. %)				Gross Domestic Product (weight % on total)				Bank balance (in GDP %)			
	2008	2009	2010	2011	2008	2009	2010	2011	2008	2009	2010	2011
EUROPEAN UNION	0.7	-4.1	1.8	1.8	21.8	21.1	20.5	20.0	-0.9	-0.2	-0.1	-0.2
Euro area	0.4	-4.1	1.7	1.6	15.5	15.0	14.6	13.8	-0.6	-0.2	0.1	0.0
Central and Eastern Europe	3.2	-3.6	4.2	3.7	3.6	3.5	3.4	3.4	-7.9	-2.8	-4.3	-5.4
Russia	5.2	-7.8	4.0	4.8	3.3	3.0	3.0	3.0	6.2	4.1	4.9	5.6
Middle East and North Africa	5.1	1.8	3.8	4.1	4.9	5.0	5.0	5.0	14.9	2.4	6.5	12.9
Sub-Saharan Africa:	5.6	2.8	5.0	5.5	2.3	2.4	2.4	2.5	0.9	-2.4	-2.4	0.4
South Africa	3.6	-1.7	2.8	3.5	0.7	0.7	0.7	0.7	-7.1	-4.1	-2.8	-4.4
ASIA												
Japan	-1.2	-6.3	3.9	1.4	6.2	5.9	5.8	5.7	3.2	2.8	3.6	2.3
Asian Countries:	7.7	7.2	9.5	8.4	21.4	23.0	24.0	25.0	5.9	4.1	3.3	3.3
China	9.6	9.2	10.3	9.6	11.7	12.9	13.6	14.3	9.6	6.0	5.2	5.7
India	6.2	6.8	10.4	8.2	4.8	5.2	5.4	5.6	-2.0	-2.8	-3.2	-3.7
USA	0.0	-2.6	2.8	2.8	20.5	20.1	19.7	19.4	-4.7	-2.7	-3.2	-3.2
Southern Central America:	4.3	-1.7	6.1	4.7	8.6	8.5	8.6	8.6	-0.7	-0.6	-1.2	-1.4
Brazil	5.2	-0.6	7.5	4.5	2.9	2.9	2.9	2.9	-1.7	-1.5	-2.3	-2.6
WORLD	2.9	-0.5	5.0	4.4	100	100	100	100	–	–	–	–

Source: ICE processing on FMI data – World Economic Outlook, April 2011

Table 0.2   Trade flow distribution for geographical macro-areas (weight percent on current price values)

Geographical areas	Exports			Imports		
	2008	2009	2010	2008	2009	2010
European Union	36.7	36.7	33.8	38.1	37.3	34.7
Euro area	26.9	26.9	24.6	25.5	25.3	23.5
Non-EU European countries	7.0	6.3	6.3	6.0	5.5	5.5
Africa	3.5	3.1	3.3	2.9	3.2	3.0
North America	12.6	12.8	12.9	17.6	17.1	17.4
Southern Central America	3.7	3.7	3.8	3.6	3.5	3.7
Middle East	6.4	5.6	6.0	3.6	4.0	3.7
Central Asia	2.1	2.1	2.3	2.8	3.0	3.0
Eastern Asia	26.4	27.9	29.9	23.7	24.7	27.1
Oceania and other territories	1.6	1.7	1.9	1.6	1.7	1.7
World	100	100	100	100	100	100

Source: ICE processing on OMC data

respectively, rates ranging from 20 percent and 19.5 percent of the world's GDP, but they register very narrow growth rates (between 1.8 percent and 2.8 percent). Other areas present a different trend in their GDP: in 2011 China had 14.3 percent of the world's GDP, with +9.6 percent from 2010 to 2011, while India, which in 2011 represented 5.4 percent of the world's GDP, registered a 10.4 percent growth between 2010 and 2011. Another interesting area in terms of GDP trend is South Central America, whose GDP represents 8.6 percent on a world basis, and its growth during 2010–2011 is 4.7 percent.

An analysis of the import/export flows (Table 0.2) also shows that the most advanced economy areas keep on catalyzing the most significant traffic volumes. In 2010 the European Union and North America economies together still hold an all-time record, with an overall rate of 46.7 percent of exports, and 52.1 percent of imports; whereas within the country scope, China is first in exports and second in imports compared to the United States, although with greater growth rates (from 2009 to 2010, +31.3 percent versus +21 percent in exports; +38.7 percent versus +22.6 percent in imports).

However, if one considers the average growth rates per single geographic area of import/export flows, the real growth trends of some

Table 0.3   Average growth rates of exports and imports per geographical macro-areas

	1980	1990	2000	2005	2007	2008	2009	2010
Average growth rates of exports								
World	7.1	6.8	10.9	14.2	15.4	15.2	−22.4	21.3
Developing economies	7.7	9.1	14.3	22.2	16.2	19.3	−20.9	27.4
Transition economies	1.4	6.7	18.3	28.6	20.8	34.3	−35.2	29.0
Developed economies	7.2	5.9	8.5	9.2	14.5	11.3	−22.4	16.5
Average growth rates of imports								
World	7.0	6.7	10.6	13.8	15.2	15.5	−23.0	21.2
Developing economies	8.1	8.7	14.1	17.7	18.4	21.6	−18.8	28.5
Transition economies	0.9	3.7	19.4	21.7	34.6	30.5	−32.9	19.8
Developed economies	6.9	6.2	8.5	11.7	12.8	11.6	−24.9	19.7

Source: UNCTAD, *Handbook of Statistics*, 2011

world areas with respect to the ones with a more advanced capitalism emerge (Table 0.3). The world as a whole is growing 14.2 percent with the developed economies growing 9.3 percent, the developing economies 19.7 percent and the transition economies 27.6 percent.

As for the outgoing FDI flows, it emerges that, with the exception of the two decades 1980–1990 and 1990–2000, the most developed economies are substantially keeping stable. The developing and transition economies, on the other hand, register macroscopic increments in all the reference decades, although the more exiguous starting bases are not to be over-looked.[3] This applies even more to the incoming FDI flows, where the presence of strong elements of attractiveness of the less developed areas is much more evident[4] (Table 0.4).

The emerging countries therefore offer important opportunities for development and, in some cases, unconventional performances for the Western businesses that have advanced and already saturated markets (Kos, 2010). Many businesses, in view of the slowdown of their domestic demand, are looking closely at these new markets for the richness of their natural resources, their strong economic development, the rise of their

Table 0.4   *Outgoing and Ingoing FDI flows from 1980 to 2010 per macro-areas (values in US $ mln)*

IDE: Outgoing flows
(US $ mln)

	1980	1990	Δ% (1980– 1990)	2000	Δ% (1990– 2000)	2005	Δ% (2000– 2005)
World	51,590	241,498	368.1	1,232,117	410.2	1,405,389	14.1
Developing economies	3,192	11,914	273.2	134,194	1,026.4	226,683	68.9
Transition economies	–	–	–	3,195	–	23,723	642.5
Developed economies	48,397	229,584	374.4	1,094,728	376.8	1,154,983	5.5

IDE: Ingoing flows
(US $ mln)

	1980	1990	Δ% (1980– 1990)	2000	Δ% (1990– 2000)	2005	Δ% (2000– 2005)
World	54,078	207,455	283.6	1,402,680	576.1	1,461,863	4.2
Developing economies	7,479	34,853	366.0	257,625	639.2	429,459	66.7
Transition economies	24	75	212.5	7,023	9,264.0	54,516	676.2
Developed economies	46,576	172,526	270.4	1,138,032	559.6	977,888	−14.1

Source: Our reprocessing of UNCTAD data, Handbook of Statistics, 2011

middle classes and their growing demographic profile. This trend will probably strengthen further on: research by McKinsey (2012) tracks four likely future scenarios among which the optimistic one foresees a global economic growth of 3.6 percent in 2021, when the emerging countries' GDP will reach 38 percent of the world's GDP, compared to the current 28 percent.

3.   THE 'MADE IN ITALY'

To understand the place of Italian businesses in the new international scenario, their industry specialization has to be considered. Since the Italian economic system is characterized by a high incidence of industrial production in its GDP with respect to other EU countries (after Germany, Italy is the second largest industrial manufacturing country in Europe), the comparative advantages of Italy are strongly concentrated in two big industry sector groups.

2007	Δ% (2005–2007)	2008	Δ% (2007–2008)	2009	Δ% (2008–2009)	2010	Δ% (2009–2010)	Δ% (2000–2010)
2,174,803	54.7	1,910,509	−12.2	1,170,527	−38.7	1,323,337	13.1	7.4
294,177	29.8	308,891	5.0	270,750	−12.3	327,564	21.0	144.1
51,581	117.4	60,386	17.1	48,802	−19.2	60,584	24.1	1,796.2
1,829,044	58.4	1,541,232	−15.7	850,975	−44.8	935,190	9.9	−14.6
1,970,940	34.8	1,744,101	−11.5	1,185,030	−32.1	1,243,671	4.9	−11.3
573,032	33.4	658,002	14.8	510,578	−22.4	573,568	12.3	122.6
91,090	67.1	120,986	32.8	71,618	−40.8	68,197	−4.8	871.1
1,306,808	33.6	965,113	−26.1	602,835	−37.5	601,906	−0.2	−47.1

By using an extensively accepted taxonomy (Pavitt, 1984), these are the 'traditional' and 'specialized suppliers' industries referenced by the so-called 'four As' of Italian manufacturing excellence – *Agroalimentare* (food farming), *Abbigliamento-moda* (fashion clothing), *Arredamento-casa* (home furniture), *Automazione meccanica* (mechanical automation).

The traditional industries manufacture consumer products related to personal care and household items (textiles, clothing, footwear, leather goods, jewelry, eyewear, sport, furniture and fittings, household tools, white goods, building materials, ceramics, food). In these sectors, Italian competitiveness is based not on mere cost-efficiency and high volumes, but rather on style elements – even in the mid-market products without a brand – and on technological innovation, the latter mainly received by other industries (new materials, avant-garde machines). In almost all these fields Italy has become a style setter by creating a synergy between luxury craftsmanship – deeply rooted in the Italian Renaissance – and entrepreneurial creativity, which enables it to enter the medium/medium–high ranges of the different markets.

In these fields, Italian products can count on a high-quality image that has gradually attracted the world's attention. However, today there is increasing competition, specifically coming from China and from various South-East Asian countries, which are distinctive for their:

● lower labor costs compared to their Western counterparts;
● use of avant-garde machines imported from abroad;
● capability for imitation (and even, frequently, their ability for real counterfeiting);
● gradual improvement of product quality;
● managerial improvement.

It is evident, then, why the Italian businesses working in those sectors – and the industrial districts to which they usually belong – have lost important market shares in the last few years, especially in the low-range market at the moment, but with the risk of also losing out in the medium-range market. In these industries, it is essential that businesses continually increase their capabilities to innovate their offers in terms of style, design, creativity, fashion and quality, without forgetting that the weak dollar imposes a strong ceiling on Euro prices to stem the aggressive competitiveness of the many countries belonging to the dollar area, China included.

The specialized supplier industries basically include all the sectors of instrumental mechanics (machine tools, machines for metalworking, packaging, building, where Italy competes with Germany on a level playing field) and specialized components production (engines, transmission and brake mechanisms, pumps, membranes, valves, tools, etc.). In particular, those industries related to consumer products production present a remarkable opportunity to adapt to the specific needs of the users–customers. With the exception of a few rare cases, these are products that adapt well to an industrial structure made up of many businesses working in conditions of monopolistic competitiveness, oriented to serving niche markets with highly specific needs and with high product differentiation.

So far, thanks to an increment in the prices of products, trading-up has enabled businesses to compensate for the decrease in exports caused by the lower quantities sold. A number of mechanics industries (packaging, valves, robots, and machine tools of various kinds), for example, invested in innovation, trying to position themselves within high-technology or tailor-made production niches to contrast with the power of Germany on the one hand, and the low-cost production coming from the Far East on the other hand. In these sectors, the overtaking of Italian businesses by the new competitors has proved less simple so far, because the production process requires experience and capabilities for technological versatility that one can only gain with time. However, in some segments of less complicated machines and equipment (including much full components production), the competition from countries like China, Korea, India, Brazil, and of some nations that recently joined the European Union (Hungary, Poland, the Czech Republic, and Slovakia) is becoming stronger and stronger.

Italy shows, conversely, growing weakness (lower market shares, a greater dependence on the internal demand from imports, a negative trade balance and low multinational presence) in the two other groups located in Pavitt's (1984) taxonomy: (1) the science-based industries, that is the high-intensity research and development sectors which are true generators of technological innovation flowing in the rest of the system (computers, electronic components, telecommunications, fine and pharmaceutical chemistry, precision mechanics, aerospace, biotechnologies, etc.); and (2) the scale-intensive industries, that is the typical oligopolistic competition sectors where intermediate consumer products are produced in series (base and mass consumer chemistry, metallurgy, motor vehicles, consumer electronics, software, etc.).

4. CHALLENGES FOR ITALIAN COMPANIES

Considering its industry specialization, the Italian industrial system has been affected by competition from the emerging countries more than other European nations. However, it has proved that it is able to bear the challenge, by increasing its presence in international markets in the last few years.

Against an extremely weak internal market (which is falling, in some industries), there is the potential offered by the emerging countries that should not just be considered as low-cost factories any more but rather, and above all, markets able to absorb high-quality products. This is mainly a consequence of the change of development model of those countries, which is no longer centered on exports but on the growth of internal consumption (remarkably driven by the urbanization processes).

This generates relevant opportunities for the manufacturing businesses of 'Made in Italy', because the income growth implies an increase in the quality request and, consequently, in the potential consumers. The increase in new priorities (for example, energy efficiency and environment sustainability) in the intermediate and investment products is bound to increase the quality needs of the demand.[5]

The data related to Italy's market shares per macro-areas and main countries (Table 0.5) shows that, between 2009 and 2010, the main increments in terms of exports were in the member states of the so-called

Table 0.5 Italy's market shares per areas and main countries (values in €m)

Areas and countries	Exports			Imports			Balances	
	2010 (1)	weight %	var. % 2009–2010	2010 (1)	weight %	var. % 2009–2010	2009	2010 (1)
European Union	193,654	57.3	15.2	201,531	54.9	17.9	−2,804	−7,877
France	39,079	11.6	15.0	30,527	8.3	15.8	7,632	8,551
Germany	43,897	13.0	18.8	58,531	15.9	17.8	−12,758	−14,634
Spain	19,581	5.8	17.4	16,660	4.5	26.8	3,539	2,921
United Kingdom	18,068	5.3	20.8	12,147	3.3	23.7	5,136	5,921
Non-European countries	40,795	12.1	19.6	37,719	10.3	12.4	536	3,076
Russia	7,908	2.3	23.0	13,053	3.6	7.5	−5,710	−5,145
Switzerland	16,041	4.7	18.3	11,908	3.2	14.2	3,135	4,134
Turkey	8,033	2.4	42.1	5,158	1.4	16.6	1,230	2,875
North Africa	13,385	4.0	15.9	24,538	6.7	21.6	−8,640	−11,153
Other African countries	4,443	1.3	−2.1	5,691	1.6	31.7	219	−1,248
North America	22,713	6.7	18.5	12,638	3.4	18.8	8,529	10,075
United States	20,333	6.0	18.9	11,140	3.0	17.7	7,636	9,194
Southern Central America	11,099	3.3	23	9,922	2.7	35.9	1,725	1,178

Brazil	3,880	1.1	44.1	3,314	0.9	37.2	278	566
Middle East	16,140	4.8	6.9	20,993	5.7	74.1	3,036	-4,853
Central and Southern Asia	5,681	1.7	11.7	8,012	2.2	45.2	-433	-2,331
India	3,387	1.0	23.8	3,823	1.0	31.6	-169	-437
Eastern Asia	24,559	7.3	20.2	44,245	12.1	40.1	-11,138	-19,686
China	8,610	2.5	29.9	28,790	7.8	48.9	-12,705	-20,180
Japan	4,032	1.2	8.5	4,288	1.2	10	-185	-257
Oceania	3,146	0.9	13.5	1,177	0.3	19.3	1,787	1,970
World	337,810	100	15.8	367,122	100	23.4	-5,876	-29,312

Source: ICE processing on Istat data. (1) non-consolidated data

'Mercosur' (that is the group including Brazil, Argentina, Uruguay, and Paraguay), with around 45 percent; Turkey (+42 percent); China (+29.9 percent); India (+23.8 percent); Russia (+23 percent); non-EU European countries (+19.6 percent); United States (+18.9 percent); North Africa (+15.9 percent); and the EU countries (+15.2 percent).

However, one has to consider the overall relevance (in absolute values and in percentages) of Italian exports in Europe, that amounted to €193,654m (57.3 percent) in 2010. The above values are similar to the data registered for the import flows (€201,531m, that is 54.9 percent), which reflects the substantial Eurocentric profile of Italy in the scope of international trade flows.

Even though exports and Italian investments in China have grown 45 percent in the last five years, the presence of Italian products in the Chinese market is still limited: in 2010, Italian exports amounted to €8,610m (lower than their sales in traditional markets like Germany, France, the United States, Spain and Great Britain, but also lower than in countries like Switzerland, Belgium, and Poland).

In spite of various success cases, the Italian enterprises on the whole have difficulty in capturing the opportunities offered by new markets; this is demonstrated by the fact that more than 50 percent of Italian exports still keep being absorbed by the European Union.

One of the reasons is surely the prevailing dimensional structure of enterprises in the Italian production system. This is, in fact, very fragmented: in Italy, 57 percent of the manufacturing industry staff work in companies with less than 50 employers, compared to 51 percent in Spain, 32 percent in France, 31 percent in Great Britain and 22 percent in Germany.

The corporate dimension has important consequences on the international presence of the Italian enterprises. Of approximately 200,000 exporters censused by Istat, almost 61 percent qualify as micro-exporters, that is enterprises selling abroad, with an annual value below €75,000 each, and an overall, non-equivalent value below 1 percent of national exports. So, more than 99 percent of national exports derive from the remaining 78,051 operators.

In more recent years, the exports generated by small enterprises have proved less dynamic than the national average, as shown by the weight loss of exporters with a number of employers lower than 50 on the total sales abroad. The change happened, of course, in favor of the biggest enterprises. This is also a consequence of the significant restoration of the Italian production system in the recent past, resulting mainly from the competitive pressure exerted by the emerging countries. This restoration has been achieved with the exclusion of the less efficient exporter enterprises in the Italian panorama, and with a general improvement in the quality of the products sold abroad. Most likely, the biggest enterprises – generally active in the industries less exposed to competition from the new protagonists in world trade – have been more able to support the costs of this transformation. In fact, the big enterprises – with foreign sales revenue greater than €5m (which represent 4.4 percent of the total Italian exporters) – produce 90 percent of Italian exports.

5.   THE DIFFICULTIES IN EMERGING MARKETS

The limits of small enterprises become particularly evident when it is necessary to face the geographically and culturally far-off markets like those in the emerging countries.

Focusing on the consumer products, for example, enterprises have to face a local manufacturing industry whose productive specializations often widely overlap the Italian ones, even though they are based on lower quality standards. Moreover, some countries (China and India first, whose dimensions are huge) have to face not just a unique market, but rather a system of local markets that differ from each other, with a fragmented trade industry and with a heterogeneous end demand in terms of purchasing power, life, and consumption styles. Here there is a need for a strong local adjustment in strategies and marketing policies, which also requires broad capabilities of reading and understanding the consumers' needs, and a great deal of flexibility and dynamism.

Moreover, the Italian businesses cannot count on the presence of large national distribution channels to act as a 'Trojan horse' to open the doors of these markets. Focusing, for example, on the food and farming products, it is clear that distribution in the Chinese market is a prerogative – besides the local retail chains – of French, German, American, or Australian chains, which obviously do not have a particular interest in promoting Italian products. The absence of national distribution channels has always held back the spread of Italian consumer products in the emerging markets. The situation improved some years ago when, thanks to the new regulations approved in some countries, the big companies began to auto-distribute their own products on the local market. However, for all the other enterprises, nothing changed; the penetration of these markets, particularly for the small enterprises that cannot count on local retail chains, is still a very difficult mission. The consequence is that – as many empirical surveys attest – the partnerships with their intermediaries are, for many enterprises, the main issue.

Italian enterprises, indeed, are unlikely to have operational support in the target market, and because of this they are not actually able to govern the distribution and selling modes of their products (from the selling price to the kind of distribution channel, the geographic sales, and the nature of the end customer). This is, of course, extremely negative because only direct knowledge of local consumer behavior can enable the enterprises to adapt their products to the local markets, to develop consistent branding and communication policies and, in the last analysis, to obtain stronger operational support in the market.

A solution that could help many of our enterprises to overcome these limitations is the use of interfirm alliances (even in the form of formal agreements like consortia). The current experiences are still limited, but this could be a path worth following, for example through the opening of collective showrooms that allow not only remarkable cost savings, but also a physical rootedness in the local market, with the possibility of gathering information on market trends, and local phenomena, while becoming autonomous from the intermediary role.

Another front on which to intervene relates to the valorization and active defense of products. In this regard, the brand – and, more widely, the company image – plays an essential role. The problem does not concern the high-range products, but rather the less famous brands and, in general, the brands not belonging to the luxury industry. In the first case, the big brands (such as Prada, Tod's, Armani, Dolce e Gabbana, etc.) also enjoy high notoriety and appreciation in many emerging countries. In these markets, the successful foreign brands are the ones able to attract consumers, proving themselves as a reference in their industry. For example, the fact that Chinese consumers buy luxury brands to show their social status tends to reward the sales of the most easily recognizable brands; leaders in their respective categories.

The situation of small and medium enterprises (SMEs) is totally different. In this scenario, what do the successful Italian mid-sized firms do to gain the emerging markets? Which are the marketing tools can they play on? For these enterprises, two models seem to assert themselves on the international markets (Coltorti et al., 2012, chapter 4). The first model – prevailing in the consumer markets – is based on the brand–communication–retail trinomial; the brand development is strengthened not only by the short distribution channel and the sales points (flagship and concept stores) – which have the double role of collecting the information from customers and of communicating to them the brand values of the enterprise image or product concept – but also by investments in communication to carry out the corporate campaigns. The second model – prevailing in the business markets – associates niche positions, with high performance and quality products, to relationship-type marketing mainly with business customers (manufacturer or traders).

6. VOLUME OVERVIEW

All the 'Made in Italy' enterprises, namely the ones that cannot make big investments in communication, have to appropriately exploit the country of origin (COO) effect, that gathers all the elements reflecting the meanings associated with the Italian origin of the products (Busacca et al., 2006). In many foreign markets, indeed, these meanings represented (and still represent) an element of positive differentiation for many enterprises working in the 'Made in Italy' industries. We refer, in particular, to SMEs focused on niche productions in fashion, house furniture, food, and instrumental mechanics industries, and whose brands are not as strong as those of the big companies.

By combining academic rigor and the desire to provide insightful managerial inputs, this volume analyses the impact of the COO effect on the international development of Italian enterprises. At the same time, the volume proposes strategies and tools that the companies might use to develop their product offerings in the international markets, and suggests public policies that might strengthen these efforts. The chapters in Part II of the volume investigate the impact of the COO effect; the chapters in Part III suggest the tools that can be used to exploit the effect.

Specifically, the book clarifies the dynamics of the emerging markets such as the Asian ones, based on the assumption that those are the areas where the core of the world economy is now located. All the findings are analysed with the support of empirical analysis conducted on consumers or companies through surveys or case studies.

The book publishes the results of a project run by seven research groups that have worked jointly for two years, coordinated by Giuseppe Bertoli and Riccardo Resciniti. Altogether, 23 of the most influential Italian scholars of international marketing, from 12 Italian universities, joined the project.

Recognized as an important competitive factor for the commercialization of a product in the foreign markets, the COO effect has been arousing interest among marketing scholars for almost 50 years (Schooler, 1965). In the latter years, this interest has been further excited by the phenomenon of the process of productive delocalization in countries different from the country of origin of the producer, and by the already widespread process of integration of services and goods markets.

The country of origin represents an extrinsic cue used by the consumers as an indicator of the quality of products of a country. The hypothesis is that, in some cases, this country (and its image) is used by the consumer as 'substitute for information', that is as an indicator of the features of the product. The COO effect represents the effect through which consumers differently evaluate (in a positive or negative way) a product/service based on its specific geographic origin (country, region, or town).

The aforementioned effect is indeed particularly important (the 'halo effect') when the customer has limited knowledge of the product or when the intrinsic cues are not available. In this case, for example, the customer who knows that Germany is famous for producing excellent cars, can decide to buy one even if he is not able to evaluate its technical features (a deductive decisional process).

Similarly, a customer who has had several positive experiences with Italian clothing in the past can decide to buy other products of the same type, coming from the same origin (an inductive decisional process), and prefer a certain 'Made in Italy' item in a following purchase (a 'synthesis effect').

With the passing of time, the studies have become enriched in method-ologies and contents, inasmuch as: (1) the COO effect has been connected to other variables related to the consumer, the product, and the socio-economic approach (the 'multi-cue approach'); (2) its increasingly sophis-ticated measurement scales have been identified; and (3) its characterized construct has been deepened and structured.

Although keeping the variety of the adopted methodological settings, the researches on the COO effect have in common the aim of investigating the positive or negative effect exerted by this construct on the evaluation and intention of a purchase of a product by the consumers.

An effective classification of the plentiful literature on the subject of COO and on the various methodological options is proposed in Part I by Michela Matarazzo in 'Country of origin effect: research evolution, basic constructs and firm implications'. This chapter is structured into three sections. The first section reviews the relevant literature related to COO issues. The second section presents the various constructs proposed in the literature. Finally, the third section discusses some managerial implica-tions and concluding comments.

In Part II, related to the impact of the COO effect, Chapter 2, 'Italy's country image and the role of ethnocentrism in Spanish and Chinese con-sumers' perceptions' (by T. Bursi, B. Balboni, S. Grappi, E. Martinelli, and M. Vignola) analyses the COO effect on consumer buying behavior. A research model testing the COO's multidimensionality – country image (CI), product country image (PCI) and country related product image (CRPI) – on the Spanish and Chinese intention to buy Italian shoes is applied, verifying the level of product/country of origin's consistency (fit), as well as the role of ethnocentrism (CE). The model is tested through a quantitative analysis, administering structured questionnaires to a sample of Spanish and Chinese consumers, and applying structural equations modeling. Consumer ethnocentrism is considered as an explanatory variable of consumers' preferences or buying intention and the research on the combined effect of CE and COO is poor. Another element of interest of the chapter is that few studies make comparison between Western countries and emerging Asian countries. Results show that COO influences the consumers' intentions to buy through a causal link within the three dimensions, while CE plays a significant, yet weak, role on COO only in the Spanish context and for the CI and CRPI dimensions. Scientific and managerial implications are derived.

The product–country image is also investigated in Chapter 3, 'Tourism experience, country image and post-visit attitudes: a study on international tourists in Italy' (by A. De Nisco, G. Mainolfi, V. Marino, and M.R. Napolitano) in the field of tourism, where it has mostly been conceptualized in term of tourism destination image (TDI). Such a construct refers to the effects of beliefs, ideas, and impressions that a person has of a particular destination. The chapter aims at understanding the relationship between country image, tourism and attitudes towards the national products by investigating: (a) the influence of tourist satisfaction on the perception of general country image (GCI) and of tourism destination image (TDI); (b) the influence of GCI on TDI; and (c) the influence of GCI and TDI on post-visit consumption attitudes towards the country as a tourism destination and towards the national products. The research framework is tested on a sample of international tourists intercepted in two international airports (Capodichino International Airport in Naples and Leonardo da Vinci Airport in Rome) at the end of their journey to Italy. On the basis of results, this study concludes with a discussion of its theoretical contribution to country image and tourism destination image literature and provides managerial implications for both public sector and national companies.

COO literature is mainly focused on consumer sectors (business to consumer). In Chapter 4, 'Italian country image: the impact on business models and relations in Chinese business-to-business markets' (by E. Cedrola and L. Battaglia), instead, the theme of COO is investigated with reference to Italian firms operating in more technical industries, such as in the mechanical or electronic sectors, which have a major presence in the international markets. Despite offering excellent quality products in these sectors, Italy has a lower perceived image than other countries such as Germany. Literature on the COO effect in business-to-business markets is much less abundant. Among theorists, two main research streams can be identified. Some believe that the COO effect has the same importance in the consumer market, while others assert that industrial customers, operating in a more informed way, are less likely to be influenced by it. The chapter, through a survey of a sample of 338 firms, aims at verifying whether this effect really matters in these markets, particularly in business relations between firms that belong to markets with high cultural distance, as in the case of China. A second objective is to identify the elements that come into play in the evaluation of Italian offers and whether there are differences of perception according to the business sector considered.

In Chapter 5, 'What is the link between "Made in" and corporate social responsibility in SMEs? The value of socially oriented behavior in the "hostile" territories' (by A. De Chiara), the theme of the COO effect is addressed with reference to small and medium enterprises, usually devoid of famous brands. The possibility of recourse to the enhancement of the geographic origin becomes for many SMEs the true differential against foreign competition, the resource on which to focus to succeed and consolidate their presence in international markets. But in situations where the land is no longer an 'ally' and 'Made in' loses value, SMEs are likely to incur a loss of competitiveness of their offer in the international markets. The chapter argues that strategies of corporate social responsibility can be a viable alternative that can be pursued by SMEs to overcome the negative effects produced by the territory and to restore the competitiveness of companies.

Part III begins with Chapter 6, 'Distribution channel governance and value of "Made in Italy" products in the Chinese market' (by D. Vianelli, P. de Luca, and Guido Bortoluzzi), which asserts that the COO advantage is not sufficient to have success in foreign markets if the governance of distribution channels is weak. A company strategy to leverage the COO of a product (or of the company itself) in international markets must take into consideration the role of distributors in order to deliver part of the value that is embedded in the given product or brand to final consumers. The chapter aims at analysing the degree of control exerted on distribution channels by small/medium-sized Italian companies entering the Chinese market. All the selected companies (a total of 78) considered belong to the furniture, food, and fashion industries: sectors in which Italian companies typically leverage the 'Made in Italy' effect, and where the role of the foreign distributor is significant to strengthen the positive value of the COO effect. An online self-administered questionnaire was used to collect results. The main results show the need for improvement in the governance of distribution channels for the Italian companies operating in China. The current use of indirect entry modes and the problematic relationships with Chinese distribution partners make it difficult to convey the value of 'Made in Italy' to the final consumer, limiting the future growth of Italian companies in China.

The Chinese market is also analysed in Chapter 7, 'Country of origin effect, brand image and retail management for the exploitation of "Made in Italy" in China' (by T. Pucci, C. Simoni, and L. Zanni). Specifically, it is suggested that 'Made in Italy' exerts a positive effect on Chinese consumers' behavior. A cross-city survey of the children's apparel market in China was conducted to test hypotheses, predicted on a sample of 1,110 respondents. The interviews were carried out in both multibrand and monobrand stores, located in ten different Chinese towns in order to understand the influence of retail strategies on the brand image of an Italian firm that operates in China through an equity joint venture with a Chinese partner. The results reveal that associations of brand image, product image and Italy's image exert a significant positive effect on purchase intention. Furthermore, the COO image is found to be a positive moderator in the relationship between brand image and purchase intention. Some store management policies – namely the use of an effective store sign and the availability of an integrated system of different store elements with a positive association to Italy – also show some effects. Conversely, other retail strategies (monobrand versus multibrand shops) have a weaker effect than expected on brand image when measured in terms of premium price effect. This suggests that managers need to maintain a stronger control on store management that, in this case, was delegated to the general manager of the equity joint venture, who is one of the shareholders, and who implemented his own vision that was not aligned with the Italian firms.

Finally, Chapter 8, 'The role of country of origin in supporting export consortia in emerging markets' (by F. Musso, B. Francioni, and A. Pagano) aims at investigating the role of the COO effect in facilitating the market penetration efforts of export consortia in emerging countries. Thus far export consortia have received limited attention in the academic literature, and the role of COO in export consortia has also been neglected. Generally the theme of COO has been widely investigated with regard to its impact on customers and to a lesser extent as a strategic option to be actively adopted and exploited by firms. The research methodology is qualitative and is based on the case-study analysis of Alpha, an Italian export consortium active in the food market in India. The case of Alpha shows that the strategic use of COO could provide advantages – in terms of image and market penetration – to export consortia, notably in new and complex markets such as India, even though various hurdles – in terms of consortium structure and functioning – have to be faced.

NOTES

1. In the last ten years, GDP in Italy has grown less than 3 percent, in France less than 12 percent, in Great Britain less than 15 percent, in Finland less than 20 percent, and in Sweden less than 22 percent.
2. For an analysis of the international scenario against which the internationalization of the Italian businesses are evaluated, see also Matarazzo (2012).
3. Between 2002 and 2009, countries such as Saudi Arabia, Hungary, India, Brazil, Russia registered the following percentage increases in outgoing FDI: 729.7 percent; 586.5 percent; 534.9 percent; 297.4 percent; 256.2 percent.
4. Among the incoming FDI increments: Hungary +7,974.90; India +1,796.70; Malaysia +693.5 percent; China +517.7 percent; Russia +299.2 percent.
5. Moreover, in the current historical phase, the internationalization efforts of 'Made in Italy' can also be supported by the Euro's weakness, able to strengthen the competitiveness of many businesses. It is a sort of unparalleled discount for the European enterprises, above all in periods of urgent budget constraints.

REFERENCES

Busacca, B., G. Bertoli and L. Molteni (2006), 'Consumatore, marca ed "effetto made in": evidenza dall'Italia e dagli Stati Uniti', *Finanza Marketing e Produzione*, 2, Juin, 5–32.

Coltorti F., R. Resciniti, A. Tunisini and R. Varaldo (2012), *Mid-Sized Manufacturing Companies: The New Driver of Italian Competitiveness*, Springer.

Draghi, M. (2011), *Considerazioni finali anno 2010*, Banca d'Italia, Assemblea ordinaria dei partecipanti, 31 maggio.

Eckhardt, J.T. and S.A. Shane (2003), 'Opportunities and entrepreneurship', *Journal of Management*, June, 29 (3), 333–349.

Kos, A.J. (2010), 'An explanatory model for the decision to enter emerging markets: a shareholder perspective', *International Journal of Management*, 27 (2), 320–325.

Matarazzo, M. (2012), *Le strategie internazionali delle medie imprese: nuovi mercati e modalità di entrata*, Milano: FrancoAngeli.

McKinsey Global Institute (2012), *Debt and Deleveraging: Uneven Progress on the Path to Growth*, January.

Pavitt, K. (1984), 'Sectoral patterns of technical change: towards a taxonomy and a theory', *Research Policy*, 13 (6), 343–373.

Schooler, R.D. (1965), 'Product bias in the Central American Common Market', *Journal of Marketing Research*, 2 (4), November, 394–397.

UNCTAD (2011), *Training Manual on Statistics for FDI and the Operations of TNCs – Volume III: Collecting and Reporting FDI/TNC Statistics: Institutional Issues*.

PART I

The studies about the country of origin effect

1. Country of origin effect: research evolution, basic constructs and firm implications

Michela Matarazzo

1. INTRODUCTION

The explosive growth of globalization over the past decades has become one of the prominent issues in business today. As consumers normally come into contact with product offerings from other countries, and as domestic firms increasingly expand their markets overseas, the notion of national product image becomes ever more salient.

Although country image, unlike brand or corporate image, is not under the marketer's control, it can have a significant impact on the effectiveness of marketing strategies, especially those operated by firms aiming to penetrate foreign markets. For this reason, country of origin (COO), or the place-related image with which buyers may associate a product and its effect on buyers' behaviour, has attracted significant research attention over the past 40 years, and this interest has recently increased as a result of the dramatic growth of foreign direct investment (FDI). The results of these studies seem to agree in highlighting that country image represents an 'extrinsic cue' that, like the price and qualitative characteristics of the product, is able to influence the choice behaviour of consumers.

It was in the early 1960s that the notion of the COO effect gained the attention of international marketing scholars and has since grown to comprise one of the most voluminous sets of literature within any disciplinary subfield. In spite of the relative novelty of the field, research in it is substantial: as already mentioned by Papadopoulos in the Foreword, as at the end of 2011 there are over 1600 published researches on this topic describing the nature and the extent of the COO effect, the circumstances in which it is more or less evident and the factors moderating it (Agrawal and Kamakura 1999). Furthermore literature contributions by several scholars (Bilkey and Nes 1982; Peterson and Jolibert 1995) have increased significantly in terms of the variety of approaches they adopt, their analytical depth, and their overall number. All this is a good indication of the importance of country image in international marketing strategies.

Papadopoulos and Heslop (2003) identify in their review several of the main themes addressed by the various studies, developing a taxonomy. They distinguish six main groups of publications, ordered below according to the number of studies they include:

1. *countries* – how people in one or more countries view products of different origin;
2. *other issues* – ethnocentrism, domestic vs foreign products, consumer patriotism, cross-national and sub-national studies, stability of national image, and 'hybrid' products resulting from globalization and multinational production (a product containing components or ingredients made in different countries);
3. *research orientation* – consumer behaviour perspectives such as the effects of familiarity and perceived risk on product/country perception, multi-cue experiments and insights from social psychology;
4. *sectors and markets* – organizational buyers, retail buyers and investors, or specific sectors, ranging from tourism to food and cars;
5. *conceptual, methodological and theoretical issues* – methodological aspects, integrative works and models, literature reviews, meta-analyses and research agendas;
6. *strategy* – general, marketing mix, particularly advertising.

Roth and Diamantopoulos (2009) highlight the complexity and multi-dimensionality of the COO construct (Bursi et al. 2012), defining three different dimensions to be considered when analysing its effects on purchase intention:

1. *country image (CI)*: which focuses on the definition of factors that contribute to create the country image, such as cognitive beliefs and affective components;
2. *product–country image (PCI)*: which considers the effect of country image on products manufactured in a certain country;
3. *product image (PI)*: which emphasizes the quality image of specific products marketed by firms associated with different countries.

The rest of the chapter is structured into three sections. The next section reviews the relevant literature regarding COO issues, followed by Section 3 which presents COO constructs. Finally, some managerial implications are discussed in Section 4 and concluding comments made in Section 5.

2. MAIN STUDIES ON COUNTRY OF ORIGIN IMAGE

As literature on COO represents a vast area of research, only very important streams of research and significant researchers from different phases of study are presented from the early conceptual and empirical studies to the current literature.

Phau and Prendergast (2000) identify three main phases in the chronological development of COO research (see Figure 1.1). The first phase covers the years 1965–1973, starting with Schooler's (1965) study of COO effects in the Central American market that, while establishing that a COO effect does exist, did not investigate the strength and direction of such effects.

The second phase, 1982–1990, beginning with Bilkey and Nes's seminal review (1982), including research on the COO phenomenon up to 1980, marked a further increase in the volume of COO research. Baughn and Yaprak (1993) considered Bilkey and Nes's widely cited article as the starting point for a better understanding of the role PCI plays in the formulation of global marketing strategies. In fact, the dramatic transformation of the world economy and the staggering growth in global strategic alliances and countertrade arrangements had reduced the applicability of pre-Bilkey and Nes studies. This second period is characterized by a development from simple single-cue studies, where COO is the only product cue to be manipulated, towards more complex investigations and multi-cue studies.

Bilkey and Nes (1982) suggest that manufacture (or design, etc.) location is viewed as one of an array of information cues available to the consumer when evaluating a product and, therefore, that single-cue models present an important limitation (Chao 1989; Ettenson et al. 1988) which not only makes it hard to estimate the size of the COO effect, but fails to provide information on how or whether the origin effect can be offset by other cues. For such reasons single-cue studies are unlikely to adequately represent the informational environment in which product evaluation takes place.

Thus, it is important to integrate COO with other information cues, both intrinsic (taste, design, performance) and extrinsic (price, brand, warranties). Some empirical studies (d'Astous and Ahmed 1999) show that COO is of higher importance than brand itself when it comes to perception and to product quality evaluation. Conversely, when customers move from perceptions to purchasing intentions, the roles are reversed. Han and Terpstra (1988) found that both source country and brand name affect consumer perceptions of product quality, but source-country stimuli

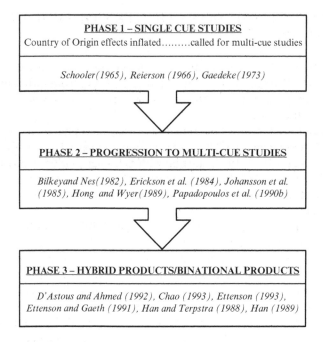

Source: Adapted from Phau and Prendergast (2000, p. 161).

Figure 1.1   Evolution of country of origin research

were found to have a more powerful effect than brand name on consumer evaluations of bi-national products involving two countries of origin. Peterson and Jolibert (1995) report a significant decrease in the COO effect on both quality perception and purchase intention when multiple cues are considered, compared to when COO is the only cue. On the basis of these arguments Agrawal and Kamakura (1999) examine the corporate perspective and conclude that COO might not necessarily lead to a competitive (dis)advantage in terms of price premium or discount. They show that marketers from different countries charge prices that are justified by differences in product quality rather than by the image effect produced by a COO cue. Another important result of their review regards the role of COO in influencing different stages of consumer behaviour; they found that, although COO plays an important role in product evaluation, the effect tends to become weaker as one moves from product quality perception to attitude formation and to behavioural intention.

The increased sourcing of production by multinational firms and their use of standardized advertising for their products (Han and Terpstra 1988;

Jaffe and Nebenzahl 1991), and the burgeoning rate of international joint ventures and other cross-national cooperative enterprises (Auster 1987), led to the prevalence of such 'hybrid' products and to consequent research into the relationship between the image of the country of manufacture and that of the country of national origin (Baughn and Yaprak 1993). Papadopoulos and Heslop (1993) reconceptualize COO in terms of PCI to account for the multidimensional character of products/brands and also the multiple places potentially involved in a global production system.[1] The term PCI has become common in the literature and has itself been subject to adaptation and refinement, for example in Askegaard and Ger's (1998) proposal of a more specific term, that is contextualized product–place image (CPPI). Unlike many COO studies, their conceptualization of CPPI takes into account the cultural context, and it is also innovative in its use of qualitative rather than quantitative methodology.

Some scholars (Samiee 1994; Jaffe, et al. 1994) distinguished between the following two key concepts:

1. consumer perception of the country with which a product/brand is identified,
2. country of manufacture.

Starting from the made-in cue, Jaffe and Nebenzhal (2006) proposed the following taxonomy taking into account different levels of analysis correspondent to the different countries where international sourcing takes place:

1. home country (HC): in what country does the consumer permanently reside?
2. design country (DC): in what country is either a part of or the entire finished product designed?
3. made-in country (MC): what country appears on the 'made-in' label?[2]
4. country of origin (CO): what country is considered by the consumer as being the source of a certain product or brand?

All except the first of the categories listed above have their corresponding image affecting consumer perceptions of brands or products related with the specific country (see Figure 1.2): this is defined as country image effect (CIE).

When it comes to making a purchase decision consumers therefore form overall images of a country's abilities to produce quality products. This overall image perception is mitigated by a corresponding perception of the country as source of a particular product line. Consequently, if there is a

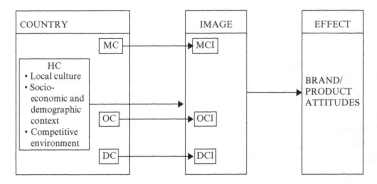

Source: Adapted from Jaffe and Nebenzahl (2006, p. 46).

Figure 1.2   Dimensions of country image effect (CIE)

great deal of variability in the perceived quality of different product categories, it may be difficult to estimate the outcome of all country image effects.

In conclusion, the focus of COO research has gradually shifted from
evaluating differences in product assessment and preferences based on the
mere notion of national origin of a product to explicitly measuring the
image of a country as product origin, that is the so-called country of origin
image (COI). The image is the representation, reputation or stereotype of
the specific country that consumers associate with the product.

Many researchers define COO image as 'perceptions' (Allred et al.
1999), others use related terms such as 'impressions' or 'associations'
(Ittersum et al. 2003), while others refer to 'stereotypes' (Verlegh and
Steenkamp 1999) or 'schemas' (Askegaard and Ger 1998) or 'beliefs'
(Kotler et al. 1993), which represent the cognitive component of 'attitudes'
(Zanna and Rempel 1988). Roth and Diamantopoulos (2009) underline
that none of these concepts is comprehensive enough to fully grasp the
domain of COI, except for the attitude theory,[3] which is a powerful tool
because it explains how countries are seen in the mind of consumers as
well as how such information affects their reactions towards a country.
It is based on a three-dimensional concept comprised of the following
(Papadopoulos et al. 1990b):

1.   cognitive – beliefs including schemas and stereotypes,[4]
2.   affective – feelings and emotions,
3.   conative – intended behaviour.

Country images incorporated in many trademarks, such as the country's
name, flag, currency, as well as in music and landmarks, people and per-

sonality, cultural and product exports (cognitive component) evoke strong emotions (affective component) and are an important driver of buyer behaviour (conative component).

Recent studies consider the above mentioned facets of attitudes as not independent from each other, but rather casually related (Mackie and Hamilton 1993; Verlegh and Steenkamp 1999). Therefore, they describe attitudes either through a two-component view (Engel et al. 1995) or a hierarchy-of-effects (or ABC) sequence (Zinkhan and Fornell 1989) which assumes 'that self-reported behaviour and stated intentions to respond . . . (are) treated as dependent effects of affective and/or cognitive variables' (Bagozzi and Burnkrant 1979, p.914). For example, a consumer decides to buy certain products from a particular country (conative component) on the basis of his beliefs (cognitive component) and emotions (affective component) about that country.

The conceptual domain of COO image is broader than that of PCI as it involves not only the evaluation of a country's products, but also other important outcomes such as investments, tourism and ties with a country. This chapter focuses exclusively on the latter: we are, in fact, interested in highlighting the literature contributions on the COO effects on buyers of traditional products and their implications for companies.

3. THE CONSTRUCTS OF COO

Research attempting to differentiate consumers on the basis of their foreign product acceptance has focused on features such as:

1. product familiarity,
2. consumer nationalism.

According to the first point, several studies assessed the role of country image in consumer choice behaviour across different sourcing countries analysing its impact (Han 2001) on:

1. consumers' attitudes towards brands,
2. consumers' intention to purchase certain brands,
3. consumers' perceptions of specific product attributes,
4. how a product category affects other categories from the same country.

Han (1989) was the first scholar who argued that PCI might be explained through the following two constructs:

- halo,
- summary.

According to the first one, when consumers evaluate a country's unfamiliar product they use their perceived country image (CI), that is based on whatever knowledge they have about the country itself, including its people, and its level of economic, political and social development.

The halo hypothesis suggests that consumers may consider not buying an unfamiliar foreign brand simply because they may make unfavourable inferences about the quality of the brand from their lack of familiarity with products from the country (Han 2001). Consumers may use country image as a halo in reducing the set of alternatives for the purchase decision, without evaluating the brand in detail (Howard and Sheth 1969).

At this stage, consumers may not have specific perceptions of attributes of the country's products, and thus their ratings of attributes are heavily affected by country image; that is, consumers may tend to infer specific attributes of a country's products in accordance with their overall perception of the CI.

Finally, consumers may infer the quality of a product category from a given country from their perceived quality of other categories or products from the same country. Findings indicating that halo processes may occur when consumers are unfamiliar with a country's products suggests that a country's initial exports and highly publicized products may improve the perception of other products associated with that country. It means that familiarity interacts with country image effect.

When consumers are not familiar with the country's products, it may therefore be hypothesized that:

1. country image is more likely to influence consumers' attitudes toward a brand, (than when they are familiar);
2. country image is more likely to have a direct effect on purchase intention (than when they are familiar);
3. there is a stronger association between country image and product attributes (than when they are familiar);
4. there is a stronger association between images of different product categories (than when they are familiar).

Han (2001) proposed a causal model specification as showed below:

CI => brand attitude => purchase intention

In support of the halo view, an empirical study by Johansson et al. (1985) showed that country image does affect the evaluation of product attributes but not the overall evaluation of products. Furthermore, their findings indicated that the overall evaluation of an automobile seemed to influence consumers' ratings on specific attributes. Another study by Erickson et al. (1984) also reported that country image affects consumers' evaluation of specific attributes rather than their overall evaluation of the product.

The halo argument implies that when consumers are familiar with the product category, their reliance on indirect evidence such as the country of origin of the product should decrease. Empirical evidence, however, does not seem to support this argument. In fact, the opposite has often been reported. Findings from the studies of Johansson et al. (1985) and Johansson and Nebenzahl (1986) indicated an increase in the propensity to use the country of origin information when product familiarity was high. Such results clearly weaken familiarity-based explanations.

In an attempt to explain these findings, Johansson (1989) proposed that country image may serve as a summary construct; that is, when consumers evaluate a country's unfamiliar products while they have experience with other products from the same country, they use this experience to form their perceived country image and, in turn, their attitudes towards the brand or the specific product. Experience is not necessarily that of the individual, but it can be indirect, influenced by the experience of others through information flows such as word-of-mouth and mass media. Han (1989) presents his proposition as:

Experience => beliefs => CI => brand attitude

Thus, CI may work like a halo for an unfamiliar foreign country, but it may become a summary construct as consumers become familiar with the country's products.

Knight and Calantone (2000) criticized Han's conceptualization for not accounting for the simultaneous processing of country image and product beliefs that takes place during consumer attitude formation. They argue that regardless of consumers' level of familiarity with a country's products, country image and product beliefs are used simultaneously and in different degrees to shape attitudes towards the product. Furthermore, country image is assumed to have an additional indirect effect on attitudes through consumers' product beliefs.

Laroche et al. (2003) propose a model similar to the 'flexible' model of Knight and Calantone (2000). The main difference lies in their conceptualization of country image as a multidimensional construct and its implications. They differentiate product beliefs, referring to consumers' beliefs about a product's intrinsic characteristics such as quality and reliability, from product evaluation referring to consumers' attitude toward the product, displayed in terms of pride of ownership, liking and intention to purchase. In order to highlight the simultaneous processing of country image and product beliefs, they propose a model that also takes into account both the halo and summary views. The direct effect of country image reflects its use as a summary construct, while the indirect effect, through product beliefs, represents consumers' use of country image as a halo.

Both halo and summary constructs stress the important dual role of CI in consumers' brand evaluations and purchase decisions. While COO information may serve as a surrogate for other information when buyers are not familiar with the product, increasing familiarity may lead to abstracting, summarizing and storing information based on the origin cue.

Lee and Ganesh (1999) identified and tested three types of familiarity in their study: product familiarity, brand familiarity and country familiarity. For both product and brand familiarity, the effects of COO information were stronger for consumers with high and low familiarity and weaker for consumers with medium familiarity. Likewise, country familiarity effects of COO information were stronger for consumers with low familiarity.

The construct of consumer nationalism is based on the notion that consumers' patriotic emotions have significant effects on attitudes and purchase intentions. It reflects a tendency for consumers to persistently prefer a domestic brand as opposed to one associated with a foreign country, often without a rational basis (e.g., when the foreign products are cheaper and/or of better quality). This type of bias, which Balabanis and Diamantopoulos (2004) refer to as 'domestic country bias', is manifested in both product perceptions and buying intentions.

Domestic goods are preferred in countries where (Phau and Prendergast 2000):

1. consumers have a strong sense of patriotism or national pride,
2. the domestic economy is threatened by foreign goods,
3. there is product service availability,
4. there is unfamiliarity with foreign products and brands.

The origin of the 'consumers' ethnocentrism' construct (CE from now on) can be traced to Sumner (1906), who introduced ethnocentrism as a general construct reflecting 'the view of things in which one's own group is the centre of everything, and all others are scaled and rated with reference to it' (p. 13). He coined this term to refer to the way people identify themselves as group members (ingroups) and distinguish themselves from others (outgroups). If we relate this to the COO effect, the nation is the ingroup of interest. CE is an application of ethnocentrism to the economic sphere that inherited the main premises and properties of ethnocentrism. Shimp and Sharma (1987) define CE as 'the beliefs held by consumers about the appropriateness, indeed morality, of purchasing foreign-made products' (p. 280). They developed a 17-item scale to evaluate consumers' ethnocentric tendencies and called it CETSCALE (for Consumers Ethnocentric Tendencies Scale). It seeks to measure the degree to which consumers feel that the purchase of foreign products is unpatriotic and immoral because it hurts the domestic economy, causing loss of jobs. Lantz and Loeb (1996) proposed to differentiate between the part of the COO effect explained by country image and the part explainable by nationalistic tendencies, using the social identity theory. They found that, when dealing with mundane, low involvement products, undifferentiated by price, country of origin is an important variable for all respondents. On the contrary, when the same categories of products present small differences in price, people with greater consumer ethnocentrism are willing to pay a higher price to buy domestic products, while those who are lower in consumer ethnocentrism are willing to switch to imported products. Papadopoulos et al. (1990a) found French, German and Dutch consumers to have the most positive views about their home products, while consumers in the US, Canada and Great Britain viewed their domestic products as better than foreign ones on some dimensions but as worse on others. Gurhan-Canli and Maheswaran (2000) extend the above mentioned findings by Shimp and Sharma by documenting that in addition to ethnocentrism, other general cultural orientation such as individualism/collectivism may also affect the purchase of foreign products. Collectivist cultures are mostly Eastern while individualist cultures are mostly Western (Hofstede 1990). They examined two countries (Japan and the United States) and found that individualists evaluated domestic products more favourably only when they were superior to competition, while collectivists evaluated domestic products more favourably regardless of their superiority. Thus they showed that COO effects vary on the basis of the diverse cultural patterns present in different countries and, consequently, COO-based strategies need to be customized according to the destination country. In addition, some studies suggest that products from countries viewed as culturally similar to the home country are preferred to products from countries that are viewed as culturally dissimilar (Crawford and Lamb 1981; Heslop et al. 1998). Schwartz (1994) identified seven value types that can be used to explain differences between cultures and provided a list of such differences for over 30 countries. Watson and

Wright (2000) investigated the situation where a domestic alternative is not available and found that in this case cultural similarity is an important consideration for highly ethnocentric consumers in the evaluation of foreign products.

Moreover Balabanis and Diamantopoulos (2004) found that the link between CE and consumer preferences appears to be variable depending on both the product category under consideration and the specific (foreign) COO involved: for some product categories and some COOs, CE may indeed act as a barrier (e.g., Italian food products); while for other product categories and/or COOs, CE may have no influence whatsoever (e.g., German furniture).

4. IMPLICATIONS FOR FIRMS

While previous literature reviews mainly emphasized the effect of COO on consumer behaviour, this paragraph focuses on how the COO cue can benefit firms associated with countries possessing positive product-country image.

Managers are reminded by the aforementioned research that country image plays an important role in consumers' market behaviour. Marketers can benefit by emphasizing and promoting PCI information when their country enjoys positive stereotypes, or by minimizing their reference to such information if their country suffers negative biases. However, while promotional use of the COO is the most evident application, it is, in a strategic sense, the least interesting one, because it involves middle management level decisions rather than top management ones. The FDI case is actually the most important one.

Alternative COO strategies relevant at firm level have to take into account these facets:

1. the association between perceived country image and brand image,
2. the 'fit' between country image and product category,
3. the International Product Life Cycle (IPLC).

As to the first point, evidence about the relative importance of brand and COO is found in a number of studies (Jaffe and Nebenzahl, 2006; d'Astous and Ahmed, 1992; Tse and Lee, 1992). These studies led to the conclusion that a strong global brand sourced in a weak image country can compensate for a negative country image.

Other studies (Phau and Prendergast 2000; Thakor and Lavack 2003) extended prior COO research by conceptualizing the COO of brand as an alternative evaluation tool as a consequence of the proliferation of products of multicountry affiliation (hybrid products).

A second finding is that for hybrid products with multiple country images, because they are made of parts sourced from more than one country, companies should highlight the country image that is likely to resonate more positively with their target market. For example, some products often carry an 'assembled in' label because the manufacturer believes that the country of assembly has a more favourable image than the countries where the parts are made. In fact, sourcing production in low wage countries that have an unfavourable country image may save costs, but may also result in negative product evaluation by consumers and, consequently, in a significant deterioration in brand value. Research has shown that this shift is mitigated by the fact that such strategic relocations are often limited to more simple products (inexpensive watches, cheaper running shoes, etc.) (Johansson and Nebenzahl, 1986). Thus the tradeoff between lower costs and potential negative consumer demand must be determined before a sourcing decision is made.

According to the second point, Roth and Romeo (1992) emphasize that country image is product-specific. They suggest a framework that matches the importance of the product category dimensions with the perceived image of the COO. For example, many prestige and status products (Swiss watches, French perfumes, Swedish crystal) owe their brand image to a strong country image for these product categories. This framework helps managers better understand when promoting a product's COO is beneficial and when it is not, as well as identifying the dimensions along which country image should be improved.

The country image dimensions taken into account are as follows:

1. Innovativeness – using new technology and engineering innovations;
2. Design – appearance, style, colours, variety;
3. Prestige – exclusivity, status, brand, reputation;
4. Workmanship – reliability, durability, craftsmanship, manufacturing quality.

Figure 1.3 shows that a product–country match should occur when important dimensions for a product category are also associated with a country's image. When there is no such linkage, a mismatch between a product category and country should exist. For example, design and prestige may be important features when consumers consider purchases of shoes (favourable match, cell 1), but relatively unimportant for the purchase of beer (favourable mismatch, cell 3). An unfavourable match occurs when the important product dimensions are not perceived as a

COUNTRY IMAGE DIMENSIONS

	Positive	Negative
Important	**I Favourable Match** Examples: • Japanese auto • German watch Strategic Implications: • Brand name reflects COO • Packaging includes COO information • Promote brand's COO • Attractive potential manufacturing site	**II Unfavourable Match** Examples: • Hungarian auto • Mexican watch Strategic Implications: • Emphasize benefits other than COO • Non-country branding • Joint venture with favourable match partner • Communication campaign to enhance country image
Not important	**III Favourable Mismatch** Examples: • Japanese beer Strategic Implications: • Alter importance of product category image dimensions • Promote COO as secondary benefit if compensatory choice process	**IV Unfavourable Mismatch** Examples: • Hungarian beer Strategic Implications: • Ignore COO – such information not beneficial

DIMENSIONS AS PRODUCT FEATURES

Source: Roth and Romeo (1992, p. 495).

Figure 1.3   Product–country matches and mismatches: examples and strategic implications

country strength (cell 2). Finally, an unfavourable mismatch (cell 4) occurs when an image dimension is both an unimportant product feature and not a perceived strength of the country.

Taking into account favourable and unfavourable (mis)matches can be very beneficial to managers who can select or omit specific product or country information in their marketing communications. Besides, it suggests that a brand that positively correlates with COO would be beneficial. In fact, when a strong, favourable match exists, a COO effect is likely to occur, positively affecting product evaluation. When a mismatch is clear, COO should have little impact on willingness to buy. Thus, willingness to buy autos and watches from Japan, Germany and the US can be enhanced by promoting COO by placing the brand's COO on the packaging, or on the product itself. In fact, willingness to buy these products appears related to these countries' overall good image, and the components of this image, workmanship, design, innovativeness and prestige are important characteristics for these product categories. Another strategic implication is related to foreign market entry, especially FDI, because favourable matches also indicate potentially attractive manufacturing sites for multinational companies. By contrast, in the case of unfavourable matches, advertising should emphasize important product benefits other than COO; as to foreign market entry strategies, a joint venture or a strategic arrangement with a partner from a favourable match country could be considered. Finally, the mismatch cells also offer interesting implications for marketers: in the favourable mismatch, one option is to alter the importance of image perceptions by associating with the product category country image dimensions which are not usually important for that product category; in the unfavourable mismatch COO should probably be ignored.

According to the IPLC, Niss (1996) suggests that promoting products or services abroad through national image is more common and helps the exporter to penetrate the market faster than by investing in brand awareness. Djursaa et al. (1991) reported a declining use of national image by Danish firms as market penetration evolves from the market entry stage, to the consolidation stage and finally to the established market penetration stage. In fact, those manufacturers that have been able to build regional or global brands over the market development stages rely less on national image. The reason can be also found in the increasing number of competitors entering a market in advanced stages and the consequent loss of first-mover advantages (Chen and Pereira 1999).

Other scholars (Amine et al. 2005) studied the use of national image over time and found that it is related to its different components. Thus, initial market entry should emphasize cognitive values suited for attracting lead users, and subsequently the attention should be focused on more emotional appeals, better suited to attract the mass market.

5. CONCLUSION

Despite the existence of many theoretical and empirical studies, perspectives for further research on this topic are many and of great interest, from both a scientific and a managerial/institutional point of view, considering also the difficulty in generalizing the results to date, and in reaching an outright consensus. The main trends are synthesized as follows.

There is increasing development of multi-cue studies which highlight that country image represents only one of the possible 'extrinsic cues', along with the price, brand, design and so on, able to influence the choice behaviour of consumers. In addition there is growing attention toward the definition of basic constructs such as halo and summary linking the COO effect to the specific characteristics of the products (high vs low familiarity).

There is continuous re-conceptualization of COO as in the case of 'hybrid' products consequent to the fragmentation of the value chain:

COO is distinguished in country of manufacture (Com), country of design (Cod) and country of assembly (Coa).

There is a conceptualization of COO of brand as an alternative tool due to the 'hybrid' products that make Com irrelevant and link consumers' perception of quality to brand, rather than product associations: perceived origin associations are evident within brand names created either through the language associated with the brand name or through advertising.

Methodologically, the main weakness in the COO literature noted in the course of this chapter is related to the paucity of studies using qualitative techniques. A majority of studies in the field, in fact, have employed quantitative techniques to measure a limited set of categories causing a lack of exploratory research into the multidimensional nature of the COO construct.

NOTES

1. Papadopoulos et al. (1988) were among the first to incorporate distinct country image measures in PCI research (in addition to measures of products simply designated as 'made in X'), and the first to attempt to model the relationship between country beliefs, product beliefs, familiarity, and product evaluation and willingness to buy, using LISREL. The term is shorthand for 'linear structural relations' and refers to structural equation models with latent variables that are the unobservable factors from measurement models.
2. In this regard the scholars make a further distinction between PC (which country is the source of identified key parts or components?) and AC (in which country does final assembly take place?).
3. Fishbein and Ajzen (1975, p. 6) define attitudes as 'a learned predisposition to respond in a consistently favourable or unfavourable manner with respect to a given object'.
4. The dimensions usually mentioned in the literature include country facet (i.e., economy, politics, culture, technology, landscape/environment and climate) and people facet (competence, creativity, standard of living, training and labour).

REFERENCES

Agrawal, J. and W.A. Kamakura (1999), 'Country of origin: a competitive advantage?', *International Journal of Research in Marketing*, **16**(4), 255–267.
Allred, A., G. Chakraborty and S.J. Miller (1999), 'Measuring images of developing countries: a scale development study', *Journal of Euromarketing*, **8**(3), 29–49.
Amine, L.S. and M.C.H. Chao (2005), 'Managing country image to long-term advantage: the case of Taiwan and Acer', *Place Branding*, **1**(2), 187–204.
Askegaard, S. and G. Ger (1998), 'Product–country images: towards a contextualized approach', in B.G. Englis and A. Olofsson (eds), *European Advances in Consumer Research*, pp. 50–58.
Auster, E.R. (1987), 'International corporate linkage: dynamic forms in changing environments', *Columbia Journal of World Business*, **22**(2), 3–6.

Bagozzi, R.P. and R.E. Burnkrant (1979), 'Attitude organization and the attitude–behaviour relationship', *Journal of Personality and Social Psychology*, **37**(6), 913–919.
Balabanis, G. and A. Diamantopoulos (2004), 'Domestic country bias, country-of-origin effects, and consumer ethnocentrism: a multidimensional unfolding approach', *Journal of the Academy of Marketing Science*, **32**(1), 80–95.
Baughn, C.C. and A. Yaprak (1993), 'Mapping country-of-origin research: recent developments and emerging avenues', in N. Papadopoulos and L.A. Heslop (eds), *Product–Country Images*, New York, US, London, UK, Norwood, Australia: International Business Press, pp. 89–115.
Bilkey, W.J. and E.B. Nes (1982), 'Country-of-origin effects on product evaluations', *Journal of International Business Studies*, **13**(1), 89–99.
Bursi, T., S. Grappi and E. Martinelli (2012), 'Effetto "country of origin"', Bologna: Il Mulino.
Chao, P. (1989), 'Export versus reverse investment: strategic implications for newly industrialized countries', *Journal of International Business Studies*, **20**(1), 75–91.
Chao, P. (1993), 'Partitioning country of origin effects: consumer evaluations of a hybrid product', **24**(2), *Journal of International Business Studies*, 291–306.
Chen, H.-C. and A. Pereira (1999), 'Product entry in international markets: the effect of country-of-origin on first mover advantage', *Journal of Product & Brand Management*, **8**(3), 218–229.
Crawford, J. and C. Lamb (1981), 'Source preferences for imported products', *Journal of Purchasing and Materials Management*, **17**, Winter, 28–33.
d'Astous, A. and S.A. Ahmed (1992), 'Multi-cue evaluation of made-in concept: a conjoint analysis study in Belgium', *Journal of Euromarketing*, **2**(1), 9–29.
d'Astous, A. and S.A. Ahmed (1999), 'The importance of country images in the formation of consumer product perceptions', *International Marketing Review*, **16**(2), 108–125.
Djursaa, M., S. Kragh and J. Möller (1991), 'Danish sells – whatever they say', *Magazine for Anglo-Danish Relations*, **4**, 10–11.
Engel, J.F., R.D. Blackwell and P.W. Miniard (1995), *Consumer Behavior*, Forth Worth: The Dryden Press.
Erickson, G.M., J.K. Johansson and P. Chao (1984), 'Image variables in multi-attribute product evaluations: country-of-origin effects', *Journal of Consumer Research*, **11**(2), 694–699.
Ettenson, R. (1993), 'Brand name and country of origin effects in the emerging market economies of Russia, Poland and Hungary', *International Marketing Review*, **10**(5), 14–36.
Ettenson, R. and G. Gaeth (1991), 'Consumer perceptions of hybrid (bi-national) products', *Journal of Consumer Marketing*, **8**(4), 13–18.
Ettenson, R., J. Wagner and G. Gaeth (1988), 'Evaluating the effect of country of origin and the "Made in USA" campaign: a conjoint approach', *Journal of Retailing*, **64**(1), 85–100.
Fishbein, M. and I. Ajzen (1975), *Beliefs, Attitude, Intention and Behaviour: An Introduction to Theory and Research*, Reading MA: Addison-Wesley.
Gaedeke, R. (1973), 'Consumer attitudes toward products made in developing countries', *Journal of Retailing*, **49**(2), 13–24.
Gurhan-Canli, Z. and D. Maheswaran (2000), 'Cultural variations in country of origin effects', *Journal of Marketing Research*, **37**(3), 309–317.

Han, C.M. (1989), 'Country image: halo or summary construct?' *Journal of Marketing Research*, **26**(2), 222–229.

Han, C.M. (2001), 'Testing the role of country image in consumer choice behavior', *European Journal of Marketing*, **24**(6).

Han, C.M. and V. Terpstra (1988), 'Country-of-origin effects for uni-national and bi-national products', *Journal of International Business Studies*, **19**(2), 235–255.

Heslop, L., N. Papadopoulos and M. Bourke (1998), 'An interregional and intercultural perspective on subculture differences in product evaluation', *Canadian Journal of Administrative Sciences*, **15**(2), 113–127.

Hofstede, G. (1990), *Cultures and Organizations: Software of the Mind*, London: McGraw-Hill.

Hong, S. and R.S. Wyer (1989), 'Effects of country of origin and product-attribute information on product evaluation: an information processing perspective', *Journal of Consumer Research*, **16**(2), 175–187.

Howard J.A. and J.N. Sheth (1969), *The Theory of Buyer Behavior*, New York, NY: John Wiley & Sons.

Ittersum, K.V., M.J. Candel and M.T.G. Meulenberg (2003), 'The influence of the image of product's region on origin of product evaluation', *Journal of Business Research*, **56**(3), 215–226.

Jaffe, E.D. and I.D. Nebenzahl (1991), 'The effectiveness of sponsored events in promoting a country's image', *International Journal of Advertising*, **10**(3), 223–237.

Jaffe, E.D. and I.D. Nebenzahl (2006), *National Image & Competitive Advantage*, Copenhagen: Copenhagen Business School Press.

Jaffe, E.D., I.D. Nebenzahl and S.I. Lampert (1994), 'Towards a theory of country-of-origin effect: an integrative paradigm', in K. Obloj (ed.), *High Speed Competition in a New Europe*, Proceedings of the European International Business Association, Warsaw.

Johansson, J.K. (1989), 'Determinants and effects of the use of "made in" labels', *International Marketing Review*, **6**(1), 47–58.

Johansson, J.K. and I.D. Nebenzahl (1986), 'Multinational production: effect on brand value', *Journal of International Business Studies*, **17**(3), 101–126.

Johansson, J.K., S.P. Douglas and I. Nonaka (1985), 'Assessing the impact of country-of-origin on product evaluations', *Journal of Marketing Research*, **22**(4), 388–396.

Knight, G.A. and R.J. Calantone (2000), 'A flexible model of consumer country-of-origin perceptions: a cross-cultural investigation', *International Marketing Review*, **17**(2), 127–145.

Kotler, P., D.H. Haider and I. Rein (1993), *Marketing Places: Attracting Investment, Industry and Tourism to Cities, States and Nations*, New York, NY: Free Press.

Lantz, G. and S. Loeb (1996), 'Country of origin and ethnocentrism: an analysis of Canadian and American preferences using social identity theory', *Advances in Consumer Research*, **23**, 374–378.

Laroche, M., N. Papadopoulos, L.A. Heslop and M. Mourali (2003), 'The influence of country image structure on consumer evaluations of foreign products', *International Marketing Review*, February.

Lee, D. and G. Ganesh (1999), 'Effects of partitioned country image in the context of brand image and familiarity: a categorization theory perspective', *International Marketing Review*, **16**(1), 18–39.

Mackie, D.M. and D.L. Hamilton (1993), 'Affect, cognition and stereotyping: concluding comments', in D.M. Mackie and D.L. Hamilton (eds), *Affect, Cognition and Stereotyping: Interactive Processes in Group Perceptions*, San Diego: Academic Press, pp. 371–383.

Niss, H. (1996), 'Country of origin marketing over the product life cycle', *European Journal of Marketing*, **30**(3), 6–22.

Papadopoulos, N. and L.A. Heslop (2003), 'Country equity and product–country images: state-of-the-art in research and implications', in S.C. Jain (ed.), *Handbook of Research in International Marketing*, Cheltenham, UK and Northampton, MA, USA: Edward Elgar, pp. 402–433.

Papadopoulos, N., L.A. Heslop and Bamossy G. (1990a), 'A comparative analysis of domestic versus imported products', *International Journal of Research in Marketing*, **7**(4), 283–294.

Papadopoulos, N., L.A. Heslop and J. Beracs (1990b), 'National stereotypes and product evaluations in a socialist country', *International Marketing Review*, **7**(1), 32–47.

Papadopoulos, N., J.J. Marshall and L.A. Heslop (1988), 'Strategic implications of product and country images: a modeling approach', *Marketing Productivity*, European Society for Opinion and Marketing Research, Lisbon, pp. 69–90.

Peterson, R.A. and A.J.P. Jolibert (1995), 'A meta-analysis of country-of-origin effects', *Journal of International Business Studies*, **26**(4), 883–900.

Phau, I. and G. Prendergast (2000), 'Conceptualizing the country of origin of brand', *Journal of Marketing Communications*, **6**(3), 159–170.

Reierson, C. (1966), 'Are foreign products seen as national stereotypes?' *Journal of Retailing*, **42**(3), 33–40.

Roth, K.P. and A. Diamantopoulos (2009), 'Advancing the country image construct', *Journal of Business Research*, **62**(7), 726–740.

Roth, M.S. and J.B. Romeo (1992), 'Matching product category and country image perceptions: a framework for managing country-of-origin effects', *Journal of International Business Studies*, **23**(3), 477–497.

Samiee, S. (1994), 'Customer evaluation of products in a global market', *Journal of International Business Studies*, **25**(3), 579–604.

Schooler, R.D. (1965), 'Product bias in the Central American common market', *Journal of Marketing Research*, **2**(4), 394–397.

Schwartz, S. (1994), 'Beyond individualism/collectivism: new cultural dimensions of values', in U. Kim, H.C. Triandis, C. Kagitcibasi, S. Choi, and G. Yoon (eds), *Individualism and Collectivism: Theory, Methods and Applications*, Thousand Oaks, CA: Sage Publications.

Shimp, T.A. and S. Sharma (1987), 'Consumer ethnocentrism: construction and validation of CETSCALE', *Journal of Marketing Research*, **24**(3), 280–289.

Sumner, W.G. (1906), *Folkways: The Sociological Importance of Usages, Manners, Customs, Mores, and Morals*, New York, NY: Ginn.

Thakor, M.V. and A.M. Lavack (2003), 'Effect of perceived brand origin associations on consumer perception of quality', *Journal of Product and Brand Management*, **12**(6), 394–407.

Tse, D. and Lee Wie-na (1992), 'Removing negative country images: effects of decomposition, branding, and product experience', *Journal of International Marketing*, **1**(4), 25–48.

Verlegh, P.W.J. and J.B.E.M. Steenkamp (1999), 'A review and meta-analysis of country-of-origin research', *Journal of Economic Psychology*, **20**(5), 521–546.

Watson, J.J. and K. Wright (2000), 'Consumer ethnocentrism and attitudes toward domestic and foreign products', *European Journal of Marketing*, **34**(9–10), 1149–1166.

Zanna, M.P. and J.R. Rempel (1988), 'Attitudes: a new look at an old concept', in D. Bar-Tal and A. Kruglansky (eds), *A Social Psychology of Knowledge*, New York, NY: Cambridge University Press, pp. 315–334.

Zinkhan, G.H. and C. Fornell (1989), 'A test of the learning hierarchy in high and low involvement situations', *Advertising Consumer Research*, **16**(1), 152–159.

PART II

The impact of the country of origin effect

2. Italy's country image and the role of ethnocentrism in Spanish and Chinese consumers' perceptions

Tiziano Bursi, Bernardo Balboni, Silvia Grappi, Elisa Martinelli and Marina Vignola

INTRODUCTION

In the past decades, increasing global competition among firms operating in different parts of the world and the related consumers' exposition to an enlarging range of foreign products and brands have stimulated increasing interest on the effect of country of origin (COO) on product evaluation in studies in various areas such as international business, marketing and consumer behaviour (Nagashima, 1977; Papadopoulos and Heslop, 1993; Kaynak and Kara, 2002). The COO effect has also attracted the attention of internationalized firms which operate in competitive domestic and foreign markets, attentive to the understanding of the similarities and differences in consumers' perceptions and evaluations of foreign products (Ahmed and d'Astous, 2007).

COO is conceptualized as a synthesis of stereotypes, skills, experience and knowledge concerning a certain country and its manufacturing capabilities. Usually COO is conveyed with the phrase 'made in' (Amine et al., 2005).

Despite the richness of the literature on the topic, empirical studies concerning the influence of COO on consumer evaluation reveal mixed and sometimes contradictory results, not only due to different combinations of product types, samples and countries where the studies were conducted (Bilkey and Nes, 1982; Roth and Romeo, 1992; Kaynak and Kara, 2002; Speece and Nguyen, 2005), but also to various interpretations of the theoretical construct.

Recently, Roth and Diamantopoulos (2009) proposed considering the COO construct as composed of three dimensions: overall country image (CI); product country image (PCI); and country-related product image (CRPI). But the authors did not verify the relationships within these facets empirically. To overcome this gap, we propose a research model – and the related hypotheses – aimed at testing the three dimensions suggested, verifying the COO effect on consumer intention to buy products originated in one specific country. The influence of the level of consistency between the product category investigated and the country in which the product is made (FIT) is measured too, as well as the role of consumer ethnocentrism (CE) on the COO's dimensions. The analysis is conducted in the context of two countries – that is, Spain and China – as representative of highly industrialized countries (HIC) and newly industrialized countries (NIC) respectively. The category under observation is shoes and the country image analysed is Italy.

The model is tested through a quantitative analysis, administering structured questionnaires to a sample ($N = 312$) of Spanish and Chinese consumers and applying structural equation modelling (LISREL 8.3).

Very few studies have analysed the effect of CRPI, PCI and CI on product evaluation within the same model. Moreover, CE has rarely been considered as an explanatory variable of consumers' preferences or buying intention (Balabanis and Diamantopoulos, 2004) and the research on the combined effect of CE and COO is poor (Bandyopadhyay et al., 2011). Although extant literature has not explicitly addressed the relationship between the overall belief about a country (CI) and the ethnocentric tendency, we consider that CE can also be reflected on the overall evaluation of a country. Additionally, the comparison within countries with different socio-economic development levels enriches the analysis (Kaynak and Kara, 2002). Specifically, few studies make comparisons between Western countries and emerging Asian countries (Ahmed and d'Astous, 2007). Prevailing literature suggests that consumers in NIC, even with high CE tendency, might evaluate products from HICs as being better than products from NICs.

This chapter, after having described the theoretical framework of the research, reviewing the literature on the COO effect and on the role of CE, presents the research's model and hypotheses, design and methodology. Results are then depicted and discussed, deriving the consequent managerial implications and underlining limitations and further research directions.

THE THEORETICAL FRAMEWORK

The Country of Origin Effect on Product Evaluation and its Determinants

Country of origin is considered an important factor that affects consumers' evaluation and purchase intentions of products sourced from foreign countries (Kaynak and Kara, 2002; Hui and Zhou, 2003; Cervino et al., 2005; Pappu et al., 2007). It is defined as 'information pertaining to where a product is made' (Zhang, 1996, p. 51) and as 'the total of all descriptive, inferential and informational beliefs one has about a country' (Martin and Eroglu, 1993, p. 193). The aim of COO studies is to understand the impact, positive or negative, that this construct might have on consumer evaluation and intention to buy products coming from foreign countries and hence the consumer perception about the relationship between country image and the image that products designed and manufactured in that country have (Roth and Romeo, 1992; Gurhan-Canli and Maheswaran, 2000; Kaynak and Kara, 2002; Hui and Zhou, 2003; Wang and Chen, 2004; Cervino et al., 2005; Hamin and Elliott, 2006; Ahmed and d'Astous, 2007; Pappu et al., 2007; Chattalas et al., 2008; Bandyopadhyay et al., 2011).

As a product comprises many different physical and symbolic attributes, according to several researchers (Han, 1989; Lee and Ganesh, 1999; Essoussi and Merunka, 2007) the image of a country as the origin of products is regarded as an extrinsic cue (pertained to the intangible products traits) often used by consumers in the process of evaluation of the product quality. This effect is known as the halo or summary effect (Han, 1989). The COO cue, as a brand and price cue, often acts as risk-mitigating information about adverse consequences arising from a product purchase (Oberecker and Diamantopoulos, 2011) and it is particularly significant when consumers have imperfect or lack of knowledge about the product; that is, when the intrinsic cue (pertaining to tangible aspects or physical characteristics of the product, such as taste, style, performance and quality) is not available (Roth and Romeo, 1992; Kaynak and Kara, 2002). In others words, the COO is a heuristic that can help consumers to make inference about quality, and affects their beliefs about product attributes. The extent to which a product's country of origin cue is utilized depends on the level of consumer involvement in its purchasing: the more consumers are motivated, the more COO is perceived as a mere informational cue and not as a measurement of overall quality (Chryssochoidis et al., 2007).

As the COO is a complex construct, the majority of surveys underline its multi-dimensionality, differently interpreted in the literature (Roth and Romeo, 1992; Martin and Eroglu, 1993; Papadopoulos and Heslop, 2002; Roth and Diamantopoulos, 2009). Some scholars proposed a broad definition employing indicators such as the economic development degree, or the political and cultural country system (Laroche et al., 2005); others suggested a product-specific definition related to a country image as a place in which the products are designed and manufactured (Nagashima, 1977;

Han, 1989; Roth and Romeo, 1992). Recently, Roth and Diamantopoulos (2009) suggested three distinct definitional domains of country image that differ in their focal image object, namely:

1. the overall image of a country, defined as country image (CI);
2. the image of countries and their products, also referred to as product–country image (PCI);
3. the images of a specific product from a country, defined as country-related product image (CRPI).

CI relates to the stereotypes and generalized opinion individuals have about a specific country. This image is formed by the country's representative product, its industrialization level and technological development, and its political, cultural and economic situation (Nagashima, 1970; Knight and Calantone, 2000; Pappu et al., 2007).

In contrast, PCI refers to the attitudes individuals hold regarding the manufacture system of the country. In other words, PCI expresses the consumer's general conscience for product quality (in term of innovativeness, design, prestige or workmanship) manufactured in a specific country (Bilkey and Nes, 1982; Han, 1989; Pisharodi and Parameswaran, 1992; Jaffe and Nabenzhal, 1993; Hamzaoui and Merunka, 2006; Oberecker and Diamantopoulos, 2011).

Finally, CRPI refers to the perceived image individuals hold at the level of a specific product category from a country (Nagashima, 1970; Martin and Eroglu, 1993; Wang and Yang, 2008). This construct may be more informative compared to CI that gives an aggregate analysis based on unspecified products from a certain country (Balabanis and Diamantopoulos, 2004).

In more recent studies, a further element of interest is the concept of FIT defined as the logical connection or perceptual distance between the country image and the product designed and manufactured in that country (Roth and Romeo, 1992; Lee and Ganesh, 1999; Hamzaoui and Merunka, 2006; Essoussi and Merunka, 2007). Evaluations of products are affected not only by the image of the country of origin but also by the perceived logical and consistent capacity of that country to manufacture a product in a specific product category (Hamzaoui and Merunka, 2006; Chryssochoidis et al., 2007). If the FIT between the country and the considered product category is positive/negative, the product image will also appear positive/negative. In other words, just as brand extension to new products can profit from the positive effect of the association with the main brand (Aaker and Keller, 1990; Park et al., 1991; Keller, 1993), in the same way the positive association with a country can be transferred to a product if the product category is logically correlated with that country (Essoussi and Merunka, 2007).

The Effect of Consumer Ethnocentrism on Country Image and Purchase Intention

The evaluation of country image cue can also be affected by some biases related to cultural orientation and national stereotypes of the consumer, such as ethnocentrism (Kaynak and Kara, 2002; Balabanis and Diamantopoulos, 2004; Ahmed and d'Astous, 2007; Chryssochoidis et al., 2007; Chattalas et al., 2008). The consumer ethnocentrism (CE) concept is the application in the economic environment of the ethnocentrism construct in which one's own group (nationally defined) is the centre and one's own culture is used as comparator; so, all others are assessed with reference to it, refusing people who are culturally dissimilar (Sumner, 1906). The concept of consumer ethnocentrism explains the phenomenon of consumer preference for domestic products, or prejudice against foreign-made products (Sharma et al., 1995). 'From the perspective of ethnocentric consumers, purchasing imported products is wrong because, in their minds, it hurts the domestic economy, causes loss of jobs, and is plainly unpatriotic' (Shimp and Sharma, 1987, p. 280). According to this concept, consumers with high ethnocentric tendency prefer to buy national products because of appropriateness, morality and sense of loyalty to their home country's products (Shimp and Sharma, 1987; Watson and Wright, 2000; Kaynak and Kara, 2002; Wang and Chen, 2004; Hamin and Elliot, 2006; Bandyopadhyay et al., 2011). CE tendency may induce consumers to overestimate the quality and value of domestic products and can explain why consumers prefer domestic over foreign products, even when they are of better quality or cheaper, for example (Chryssochoidis et al., 2007). Conversely, consumers with low ethnocentric tendency evaluate foreign products on their qualities and on the basis of the utility they offer, rather than where they are made or, if considered, this condition is evaluated in a favourable manner when they are manufactured in a country with a positive image (Shimp and Sharma, 1987). Therefore the concept of CE supports the understanding of how consumers compare domestic with foreign-made products and how their judgement may be subjected to biases and errors (Kaynak and Kara, 2002; Balabanis and Diamantopoulos, 2004).

The more importance a consumer places on where a product is manufactured (home country vs. foreign country), the higher his/her ethnocentric tendency (Wang and Chen, 2004). The intensity and magnitude of the CE effect on foreign products varies not only across countries of a similar culture (Kaynak and Kara, 2002; Hamin and Elliott, 2006), but also across groups within the same country with regards to age, gender, education, income, cultural openness, patriotism, conservatism, collectivism/individualism (Sharma et al., 1995; Watson and Wright, 2000; Javalgi et al., 2005; Ahmed and d'Astous, 2007; Chryssochoidis et al., 2007; Bandyopadhyay et al., 2011). On the basis of these arguments, the country image effect on the intention to buy foreign products can be differently evaluated in relation to CE (Sharma et al., 1995; Wang and Chen, 2004; Bandyopadhyay et al., 2011). For consumers with high ethnocentric tendency, the COO cue has a larger effect on product evaluation and on purchase intentions to buy foreign products than it does on less ethnocentric consumers: the former generally pay more attention to the COO cue, perceiving the consumption of imported products as socially undesirable (Chattalas et al., 2008).

The combined effect of CE and country image can vary also when we compare consumers from highly industrialized countries (HICs) and newly industrialized countries (NICs; Watson and Wright, 2000; Bandyopadhyay et al., 2002; Kaynak and Kara, 2002; Wang and Chen, 2004; Javalgi et al., 2005; Hamin and Elliot, 2006; Ahmed and d'Astous, 2007; Chryssochoidis et al., 2007; Bandyopadhyay et al., 2011). Consumers in HICs tend to prefer products manufactured in the home country or in countries viewed as culturally, politically and economically similar to their own (Watson and Wright, 2000, p. 1150; Balabanis and Diamantopoulos, 2004; Wang and Chen, 2004; Hamin and Elliott, 2006). They perceive domestic products (or products from perceived similar countries) of higher quality than imported products, especially from NICs. The inverse is true for consumers in NICs, in particular when they import products from countries with a high image (often HICs) and these products are perceived as status symbols (Wang and Chen, 2004; Hamin and Elliott, 2006) or of higher quality, as the former display the ability to manufacture products requiring a certain level of acquired skill and technology (Balabanis and Diamantopoulos, 2004; Ahmed and d'Astous, 2007).

Conversely, Hamin and Elliott (2006) point out that Indonesian respondents with higher CE perceive locally designed and made products to be of higher quality and thus prefer to buy them. In contrast, respondents with lower CE prefer products designed and manufactured in foreign countries. In the same way, other studies find that, for consumers from NICs, COO and CE should generate opposite influences on the evaluation of foreign products (Bandyopadhyay et al., 2011). On the one hand, the COO effect implies a positive influence for products made in advanced countries and a negative influence for products sourced in less developed countries; on the other hand the CE tendency encourages local products.

THEORETICAL MODEL AND RESEARCH HYPOTHESES

Having delineated the conceptual nature of country image, product–country fit and consumer ethnocentrism, we propose a theoretical model linking CE and FIT to the key outcome variables – different domains of country image (CI, PCI and CRPI) and intention to buy.

The domains of COOs have to be considered simultaneously because 'overall country image gives the least amount of information to the marketer since it cannot tell him whether there is variation between product categories of a given country' (Chasin et al., 1988, p. 15). The relationship between the different domains of country image has been well established in prior research, even though they have not been conceptualized and empirically tested within the same theoretical model (Roth and Diamantopoulos, 2009). Some authors have analysed the combined effect of CRPI and PCI (Lee and Ganesh, 1999; Ahmed et al., 2004) or of CI and CRPI (Li et al., 1997; Lee and Ganesh, 1999; Knight and Calantone, 2000; Laroche et al., 2005; Essoussi and Merunka, 2007) on product evaluation. Therefore the CRPI dimension has been the most considered in the COO works. Several authors (for example, Liu and Johnson, 2005; Wang and Yang, 2008) have focused on the CRPI-specific impact on consumers' preferences. Wang and Yang (2008) state that CRPI has a positive influence on purchase intention. Nevertheless, very few empirical studies have analysed the effect of CRPI, PCI and CI on product evaluation within the same model (Papadopoulos and Heslop, 2003) as, for example, has Lee and Ganesh's (1999) work. The authors found a positive combined effect of CRPI, PCI and CI on consumer evaluation of television, reporting a number of interactions among the three domains.

Thus we expect that the general beliefs about a country (CI) – in terms of a country's overall economic, social, technological and political aspect – affect consumer perceptions of the country's products (PCI; Roth and Romeo, 1992; Lee and Ganesh, 1999; Pappu et al., 2007), and both these constructs affect the image of a specific product category from a country (CRPI; Wang and Lamb, 1983; Pisharodi and Parameswaran, 1992).

So, our research hypotheses are as follows:

Hypothesis 1:   CI has a positive impact on PCI

Hypothesis 2:   PCI has a positive impact on CRPI

Hypothesis 3:   CI has a positive impact on CRPI

Product–country FIT represents another key antecedent of CRPI. In fact, consumers tend to associate a specific product category with a country (for example, Turkey and carpets). It implies that the connection perceived by a consumer between a country and a product category will influence perceived product image (Roth and Romeo, 1992; Essoussi and Merunka, 2007). So, the higher the logical connection between a country and a product category, the higher its perceived product quality. Thus we hypothesize that:

Hypothesis 4:   FIT has a positive impact on CRPI

Recently some researchers have explored the relationship between different domains of country image and consumer ethnocentrism (CE; Watson and Wright, 2000; Balabanis and Diamantopoulos, 2004; Bandyopadhyay et al., 2011). These authors found that CE has a negative impact on evaluation of products from a foreign country, as captured by the PCI, and on the evaluation of a specific product from a country, as captured by CRPI (Watson and Wright, 2000; Hamin and Elliott, 2006; Chryssochoidis et al., 2007; Bandyopadhyay et al., 2011; Oberecker and Diamantopoulos, 2011). Although extant literature has not explicitly addressed the relationship between the overall belief about a country (CI) and the ethnocentric tendency, we consider that consumers' ethnocentrism can also be reflected on the overall evaluation about a country. Since foreign countries represent out-groups in the conceptualization of CE (Sharma et al., 1995), we expect CE to have a negative impact not only on foreign product evaluations but also on the overall impression about a country (CI). So, we hypothesize that:

Hypothesis 5:   CE has a negative impact on CI

Hypothesis 6:   CE has a negative impact on PCI

Hypothesis 7:   CE has a negative impact on CRPI

CE's literature states that CE can affect the intention to buy foreign products (Sharma et al., 1995; Wang and Chen, 2004; Bandyopadhyay et al., 2011). Since CE influences consumers' preferences by affecting the formation of positive or negative assessments on products associated with a particular country (Chryssochoidis et al., 2007), we expect that the evaluations of CRPI will directly affect intention to buy (INT; Roth and Romeo, 1992; Heslop et al., 2004; Wang and Yang, 2008), while the relationship between CE and INT is totally mediated by CRPI. Thus we hypothesize that:

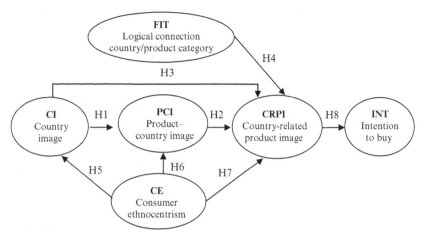

Figure 2.1   The theoretical model

Hypothesis 8:   CRPI has a positive influence on INT

Figure 2.1 shows the theoretical model and our hypotheses.

RESEARCH DESIGN AND METHODOLOGY

Research Design

In this study we adopt a single-cue approach in which the place of origin is the only displayed information, instead of a multi-cue approach in which other information, such as brand and price, are given. In fact, we aim to study the effect of COO separately from other effects.

We adopt an approach that compares consumers' perceptions in one HIC – namely Spain – with those of consumers in one NIC – that is, China. These countries were chosen not only because of the large differences between them in terms of per capita incomes, cultural heritage and industrial development, but also because of the specific product category observed (Ahmed and d'Astous, 2007, pp. 241–245); that is, footwear. This is a conspicuous product (Wang and Chen, 2004; Hamin and Elliott, 2006), available in domestic manufacturing of the countries observed (Balabanis and Diamantopoulos, 2004). The existence of domestic alternatives is important in studying the role of CE in affecting consumer preferences, since 'if a domestically manufactured product is not available, the ethnocentric consumer will have no choice but to purchase imported goods' (Watson and Wright, 2000, p. 1153). It is also a typical symbol of 'made in Italy'.

Methodology

We used the questionnaire technique to collect data. We asked respondents to estimate, on a seven-point Likert scale, their personal degree of agreement with the statements detailed in the questionnaire. To generate the items, we conducted an extensive literature review (see Table 2.1). Then the questionnaire was back-translated (Italian to English; English to Spanish/Chinese). Questionnaires were administered face-to-face, with randomly selected actual consumers, in a number of towns for each country investigated.

The two samples of consumers are analysed separately. The first sample is composed of Spanish consumers, the second of Chinese consumers (see Table 2.2).

EMPIRICAL RESULTS

Table 2.3 shows means and standard deviations of each of the variables of the proposed model, separately for the two analysed countries. Each variable corresponds to the mean of the scores of each single item belonging to that variable.

Both Chinese and Spanish consumers have an overall positive image of Italy as a country, showing a CI rating above 4. In particular, Chinese consumers show a slightly higher level of CI (4.56) compared to Spanish consumers (4.30). The difference between the consumers' perception of the two analysed countries increases for the other two dimensions of the COO construct: PCI and CRPI. Chinese consumers acknowledge a much better ability and expertise of Italy as a manufacturer (PCI equals to 4.68) compared to Spanish people (3.61). Moreover, the excellent and good reputation of Italy as a shoe manufacturer (CRPI) is fully acknowledged by Chinese consumers (4.73), whereas Spanish consumers rate this characteristic on a much lower level (3.20).

Both Chinese and Spanish consumers evaluate the variable FIT on a level around the mean value of the measurement scale, even though in this case Chinese consumers also show a higher predisposition (3.60), compared to Spanish (3.36), to acknowledge the congruity between the product (shoes) and the country of origin (Italy). As regards the ethnocentrism characterising the two samples, in both cases this variable is not very high (China = 3.08; Spain = 3.38). Finally, consistent with previous

Table 2.1   Items of the questionnaire

Variables	Items	References
CI	This country has a high level of technological research	Martin & Eroglu (1993),
	This country is a producer of high-quality products	Pappu et al. (2007)
	This country has a high standard of living	
	This country has high labour costs	
	This country has an excellent welfare system	
	This country has high levels of industrialization	
	This country has a government free of military influence	
	This country has a highly developed economy	
	This country has a good level of education (literate)	
	This country has a free-market system	
	This country is a democratic country	
PCI	Excellent quality workmanship	Martin & Eroglu (1993),
	Technically advanced	Häubl (1996),
	Innovative	Pappu et al. (2007)
	Pride in ownership products from this country	
	Supported by lots of advertising	
	Recognizable brand names	
	Reliable	
	Expensive	
	High status	
	Excellent finish	
	Dependable	
	Up-market	
CRPI	Excellent quality workmanship	Martin & Eroglu (1993),
	Technically advanced	Pappu et al. (2007)
	Innovative	
	Pride in ownership products from this country	
	Supported by lot of advertising	
	Recognizable brand names	
	Reliable	
	Expensive	
	High status	
	Excellent finish	
	Dependable	
	Up-market	

Table 2.1   (continued)

Variables	Items	References
FIT	Illogical/logical Unnatural/natural Inappropriate/appropriate	Hamzaoui & Merunka (2006), Essoussi & Merunka (2007)
CE	A good citizen does NOT buy foreign products It is NOT right to purchase foreign products because it puts out of jobs We should purchase products manufactured in our country instead of letting other countries get rich off us We should buy from foreign countries only those products that we cannot obtain within our own country	Shimp & Sharma (1987), Ouellet (2007)
INT	I would be willing to buy Italian shoes in case I need that product I would like to own Italian shoes I will likely buy Italian shoes in my next buying of shoes	Roth & Romeo (1992), Wang & Yang (2008)

Table 2.2   *The demographic characteristics of the respondents*

	Spain	China
Sample	162	150
Gender		
% men	46.3	55.4
% women	53.7	44.6
Age	40.39 (std: 16.22)	29.46 (std: 8.54)

evaluations, interviewees show a high intention to buy the product (Italian shoes). This is particularly true for Chinese consumers (4.25) compared to Spanish consumers (3.66).

A structural equation model was then used to test our proposed theoretical framework. The LISREL 8.7 program was employed for this purpose (Jöreskog and Sörbom, 1999). In all cases the reliabilities of the measures are above the recommended value of 0.70 (Nunnally and Bernstein, 1994;

Table 2.3   Means (std. deviations) and analysis of variance (ANOVA) results

	China	Spain	F-value, p.
CI	4.65 (0.99)	4.30 (0.95)	$F(1, 307) = 10.10$ $p < 0.05$
PCI	4.68 (1.00)	3.61 (1.00)	$F(1, 308) = 89.25$ $p < 0.05$
CRPI	4.73 (1.13)	3.20 (1.04)	$F(1, 310) = 156.38$ $p < 0.05$
FIT	3.60 (1.46)	3.36 (1.40)	$F(1, 308) = 58.77$ $p < 0.05$
CE	3.08 (1.59)	3.38 (1.90)	$F(1, 307) = 2.22$ $p > 0.05$
INT	4.25 (1.49)	3.66 (1.52)	$F(1, 310) = 11.81$ $p < 0.05$

Table 2.4   Results (standardized values)

		Causal links		China	Spain
H1	CI	→	PCI	0.67	0.74
H3	CI	→	CRI	−0.05*	−0.06*
H2	PCI	→	CRPI	0.72	0.79
H4	FIT	→	CRPI	0.34	0.29
H5	CE	→	CI	−0.11*	−0.17
H6	CE	→	PCI	−0.02*	−0.10*
H7	CE	→	CRPI	−0.06*	−0.15
H8	CRPI	→	INT	0.66	0.71
		R^2 CI		0.01**	0.03**
		R^2 PCI		0.45	0.53
		R^2 CRPI		0.59	0.68
		R^2 INT		0.44	0.51

Notes:
*   The link is not statistically significant
**   The R^2 of the variable CI is low because we hypothesized only one causal link between this variable and its antecedent; i.e., CE.

α CI: 0.90; α PCI: 0.94; α PRCI: 0.96; α FIT: 0.92; α ethnocentrism: 0.92; α INT: 0.88).

The proposed model has been analysed separately for the two samples. Results of the estimate of the proposed model are detailed in Table 2.4. Regarding the global fit of the model (Spain = chi² (937): 3235.60; root mean square error of approximation (RMSEA): 0.08; NNFI: 0.87; CFI: 0.87; China = chi²(937): 1956.96; RMSEA: 0.08; NNFI: 0.94; CFI: 0.95) the goodness-of-fit measures prove that the model fits the data well and the average variance extracted for the latent variables were adequate in each sample.

Findings show how all significant relationships between latent constructs are in the hypothesized direction, providing evidence supporting the hypothesized model. Results highlight the importance in both contexts of the relationships between CI, PCI, CRPI and INT, corroborating the effect exerted by the country of origin of a product on Spanish and Chinese consumers' intention to buy that product (that is, Italian shoes), as well as the effect of FIT on CRPI. So, H1, H2, H4 and H8 are verified. On the contrary, in this study the relationship between CI and CRPI is not statistically significant in both contexts (H3 is rejected), and CE seems to play a role, negative, only in the Spanish context, affecting the variables CI and CRPI. Thus H5 and H7 are only partially verified and H6 is rejected.

DISCUSSION AND MANAGERIAL IMPLICATIONS

The study reported in this chapter contributes to the evolution of the scientific knowledge on the COO effect proposing and testing a theoretical model enabling the appreciation of the contribution of the COO construct's dimensions on consumers' intention to buy products and proving its applicability to different country contexts. The relationship between the constructs has resulted in a linear causal link as CI does not reveal any significant effect on CRPI. Thus the rejection of H3 supports an incremental stage view in the impact of COO on consumer buying intentions. Standardized values are particularly high, giving evidence of the strength of these relationships. Our results also confirm the positive contribution of FIT on CRPI, showing that the congruity between one product and its origin contributes to reinforce the impact of COO on consumer intention to buy products.

Our research outcomes are also particularly interesting because we compare the different impact of CE on the COO dimensions within two countries featuring very different socio-economic contexts. The prevailing literature widely recognizes the higher consumer evaluation associated with products that originate from HICs compared with those sourced from NICs (Kaynak and Kara, 2002; Balabanis and Diamantopoulos, 2004; Wang and Chen, 2004; Ahmed and d'Astous, 2007). For some authors this evaluation is related to the level of CE (Wang and Chen, 2004; Ahmed and d'Astous, 2007). Wang and Chen (2004) point out that, even if CE and CI are both considered to assess consumer behaviour, the former is a significant interpreter of intention to buy only when the product has been manufactured in NICs. On the contrary, the ethnocentric tendency is less significant when the consumer estimates a product originated from a country with a higher positive image (generally, HICs). 'In other words, in a developing country, a consumer with strong ethnocentric tendencies may not necessarily perceive domestic products as being of higher quality than imports, even though she/he rejects foreign products on moral grounds' (Wang and Chen, 2004, p. 293).

In our model, this CE effect is reflected to product image (CRPI) rather than intention to buy. It means that the impact of CE on CRPI is weak (in our study it is non-significant) in China because Chinese consumers do not perceive domestic products of higher quality than imported ones. They ascribe to Italian shoes symbolic meanings of social status.

In the same way, the effect of ethnocentrism is counteracted for Spanish consumers who tend to have a better opinion of their products. This perception enhances the negative influence of the ethnocentric tendency on the image of Italian shoes (CRPI). In sum, the effect of the CE tendency on the evaluation of foreign products is insignificant in China (NIC) and significant in Spain (HIC; Wang and Chen, 2004).

Chinese and Spanish consumers have an overall positive image of Italy as a country, while people from an emerging country like China possess a better perception of Italy as a manufacturer, of shoes in particular. The evaluations around the mean value of the measurement scale given by Spanish consumers could be explained by the fact that the production of shoes in Spain is quite important as an industry. Spanish consumers tend to give a higher evaluation of their own ability to produce products in general and this acts as a reinforcement of the prejudice. Accordingly, findings show that CE acts as a bias for Spanish people but not for Chinese consumers.

Managers of both local and foreign brands can make use of these findings to position their offerings appropriately in China and Spain. These are interesting markets not only for the internal capacity of absorption of the local demand, but also because they are quite important countries of production of the specific product category under observation, namely shoes. Our findings offer in particular useful information to the Italian companies interested in extending and consolidating their presence in foreign markets, specifically the Chinese and Spanish ones. In the former market, Italian companies should show the Italian origin of the products, especially by planning communication strategies and/or product policies able to immediately represent the country derivation, for example employing Italian names, colours and symbols. On the other hand, in the Spanish market Italian entrepreneurs should choose to push on different marketing strategies and tools. Accordingly, the decision to de localize the production in China to take advantage of the local demand should be taken with caution.

Last but not least, our findings could be particularly interesting for the national institutions supporting and promoting the development of Italian companies internationally. National and local agencies, entrepreneurs' unions and so forth could in fact possess the economic capacity and marketing vision and ability to effectively use marketing tools in order to create collective brands and support their national production with large communication campaigns leading to Italian origin, in particular in the product category sector under investigation – that of shoes – composed of numerous very low-scale enterprises.

LIMITATIONS AND FURTHER RESEARCH DIRECTIONS

The study reported in this chapter contributes to the advancement of the COO literature. Nevertheless, it also possesses some limitations that should be considered in conducting future research.

Methodologically, we adopt a single-cue approach as we aim at giving a comprehensive view of the relationships within the three dimensions of the COO's construct and the buying behaviour of Spanish and Chinese consumers. But when COO is the only information cue observed, its effect on consumer attitudes might be diluted (Agrawal and Kamakura, 1999). So, to achieve a better understanding of this topic, future research should take into account other features – such as price, quality, brand, and so on – rather than solely the country of origin (Insch and McBride, 2004). Moreover, in the study described in this chapter Italy's country image has been considered as a unique construct, without distinguishing between the different dimensions that constitute it: economic, political and technological (Martin and Eroglu, 1993). Measuring the importance of these dimensions could improve the knowledge of the CI construct's formation.

Subsequently, our research focuses only on the cognitive dimensions of COO cues, while some studies also encompass affective facets, like consumer affinity (Oberecker et al., 2008).

The scientific and managerial implications derived from our findings could also vary in relation to possible moderating factors, such as the level of familiarity with the countries observed and the product investigated, as well as some demographic variables (education, age, gender, and so on). As our study did not take these moderators into account, it could be interesting to include them in future papers. Accordingly, the antecedents of the CE construct – that is, demographic variables, consumer affinity and involvement, perceived economic threat, and so forth (Sharma et al., 1995; Watson and Wright, 2000; Javalgi et al., 2005; Ahmed and d'Astous, 2007; Oberecker and Diamantopoulos, 2011) – could also be considered.

Finally, we are aware that the results of this study could also be addressed by the specific product category observed (Balabanis and Diamantopoulos, 2004, p. 82). Thus applying the model to some other merchandise with different levels of complexity and consumer decision-making process involvement and commitment could strengthen the model validity (Ittersum et al., 2003). Hence country image can vary by the countries investigated: extending the analysis to other national contexts could allow a better generalization of these results.

REFERENCES

Aaker, D.A. and K.L. Keller (1990), 'Consumer evaluations of brand extensions', *Journal of Marketing*, **54** (1), 27–41.

Agrawal, J. and W. Kamakura (1999), 'Country of origin: a competitive advantage?', *International Journal of Research in Marketing*, **16** (4), 255–267.

Ahmed, S.A. and A. d'Astous (2007), 'Moderating effect of nationality on country-of-origin perceptions: English-speaking Thailand versus French-speaking Canada', *Journal of Business Research*, **60** (3), 240–248.

Ahmed, Z., J.P. Johnson, X. Yang, C. Fatt, H. Teng and L.C. Boon (2004), 'Does country of origin matter for low-involvement products?', *International Marketing Review*, **21** (1), 102–120.

Amine, L.S., M. Chao and M. Arnold (2005), 'Exploring the practical effects of country of origin, animosity, and price-quality issues: two case studies of Taiwan and Acer in China', *Journal of International Marketing*, **13** (2), 114–150.

Balabanis, G. and A. Diamantopoulos (2004), 'Domestic country bias, country-of-origin effects, and consumer ethnocentrism: a multidimensional unfolding approach', *Journal of Academy of Marketing Science*, **32** (1), 80–95.

Bandyopadhyay, S., N. Wongtada and G. Rice (2011), 'Measuring the impact of inter-attitudinal conflict on consumer evaluations of foreign products', *Journal of Consumer Marketing*, **28** (3), 211–224.

Bilkey, W.J. and E. Nes (1982), 'Country-of-origin effects on product evaluations', *Journal of International Business Studies*, **8** (1), 89–91.

Cervino, J., J. Sanchez and J.M. Cubillo (2005), 'Made in effect, competitive marketing strategy and brand performance: an empirical analysis of Spanish brands', *The Journal of American Academy of Business, Cambridge*, **2**, 237–243.

Chasin, J.B., H.H. Hartmut and D.J. Eugene (1988), 'Stereotyping, buyer familiarity and ethnocentrism: a cross-cultural analysis', *Journal of International Consumer Marketing*, **1** (2), 9–25.

Chattalas, M., T. Kramer and H. Takada (2008), 'The impact of national stereotypes on the country of origin effect: a conceptual framework', *International Marketing Research*, **25** (1), 54–74.

Chryssochoidis, G., A. Krystallis and P. Perreas (2007), 'Ethnocentric beliefs and country-of-origin (COO) effect: impact of country, product and product attributes on Greek consumers' evaluation of food products', *European Journal of Marketing*, **41** (11/12), 1518–1544.

Essoussi, L.H. and D. Merunka (2007), 'Consumers' product evaluations in emerging markets: does country of design, country of manufacturer, or brand image matter?', *International Marketing Review*, **24** (4), 409–426.

Gurhan-Canli, Z. and D. Maheswaran (2000), 'Cultural variations in country-of-origin effects', *Journal of Marketing Research*, **37** (3), 309–317.

Hamin, H. and G. Elliot (2006), 'A less-developed country perspective of consumer ethnocentrism and "country of origin" effects: Indonesian evidence', *Asia Pacific Journal of Marketing and Logistics*, **18** (2), 79–92.

Hamzaoui, L. and D. Merunka (2006), 'The impact of country of design and country of manufacture on consumer perceptions of bi-national products' quality: an empirical model based on the concept of fit', *Journal of Consumer Marketing*, **23** (3), 145–155.

Han, C.M. (1989), 'Country image: halo or summary construct?', *Journal of Marketing Research*, **26** (2), 222–229.

Häubl, G. (1996), 'A cross-national investigation of the effects of country of origin and brand name on the evaluation of a new car', *International Marketing Review*, **13** (5), 76–97.

Heslop, L.A., N. Papadopoulos, M. Dowdels, M. Wall and D. Compeau (2004), 'Who controls the purse strings: a study of consumers' and retail buyers' reactions in an America's FTYA environment', *Journal of Business Research*, **57** (210), 1177–1188.

Hui, M. and L. Zhou (2003), 'Country-of-manufacture effects for known brands', *European Journal of Marketing*, **37** (1–2), 133–153.

Insch, G.S. and J.B. McBride (2004), 'The impact of country-of-origin cues on consumer perceptions of product quality: a bi-national test of the decomposed country-of-origin construct', *Journal of Business Research*, **57** (3), 256–265.

Ittersum, K.V., M.J. Candel and M.T.G. Meulenberg (2003), 'The influence of the image of a product's region of origin on product evaluation', *Journal of Business Research*, **56** (3), 215–226.

Jaffe, E.D. and I.D. Nebenzahl (1993), 'Global promotion of country image: do the Olympics count?', in N. Papadopoulos and L.A. Heslop (eds), *Product–Country Images: Impact and Role in International Marketing*, New York: International Business Press, pp. 433–452.

Javalgi, R.G., V.P. Khare, A.C. Gross and R.F. Scherer (2005), 'An application of the consumer ethnocentrism model to French consumers', *International Business Review*, **14** (3), 325–344.

Jöreskog, K.G. and D. Sörbom (eds) (1999), *LISREL 8. Structural Equation Modelling with the SIMPLIS Command Language*, Lincolnwood: Scientific Software International.

Kaynak, E. and A. Kara (2002), 'Consumer perceptions of foreign products: an analysis of product-country images and ethnocentrism', *European Journal of Marketing*, **36** (7/8), 928–949.

Keller, K.L. (1993), 'Conceptualizing, measuring, and managing customer-based brand equity', *Journal of Marketing*, **57** (1), 1–17.

Knight, G.A. and R.J. Calantone (2000), 'A flexible model of consumer country-of-origin perceptions: a cross-cultural investigation', *International Marketing Review*, **17** (2), 127–45.

Laroche, M., N. Papadopoulos, L. Heslop and J. Bergeron (2005), 'Effect of subcultural differences on country and product evaluations', *International Marketing Review*, **22** (1), 96–115.

Lee, D. and G. Ganesh (1999), 'Effects of partitioned country image in the context of brand image and familiarity', *International Marketing Review*, **16** (1), 18–39.

Li, Z.G., S. Fu and L.W. Murray (1997), 'Country and product images: the perceptions of consumers in the People's Republic of China', *Journal of International Consumer Marketing*, **10** (1/2), 115–139.

Liu, S.S. and K.F. Johnson (2005), 'The automatic country-of-origin effect on brand judgments', *Journal of Advertising*, **34** (1), 87–98.

Martin, I.M. and S. Eroglu (1993), 'Measuring a multi-dimensional construct: country image', *Journal of Business Research*, **28** (3), 191–210.

Nagashima, A. (1970), 'A comparison of Japanese and US attitudes toward foreign products', *Journal of Marketing*, **34** (1), 68–74.

Nagashima, A. (1977), 'Comparative "made in" product image survey among Japanese businessmen', *Journal of Marketing*, **41** (3), 95–100.

Nunnally, J.C. and I.H. Bernstein (1994), *Psychometric Theory* (3rd edn), New York: McGraw-Hill.

Oberecker, E.M. and A. Diamantopoulos (2011), 'Consumers' emotional bonds with foreign countries: does consumer affinity effect behavioral intentions?', *Journal of International Marketing*, **19** (2), 45–72.

Oberecker, E.M., P. Riefler and A. Diamantopoulos (2008), 'The consumer affinity construct: conceptualization, qualitative investigation, and research agenda', *Journal of International Marketing*, **16** (3), 23–56.

Ouellet, J.F. (2007), 'Consumer racism and its effects on domestic cross-ethnic product purchase: an empirical test in the United States, Canada, and France', *Journal of Marketing*, **71** (1), 113–128.

Papadopoulos, N. and L.A. Heslop (eds) (1993), *Product–Country Images: Impact and Role in International Marketing*, New York: International Business Press.

Papadopoulos, N. and L.A. Heslop (2002), 'Country equity and country branding: problems and prospects', *Journal of Brand Management*, **9** (4/5), 294–314.

Papadopoulos, N. and L.A. Heslop (2003), 'Country equity and product–country images: state-of-the-art in research and implications', in S.C. Jain (ed.), *Handbook of Research in International Marketing*, Cheltenham, UK and Northampton, MA, USA: Edward Elgar, pp. 402–433.

Pappu, R., P.G. Quester and R.W. Cooksey (2007), 'Consumer-based brand equity: improving the measurement – empirical evidence', *Journal of Product & Brand Management*, **14** (2–3), 143–54.

Park, W., S. Milberg and R. Lawson (1991), 'Evaluation of brand extensions: the role of product feature similarity and brand concept consistency', *Journal of Consumer Research*, **18** (2), 185–193.

Pisharodi, R.M. and R. Parameswaran (1992), 'Confirmatory factor analysis of a country-of-origin scale: initial results', *Journal of Advertising Consumer Research*, **19** (2), 706–714.

Roth, K.P. and A. Diamantopoulos (2009), 'Advancing the country image construct', *Journal of Business Research*, **62**, 726–40.

Roth, M.S. and J.B. Romeo (1992), 'Matching product category and country image perceptions: a framework for managing country-of-origin effects, behavioral intentions model', *Journal of International Business Studies*, **23** (3), 477–497.

Sharma, S., T.A. Shimp and J. Shin (1995), 'Consumer ethnocentrism: a test of antecedents and moderators', *Journal of the Academy of Marketing Science*, **23** (1), 26–37.

Shimp, T.A. and S. Sharma (1987), 'Consumer ethnocentrism: construction and validation of the CETSCALE', *Journal of Marketing Research*, **24** (3), 280–289.

Speece, M. and D.P. Nguyen (2005), 'Countering negative country-of-origin with low prices: a conjoint study in Vietnam', *Journal of Product & Brand Management*, **14** (1), 39–48.

Sumner, W.G. (1906), *Folkways: The Sociological Importance of Usages, Manners, Customs, Mores and Morals*, New York: Ginn & Co.

Wang, C.L. and Z.X. Chen (2004), 'Consumer ethnocentrism and willingness to buy domestic products in a developing country setting: testing moderating effects', *Journal of Consumer Marketing*, **21** (6), 391–400.

Wang, C. and C. Lamb (1983), 'The impact of selected environmental forces upon consumers' willingness to buy foreign products', *Journal of the Academy of Marketing Science*, **11** (2), 71–84.

Wang, X. and Z. Yang (2008), 'A meta-analysis of effect sizes in international marketing experiments', *International Marketing Review*, **25** (3), 276–291.

Watson, J.J. and K. Wright (2000), 'Consumer ethnocentrism and attitudes toward domestic and foreign products', *European Journal of Marketing*, **34** (9/10), 1149–1166.

Zhang, Y. (1996), 'Chinese consumers' evaluation of origin products: the influence of culture, product type, and product presentation format', *European Journal of Marketing*, **30** (12), 50–69.

3. Tourism experience, country image and post-visit intentions: a study on international tourists in Italy

**Alessandro De Nisco, Giada Mainolfi,
Vittoria Marino and Maria Rosaria Napolitano**

1. INTRODUCTION

Country image is recognized as one of the most relevant research streams in the international marketing literature. Recent reviews estimate the number of journal articles published in this field at over the 1000 mark with an increase of about 150 percent over less than a decade (Roth and Diamantopoulos, 2009; Papadopoulos, 2011). Results from this large body of knowledge seems to provide reliable support to the notion that country image can be considered as an extrinsic cue, similar to price and brand name, which can be used by consumers to draw inferences in making product evaluations (Eroglu and Machleit, 1989; Kotler and Gertner, 2002). In such instances, research dealing with the effects of country image on buyers' behavior toward products associated with various origins is usually referred as product country image (PCI) (Papadopoulos, 2004).

The role of place image on consumer behavior has also been investigated in the field of tourism, where it has mostly been conceptualized in term of tourism destination image (TDI). Such construct refers to the effects of beliefs, ideas and impressions that a person has of a destination (Kotler et al., 1993). Starting from the 1970s, research on TDI has resulted in more than 200 published articles (Elliot et al., 2011). According to a review from Gallarza et al. (2002) the most investigated topics include the conceptualization and measurement of destination image (Hunt, 1975; Echtner and Ritchie, 1993), the influence of image on traveler choice (Woodside and Lysonski, 1989; Pearce, 1982), its formation (Baloglu and McCleary, 1999; Gartner, 1993), and destination image management policies (Echtner and Ritchie, 2003).

Although both PCI and TDI are well developed research streams and they both investigate how perceived images affect consumer decisions, so

65

far academic literature is still lacking in clarifying the nature of interaction between them. The relationship between country image, tourism and national products has been investigated by Kleppe and Mossberg (2005) – albeit found adopting an empirical approach – and by Hallberg (2005), who found that international travel experiences lead to changes in consumers' attitudes toward products made in the sojourn country. In a recent work Elliot et al. (2011) stated that components of country image (affective and cognitive) are able to affect both product attitudes and destination beliefs and that such beliefs, in turn, play a significant role in influencing product and destination receptivity. However, although such studies contribute to shed some light on the existence of a 'cross' effect between country image, tourism and attitudes towards the national products, at present it could be argued that the overall understanding of the nature and role of such relationship remain still unclear.

This chapter aims at extending this stream of research by investigating: (a) the influence of tourist satisfaction on perception of general country image (GCI) and of tourism destination image (TDI); (b) the influence of GCI on TDI and (c) the influence of GCI and TDI on post-visit behavioural intentions towards the country as a tourism destination and toward its national products.

The proposed research framework is tested on a sample of international tourists intercepted in two international airports (Naples and Rome) at the end of their journey to Italy. On the basis of results, this chapter concludes with discussion of its theoretical contribution to country image and tourism destination image literature and provides managerial implications for both public sector and national companies.

2. THEORETICAL BACKGROUND AND HYPOTHESES

From the theoretical point of view, the research model proposed in this study builds on literature dealing with the influence of travel experience on place image formation (Papadopoulos and Heslop, 1986; Gartner and Hunt, 1987; Echtner and Ritchie, 1993; Hallberg, 2005) and with the relationship between country image and post-visit attitudes (Mansfeld, 1992; Bigné et al., 2001). Moreover it extends concepts and issues included in the 'integrative model of place image' recently developed by Elliot et al. (2011).

The structure of the model is represented in Figure 3.1. The main underlining hypothesis is that perceived results of tourism experience have a positive influence on the general components of country image (cogni-

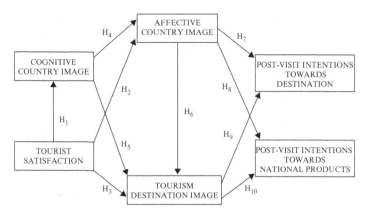

Figure 3.1   The theoretical model and research hypotheses

tive and affective) and on the specific components of tourism destination image and that such images, in turn, are able to predict post-visit intentions toward the country. As a consequence, constructs presented in the model are: (a) tourism satisfaction (TS), defined as 'the extent of overall pleasure or contentment felt by the visitor, resulting from the ability of the trip experience to fulfil the visitor's desire, expectations and needs in relation to the trip' (Chen and Tsai, 2007); (b) general country image (GCI), defined as 'a generic construct consisting of generalized images created not only by representative products but also by the degree of economic and political maturity, historical events and relationships, culture and traditions, and the degree of technological virtuosity and industrialization' (Roth and Diamatopoulos, 2009, p.727) and identified through the cognitive components (cognitive country image) and the affective components (affective country image) (Allred et al., 1999; Roth and Diamantopoulos, 2009; Elliot et al., 2011); (c) tourism destination image (TDI), which includes the beliefs and judgements regarding the country as a tourism destination (Echtner and Ritchie, 2003); and (d) post-visit intentions, evaluated both in term of intention to return and positive word of mouth towards the country as a tourism destination and in term of post-visit consumption attitudes towards the national products. In the following sections we illustrate the research hypotheses and we describe the related theoretical assumptions.

2.1   The Influence of Tourism Satisfaction (TS) on the General Country Image (GCI) and on Tourism Destination Image (TDI)

Whereas the influence of familiarity on perception of country image and product evaluation has been extensively investigated in the product country image literature (Han, 1989; Johansson, 1989; Knight and Colantone, 2000; Jaffe and Nebenzahl, 2001), there are very few studies dealing with the effect of tourism experience on country image perception (Jaffe and Nebenzahl, 2001). Research on this topic has examined the image differences between travelers who have visited a destination (visitors) and those who did not (Chon, 1991; Fakeye and Crompton, 1991; Hu and Ritchie, 1993). Other research has investigated image modifications due to actual destination experience (overt behavior) through a longitudinal approach aiming to compare pre- and post-trip perceptions. For example, Pearce (1982) compares tourists' images of two Mediterranean countries across a pre- and post-visit stage and found that travelers changed some of their perceptions after visiting them. Papadopoulos and Heslop (1986) studied the possible relationship between the international travel experience and visitors' attitudes and found that, under certain circumstances, international travel can lead to positive attitudes towards the sojourn country and its products. Finally, Hallberg (2005) analysed the effect of travel experience on cognitive and affective attitudes towards the sojourn country and found a positive correlation with intention to purchase the national products and related consumption behavior (i.e. information seeking, frequency of purchasing, etc.).

General results from these studies show that when individuals actually visit a place the image that they form after the visit tends to be more realistic and complex and that such an image is able to affect attitudes toward the country. However, so far there are no studies aiming to investigate how perceived quality of the tourism experience is able to influence evaluation of country image. Moreover, research on this topic does not clarify how international travel is able to affect the specific components related to both general country image and to specific tourism destination image.

Following the above, in our study we hypothesize the existence of a causal link between tourism satisfaction (TS), cognitive and affective components of general country image (GCI) and tourism destination image (TDI), which refers to judgements pertinent to the image of the country as a tourism destination.

Therefore we hypothesize that:

H_1: *Tourist satisfaction has a positive influence on the cognitive components of the general country image.*

H_2: *Tourist satisfaction has a positive influence on the affective components of the general country image.*

H_3: *Tourism satisfaction has a positive influence on tourist destination image.*

2.2 The Influence of General Country Image (GCI) on Tourism Destination Image (TDI)

Both literature on PCI and literature on TDI provide support to the notion that country image is a multi-dimensional construct. In PCI, a number of authors suggest that country image construct comprises: a cognitive component, which includes consumers' beliefs about a particular country; an affective component, that describes the country's emotional value to the consumer; and a conative component, which captures consumers' behavioral intentions toward the sourcing country (Laroche et al., 2005; Papadopoulos et al., 1990; Parameswaran and Pisharodi, 1994). Moreover, the overall body of PCI research supports the existence of a hierarchical relationship between the components of general country image and specific product beliefs (e.g. Papadopoulos, 1986; Parameswaran and Yaprak, 1987; Knight and Colantone, 2000; De Nisco, 2006; Mainolfi, 2010; Roth and Diamantopoulos, 2009).

Although based on more limited empirical evidence, studies on tourism destination image show very similar patterns. As stated by Baloglu and McCleary (1999) and by Beerli and Martin (2004), destination image can be considered as the consequence of two closely interrelated components: the perceptive/cognitive evaluations, which refers to the individual's own knowledge and beliefs about the object, and affective appraisals, which refers to the individual's feelings towards the object. In addition, the literature shows consensus about the cognitive component being an antecedent of the affective component (Russel and Pratt, 1980; Baloglu and McCleary, 1999; Kim and Yoon, 2003) and about the effect of affective and cognitive components on destination beliefs. (Gartner, 1993; Beerli and Martin, 2004; Nadeau et al., 2008; Elliot et al., 2011).

Arising from the above, in this chapter we consider GCI as the result of cognitive and affective components and as an antecedents of TDI. Moreover, we assume the existence of a causal relationship between cognitive and affective components of GCI.

We therefore hypothesize that:

H_4: *The cognitive component of country image has a positive effect on the affective component of country image.*

H_5: *The cognitive component of country image has a positive influence on the tourism destination image.*

H_6: *The affective component of country image has a positive influence on the tourism destination image.*

2.3   The Influence of General Country Image (GCI) and Tourism Destination Image (TDI) on Post-Visit Behavioral Intentions

The notion that components of country image are able to affect consumption intentions constitutes a fundamental principle in PCI and in TDI literature. As for the former, results seems to suggest that affective components of country image play a more significant role in influencing consumers' evaluation of national products than cognitive components (Parameswaran and Pisharodi, 1994; Laroche et al., 2005; Roth and Diamantopoulos, 2009). Such an assumption is also consistent with various studies in other disciplines such as advertising or retailing, showing that emotions can lead to much stronger reactions than pure cognitions (Donovan and Rossiter, 1982; Aylesworth and MacKenzie, 1998; Schoefer and Diamantopoulos, 2008). As for the latter, tourism image has been found in a number of studies to be a direct antecedent of intention to return and willingness to recommend the destination (Court and Lupton, 1997; Bigné et al., 2001; Park and Njite, 2010). In spite of the consistent similarities in results, only a few studies have investigated whether any 'cross' effects exist; that is, whether components of general country image are able to influence travel choices and, vice versa, whether perception of destination image affects consumption attitudes towards the national products.

However, results from this limited body of research seem to provide a significant support to this relationship, even if the nature and role of place image remains fragmented. For example, Papadopoulos and Heslop (1986) compared Canadians who had traveled to a country with those who had not and found that the two groups differed in how they evaluated that country's products but they did not investigate the effect on attitudes towards the destination. On the other hand, the link between general country image and destination attitudes was explored by Nadeu et al. (2008), but they did not include product measures in their study. The only research that aims to provide a clear picture about the potential interactions between tourism, products and country image is the one by Elliot et al. (2011). Their empirical results show that affective country image exerts a positive influence on both product receptivity and on destination receptivity. In addition, they provide evidence of a direct effect from product belief to product receptivity and from destination belief to destination receptivity and find a crossover effect from product beliefs to destination receptivity but not the other way around. However, results from their study could be affected by the specific target countries (Japan and USA) and by the specific sample involved in their survey (consumers attending a major travel show in South Korea). As a consequence authors suggest that 'different sample and target country combinations may produce different results' (Elliot et al., 2011, p. 11).

Following the above, in this chapter we hypothesize that affective components of general country image and specific components of tourism destination image are able to influence tourists' post-visit behavioral intentions toward the country as a destination – in terms of intention to visit the country again and of positive word of mouth – and lead to more positive intentions toward the national products, in terms of willingness to purchase and positive word of mouth.

We therefore propose that:

H_7: *The affective component of country image has a positive influence on post-visit behavioural intentions toward the sojourn country.*

H_8: *The affective component of country image has a positive influence on post-visit consumption behavioural intentions toward the products made in the sojourn country.*

H_9: *The tourism destination image has a positive influence on post-visit behavioural intentions toward the sojourn country.*

H_{10}: *The tourism destination image has a positive influence on post-visit behavioural intentions toward the sojourn country.*

3. METHODOLOGY AND RESULTS

In order to test the proposed model a survey was conducted in two international airports (Naples and Rome) on a sample of foreign tourists intercepted in the departure area before leaving Italy. Respondents were identified via random systematic sample by trained students, and interviews were based on a self-report questionnaire. A preliminary question served to select respondents who were in Italy for tourism purposes. The research instrument was a structured questionnaire written in English and organized in three sections: (i) tourist experience, place image and post-visit intentions; (ii) attitudes and familiarity towards the Italian products; (iii) general demographic information. The questionnaire was preliminarily tested on a small sample and minor changes were made in the measures according to results.

At the end of the survey, 542 questionnaires were coded for data analysis. The sample demographics indicate that respondents were both male (51.2 percent) and female (48.8 percent). The largest proportion of the respondents were aged between 35–44 (34.9 percent) and 25–34 (27.7 percent). The most represented countries include England (22.2 percent), USA (12.8 percent), France (10 percent), Germany (8.4 percent), Spain (7.8 percent) and Russia (5.2 percent). In terms of destination familiarity, a significant portion of respondents (36.9 percent) was in Italy for the first time, 26.2 percent had visited the country once in the past, while only 8.4 percent had been to Italy more than five times. In terms of products' consumption behavior, 53.7 percent of respondents reported that country of origin is 'very important' in their consumption choices and 38.9 percent 'somewhat important'. Almost 80 percent of respondents (79.7 percent) had already bought or tried Italian products in the past.

Model constructs were measured on the basis of scales adapted from similar studies in the field of tourist satisfaction, product–country image and tourism destination image (Table 3.1). Namely, tourist satisfaction was assessed through an eight point Likert scale built on the basis of items provided by Baker and Crompton (2000) and Bigné et al. (2001). Components of country image – cognitive country image (CCI), affective country image (ACI) and tourism destination image (TDI) – as a consequence of the tourism experience were measured on the basis of contributions provided by Papadopoulos et al. (1988) and Elliot et al. (2011). Finally, post-visit behavioral intentions were measured through measures provided by Cronin et al. (2000), Bigné et al. (2000) and Elliot et al. (2011).

According to Anderson and Gerbing (1988) a two-stage approach was followed in which the measurement model was first confirmed and then tested. In the first stage, it was assessed the internal consistency and reliability of composite measures (Table 3.1). Results provided adequate support to measurement choice: Cronbach's Alpha ranged from 0.71 to 0.86 suggesting that all the latent measures were acceptably reliable. Additionally, with the exception of affective country image, the average variance extracted (AVE) reached the suggested value of 0.50 (Fornell and Larker, 1981; Bagozzi and Yi, 1988).

After confirming the measurement model, the structural model was then tested with maximum likelihood simultaneous estimation procedure. With the exception of χ^2 the main indices show that data fit the structural model reasonably well: namely, AGFI = 0.82, CFI = 0.93 and NNFI = 0.91. As shown in Table 3.2, all the paths are in the hypothesized direction of the proposed model. Namely, tourist satisfaction plays a significant role in influencing perception of country image: empirical findings show that a higher level of tourist satisfaction is strongly related to the improvement of cognitive country image (maximum likelihood estimate = 0.55, t-value = 9.00), affective country image (0.17, 2.68) and destination image (0.41, 2.57), providing support to H_1, H_2 and H_3.

Table 3.1   Model measures and validity check

	Mean (Stand. dev.)	Cronbach Alpha	AVE
Tourist satisfaction		0.80	0.53
In general, I'm very satisfied with this travel experience in Italy	5.98 (0.98)		
This travel experience definitely exceeded my expectations in terms of overall quality and satisfaction	5.66 (0.98)		
In comparison to other similar places I've visited before, Italy is a much better destination for tourism and leisure	5.57 (1.15)		
My choice to make this travel to Italy was a wise one	5.91 (1.26)		
This travel experience in Italy was well worth my time and effort	5.91 (0.93)		
Cognitive country image		0.75	0.50
High quality of life	5.40 (0.93)		
High technology level	5.19 (1.01)		
Advanced education level	5.01 (0.96)		
High wealth	5.30 (0.93)		
Affective country image		0.71	0.46
Friendly people	5.93 (0.97)		
Trustworthy people	5.67 (0.88)		
Pleasant place	5.35 (0.91)		
Safe environment	5.30 (1.01)		
Tourism destination image		0.76	0.55
Attractive scenery	6.27 (0.83)		
High-quality attractions	6.04 (0.88)		
Lots to see and do for tourism	6.14 (0.95)		
Well organized tourism services	5.35 (1.13)		
Post-visit intentions toward the destination		0.78	0.78
I will surely visit Italy again in the future	6.14 (0.99)		
Once at home, I will suggest that my friends visit Italy	6.19 (0.99)		
Post-visit intentions toward Italian products		0.86	0.75
Once at home, I would like to buy more Italian products	4.64 (1.40)		
Once at home, I will suggest that my friends buy Italian products	5.60 (1.37)		

Table 3.2   The hypothesized relationships: standardized coefficients and fit statistics

	Hypothesized Relationships	Standard Coefficients (t-values)	Results
H_1	Tourist satisfaction – cognitive country image	0.55 (9.00)	Supported
H_2	Tourist satisfaction – affective country image	0.17 (2.68)	Supported
H_3	Tourist satisfaction – destination image	0.41 (2.57)	Supported
H_4	Cognitive country image – affective country image	0.67 (7.96)	Supported
H_5	Cognitive country image – destination image	0.33 (2.86)	Supported
H_6	Affective country image – destination image	−0.33 (−0.29)	Not supported
H_7	Affective country image – post-visit intentions toward the destination	0.25 (4.37)	Supported
H_8	Affective country image – post-visit intentions toward the national products	0.23 (3.64)	Supported
H_9	Destination image – post-visit intentions toward the destination	0.38 (6.00)	Supported
H_{10}	Destination image – post-visit intentions toward the national products	0.21 (3.35)	Supported

Fit Statistics:
$\chi^2 = 884.08$ (d.f. 174; $p<0.001$)
AGFI = 0.82; CFI = 0.93; NNFI = 0.91

Consistent with expectations, parameter estimates from path analysis show a significant causal relationship between components of general country image and specific country image. Specifically, tourists' perception of cognitive country image has a positive influence on both affective country image (0.67, 7.96) and on destination image (0.33, 2.86); such results confirm H_4 and H_5. In contrast, H_6 is rejected as the affective country image does not affect destination image (−0.33, n.s.); this result provides support to findings provided by Elliot et al. (2011).

As for the relationship between components of country image and post-visit behavioral intentions, the overall pattern of results provides full confirmation to all the hypothesized relationships. Namely, a positive perception of affective country image and destination image does influence both behavioral intentions towards Italy as a tourism destination (0.25, 4.37; 0.38, 6.00) and desires to buy Italian products (0.23, 3.64; 0.31, 3.35). Such findings support H_7, H_8, H_9 and H_{10}.

4.   CONCLUSIONS AND IMPLICATIONS

The relationship between tourism and country image is of relevant interest both in place marketing literature and for public and private practitioners. The ability of a country to provide high-quality tourism experiences may lead to significant improvements in perceived country image which, in turn, is able to affect post-visit attitudes. Arising from the current findings provided by research on tourist satisfaction, product–country image and tourist destination image, our study proposes and tests a theoretical framework aiming to investigate: (a) the influence of tourism experience on cognitive and affective components of general country image and on specific components of tourism destination image; (b) the relationship between general country image and tourism destination image; and (c) the existence of a 'cross' effect between tourism and consumption intentions towards the national products.

Results from the survey conducted on a sample of international tourists intercepted at the end of their journey in Italy provides support for all the hypothesized relationships with the exception of the link between affective country image and tourism destination image. Such results suggest that general country image and tourism destination image are able to mediate the effect of tourism satisfaction on post-visit behavioural intentions. Moreover, our study supports the notion that a high-quality tourist experience is able to affect not only intention to return and willingness to recommend the country as a tourism destination but is also able to induce more positive intentions toward the products made in the sojourn country. In this way, the existence of a significant interaction between tourism and product image is confirmed.

Following the above, the research model and results presented in this chapter are able to suggest several theoretical and managerial implications. From the research point of view, this is the first study to provide a comprehensive framework aiming to investigate the relationship between tourism satisfaction, country image and post-visit intentions. Previous research on this topic has investigated the image differences between travelers who have visited a destination and those who did not (Fakeye and Crompton, 1991; Milman and Pizam, 1995) or image modifications due to actual destination experience (Pearce, 1982; Papadopoulos and Heslop, 1986; Hallberg, 2005) but none of them have assessed how the results of the tourism experience affect the relationship between the components of country image and post-visit consumption intentions. Moreover, this is one of the few studies to consider country image as a consequence rather than an antecedent of tourism satisfaction. In this way, the proposed model is the first to capture the mediating role of country image on the relationship between tourist experience and post-visit intentions. Finally, this is one of the few studies to investigate the link between tourism, country image and national products in the Italian context. In spite of the significant correlation between the image of Italy, tourism and the promotion of national products so far there is no empirical evidence about the underlying mechanisms of such relationships.

From the managerial point of view, results from our study are able to identify a potentially innovative area of collaboration between national governments and companies for the development of integrated marketing strategies aiming to connect the general country image to the destination image and product image. For example, local companies with a strong image linkage with the country of origin could target the most relevant international tourism markets in their country selection strategies in order to take advantage of the positive perception of the general country image and destination image of Italy. Moreover, they could integrate components of affective country image and tourism destination image in advertising strategies toward such countries. At the other end, national governments could incorporate the image of national products in their 'nation brand' advertising campaigns with the aim of promoting the country and attracting international tourists. Finally, the significant influence of tourist satisfaction on the perception of country and destination image and on related post-visit behavioral intentions provides greater consideration to the role of service quality, not only as a measure of tourism performance but also as an instrument for country promotion.

While this chapter is one of the few to examine the link between tourism satisfaction, country image and post-visit attitudes, it also has a few limitations which, in conjunction with the findings, serve to suggest directions for further research. First, this is a single-country study. Because different contexts were not considered, the validity of the results is limited to the country under investigation. Second, our model does not incorporate familiarity towards the country as a tourism destination. Therefore, results may differ between tourists who have already visited the country one or more times in the past and first-time visitors. Also, familiarity with the national products was not considered. As a consequence, a further study could analyse the moderating role of product and destination familiarity in the relationship between tourist satisfaction, country image perception and post-visit intentions. Third, the model does not assess tourists' heterogeneity with respect to demographic and psychographic variables: since such variables have been found to affect both the relationship between country image and product attitudes (Chao and Rajendran, 1993; Gurhan-Canli and Maheswaran, 2000) and on destination image formation (Baloglu, 1999) they might be the object of subsequent investigation. Finally, another possible area of enquiry is attitude changes over time. For example, a follow-up study could assess tourists' post-travel consumption behavior in order to assess if a positive tourism experience is able to produce long-term effects. Results from this study could provide additional insights into how national companies and policy makers can collaborate in marketing strategies aiming to provide more concrete exposure of national products/brands and tourism destinations in connection with consumers' international travel.

REFERENCES

Allred, A., Chakraborty G. and S.J. Miller (1999), 'Measuring images of developing countries: a scale development study', *Journal of Euromarketing*, **8** (3), 29–49.

Anderson, J.C. and D.W. Gerbing (1988), 'Structural equation modeling in practice: a review and recommended two-step approach', *Psychological Bulletin*, **103** (3), 411–423.

Aylesworth, A.B. and S.B. MacKenzie (1998), 'Context is key: the effect of program-induced mood on thoughts about the ad', *Journal of Advertising*, **27** (Summer), 17–33.

Bagozzi, R. and Y. Yi (1988), 'On the evaluation of structural equation models', *Academy of Marketing Science*, **16** (1), 74–94.

Baker, D.A. and J.L. Crompton (2000), 'Quality, satisfaction and behavioural intentions', *Annals of Tourism Research*, **27** (3), 785–804.

Baloglu, S. (1999), 'A path analytic model of visitation intention involving information sources, socio-psychological motivations and destination images', *Journal of Travel & Tourism Marketing*, **8** (3), 81–90.

Baloglu, S. and K.W. McCleary (1999), 'A model of destination image formation', *Annals of Tourism Research*, **26** (4), 868–897.

Beerli, A. and J.D. Martín (2004), 'Factors influencing destination image', *Annals of Tourism Research*, **31** (3), 657–681.

Bigné, J.E., Sanchez M.I. and J. Sanchez (2001), 'Tourism image, evaluation variables and after purchase behaviour: inter-relationship', *Tourism Management*, **22** (6), 607–616.

Chao, P. and K.N. Rajendran (1993), 'Consumer profiles and perceptions: country-of-origin effects', *International Marketing Review*, **10** (2), 22–39.

Chen, C.F. and D.C. Tsai (2007), 'How destination image and evaluative factors affect behavioral intentions?', *Tourism Management*, **28**, 1115–1122.

Chon, K. (1991), 'Tourism destination image modification process: marketing implications', *Tourism Management*, **12** (1), 68–72.

Cronin, J.J., M.K. Brady and G.T.M Hult (2000), 'Assessing the effects of quality, value, and customer satisfaction on consumer behavioural intentions in service environments, *Journal of Retailing*, **76** (2), 193–218.

Court, B. and R.A. Lupton (1997), 'Customer portfolio development: modelling destination adopters, inactives and rejecters', *Journal of Travel Research*, **36** (1), 35–43.

De Nisco, A. (2006), 'Country-of-origin e buyer behaviour: una meta-analisi della letteratura internazionale', *Mercati e Competitività*, **4**, 81–102.

Donovan, R.J. and J.R. Rossiter (1982), 'Store atmosphere: an environmental psychology approach', *Journal of Retailing*, **58** (1), 34–57.

Echtner, C. and B. Ritchie (1993), 'The measurement of destination image: an empirical assessment', *Journal of Travel Research*, **31** (4), 3–13.

Echtner, C. and B. Ritchie (2003), 'The meaning and measurement of destination image', *Journal of Tourism Studies*, **14** (1), 37–48.

Elliot, S., N. Papadopoulos and S. Kim (2011), 'An integrated model of place image: exploring tourism destination image and product–country image relationships', *Journal of Travel Research*, **20** (10), 1–15.

Eroglu, S.A. and K.A. Machleit (1989), 'Effects of individual and product-specific variables on utilizing country-of-origin as a product quality cue', *International Marketing Review*, **6** (6), 27–52.

Fakeye, P.C. and J.L. Crompton (1991), 'Images differences between prospective, first-time and repeat visitors to the Lower Rio Grande Valley', *Journal of Travel Research*, **30** (2), 10–16.

Fornell, C. and D.F. Larker (1981), 'Evaluating structural equation models with unobservable variables and measurement error', *Journal of Marketing Research*, **18** (February), 39–50.

Gallarza, M.G., I.G. Saura and H.C. García (2002), 'Destination image: towards a conceptual framework', *Annals of Tourism Research*, **29** (1), 56–72.

Gartner, William C. (1993), 'Image formation process', in M. Ulysal and D. R. Fesenmaier (eds), *Communication and Channel Systems in Tourism Marketing*, New York, NY: Haworth Press, pp. 191–215.

Gartner, W.C. and J.D. Hunt (1987), 'An analysis of state image change over a twelve-year period (1971–1983)', *Journal of Travel Research*, **26** (Fall), 15–19.

Gurhan-Canli, Z. and D. Maheswaran (2000), 'Cultural variations in country-of-origin', *Journal of Marketing Research*, **37** (3), 309–317.

Hallberg, Annika (2005), *Post-Travel Consumption. Country-of-Origin effects of international travel experiences*, Göteborg: Göteborg University.

Han, C.M. (1989), 'Country image: halo or summary construct?', *Journal of Marketing Research*, **26** (May), 222–229.

Hu, Y.Z. and B. Ritchie (1993), 'Measuring destination attractiveness: a contextual approach', *Journal of Travel Research*, **32**, 25–35.

Hunt, J. D. (1975), 'Image as a factor in tourism development', *Journal of Travel Research*, **13** (3), 1–7.

Jaffe, Eugene D. and Israel D. Nebenzahl (2001), *National Image and Competitive Advantage*, Copenhagen: Copenhagen Business School Press.

Johansson, J.K. (1989), 'Determinants and effects of the use of made in labels', *International Marketing Review*, **6** (1), 47–58.

Kim, S. and Y. Yoon (2003), 'Hierarchical effects of affective and cognitive components on tourism destination image', *Journal of Travel and Tourism Marketing*, **14** (2), 1–22.

Kleppe, I.A. and L.L. Mossberg (2005), 'Country and destination images: similar or different image objects', *The Service Industries Journal*, **25** (4), 493–503.

Knight, G. and R.J. Calantone (2000), 'A flexible model of consumer country-of-origin perceptions', *International Marketing Review*, **17** (2), 127–145.

Kotler, P. and D. Gertner (2002), 'Country as brand, product, and beyond: a place marketing and brand management perspective', *Brand Management*, **9** (4–5), 249–261.

Kotler, P., D.H. Haider and I. Rein (1993), *Marketing Places*, New York, NY: Free Press.

Laroche, M., N. Papadopoulos, L.A. Heslop and M. Mourali (2005), 'The influence of country image structure on consumer evaluations of foreign products', *International Marketing Review*, **22** (1), 96–115.

Mainolfi, G. (2010), *Il modello della Country Reputation. Evidenze empiriche e implicazioni strategiche per le imprese del Made in Italy nel mercato cinese*, Turin, Italy: Giappichelli Editore.

Mansfeld, Y. (1992), 'From motivation to actual travel', *Annals of Tourism Research*, **19** (3), 399–419.

Milman, A. and A. Pizam (1995), 'The role of awareness and familiarity with a destination: the Central Florida case', *Journal of Travel Research*, **33** (3), 21–27.

Nadeau, J., L.A. Heslop, N. O' Reilly and P. Luk (2008), 'Destination in a country image context', *Annals of Tourism Research*, **35** (1), 84–106.

Papadopoulos, N. (1986), 'Development and organization of a cross-national study: the country-of-origin effect', in Nicolas Papadopoulos and M.F. Bradley (ed.), *Proceedings of the Workshop on International Strategy*, Brussels: European Institute for Advanced Studies in Management.

Papadopoulos, N. (2004), 'Place branding: evolution, meaning and implications', *Place Branding*, **1** (1), 36–49.

Papadopoulos, N. (2011), 'Of places and brands', in Andy Pike (ed.), *Geographies of Brands and Branding*, Cheltenham, UK and Northampton, MA, USA: Edward Elgar Publishing, pp. 25–43.

Papadopoulos, N. and L.A. Heslop (1986), 'Travel as a correlate of product and country images', in Thomas E. Muller (ed.), *Marketing*, Administrative Sciences Association of Canada, Marketing Division, pp. 191–200.

Papadopoulos, N., L.A. Heslop and G. Bamossy (1990), 'A comparative image analysis of domestic versus imported products', *International Journal of Research in Marketing*, **16** (7), 283–294.

Papadopoulos, N., J.J. Marshall, L.A. Heslop, G. Avlonitis, F. Bliemel and F. Graby (1988), 'Strategic implications of product and country images: a modeling approach', *Proceedings of the 41st ESOMAR Marketing Research Congress*, Lisbon, Portugal, pp. 69–90.

Parameswaran, R. and A. Yaprak (1987), 'A cross-national comparison of consumer research measures', *Journal of International Business Studies*, **18** (1), 35–49.

Parameswaran, R. and M.R. Pisharodi (1994), 'Facets of country-of-origin image: an empirical assessment', *Journal of Advertising*, **23** (1), 43–56.

Park, Y. and D. Njite (2010), 'Relationship between destination image and tourists' future behavior: observations from Jeju Island, Korea', *Asia Pacific Journal of Tourism Research*, **15** (1), 1–20.

Pearce, P.L. (1982), 'Perceived changes in holiday destinations', *Annals of Tourism Research*, **9**, 145–164.

Roth, K.P. and A. Diamantopoulos (2009), 'Advancing the country image construct', *Journal of Business Research*, **62** (7), 726–740.

Russell, J. and G. Pratt (1980), 'A description of the affective quality attributed to environments', *Journal of Personality and Social Psychology*, **38** (August), 311–322.

Schoefer, K. and A. Diamantopoulos (2008), 'The role of emotions in translating perceptions of (in)justice into postcomplaint behavioral responses', *Journal of Service Research*, **11** (1), 91–103.

Woodside, A.G. and S. Lysonski (1989), 'A general model of traveler destination choice', *Journal of Travel Research*, **28**, 8–14.

4. Italian country image: the impact on business models and relations in Chinese business-to-business markets

Elena Cedrola and Loretta Battaglia

1. INTRODUCTION

Italy is renowned around the world for its design, fashion, Mediterranean cuisine and other Made in Italy products. These products are often associated with known and famous brands, especially in the luxury sector, but many less well-known Italian firms operating in more technical industries, such as in the mechanical or electronic sectors, have a major presence in international markets. These traditional Made in Italy sectors as well as the specialized product sectors create the so-called '4Fs' of Italian excellence (Fortis 2005). The first group together traditional consumer goods linked to the person and the home. Specialized product sectors include the automation–mechanical–rubber–plastics sector. Despite offering excellent quality products in these sectors, Italy has a lower perceived image than other countries such as Germany.

Country of origin (COO) literature is mainly focused on consumer sectors. The abundance of literature on the subject in the industrial sector is lower, and among theorists two main research streams can be identified. Some believe that COO has the same importance in the consumer market, while others assert that industrial customers operating in a more informed way are less likely to be influenced by it.

This chapter falls within this debate, with the aim of verifying if the COO effect really matters in business-to-business (BTB) relations, particularly in business relations between firms that belong to markets with high cultural distance. We selected China with reference to this investigation. A second objective is to identify the elements that come into play in the evaluation of Italian offers and whether there are differences of perception according to the business sector considered.

The methodology used foresees a study developed over three stages (the first stage is quantitative, the second and third stages are qualitative) on a sample of 338 firms in the first quantitative phase and 14 in the subsequent qualitative phases.

2. COO: A BRIEF REVIEW OF THE LITERATURE WITH A FOCUS ON BTB

Over 300 articles have been published on the COO effect in the last 35 years (Nebenzahl et al. 2003), rendering it one of the main themes in international marketing literature. Although some of the literature on national stereotypes and perceptions relating to certain foreign countries was already written in the 1930s and 1940s, it is only since the early 1960s that the concept of the COO effect has received attention from scholars.

The decade from the early 1960s to the early 1970s is characterized by exploratory studies where the existence of the COO effect and its influence on the supply of foreign exchange is explored. The goal of this early research was primarily to demonstrate that information on the geographical origin of a product influences the purchasing evaluation process (Bilkey and Nes 1982).

From the early 1980s to the early 1990s, researchers began to examine the phenomenon in relation to the intrinsic and extrinsic characteristics of the product (Papadopoulos and Heslop 1993), and the perceived purchasing risk.

Research from the 1990s and 2000s had a very strong empirical focus. The main studies demonstrate that:

1. consumers are influenced by more than one attribute of the good (Verlegh and Steenkamp 1999; Peterson and Jolibert 1995);
2. COO has stronger influence in the early stages of the decision-making process;
3. information on geographical origin is often used as an indication to ascribe an overall value to the product's brand (Agrawal and Kamakura 1999; Usunier and Lee 2009).

With regard to recent literature instead, all sources appear to share the belief that the image of the COO can in specific circumstances act as a summary evaluation of the characteristics of the supply system (Giraldi 2009). However current scenarios seem to require further considerations on the role that the COO effect can play in achieving international competitive advantage. In fact COO can be separated into three elements: COM (country of manufacture), COD (country of design) and COB (country of brand). Each of these definitions can have different meanings by type of customer, product and culture.

Different perspectives emerge from the literature review that can be summarized into three macro areas: consumer, product and brand.

The first strand (consumer) examines the dynamics of COO in relation to the distinctive features that characterize foreign customers (Sharma and Shimp 1987). The various research results provide evidence that the influence of the COO of the foreign good is inversely proportional to the degree of customer involvement in the purchasing process. In the case of high involvement purchases the acquirer will attribute less importance to COO inasmuch as other factors such as price, quality, design and technology come into play in assessing the offer (Valdani and Bertoli 2003). A negative correlation also exists between the influence of COO and level of knowledge and experience in relation to a product category (Schaefer 1997): experts base their assessments on product attributes, whereas novices tend to give credence to the COO effect (Han 1989). Furthermore socio-demographic characteristics also play a significant role: for example, level of income and education have a direct relation with purchasing decisions, orienting the preferences of those with higher incomes and education towards foreign rather than local goods. According to studies by Hsieh (2004), knowledge of a product's country of origin has less influence in more developed countries than in less developed countries. This is explained by the fact that efforts to differentiate products are greater in countries with a high level of economic development; thus COO is only one of several types of information available to consumers.

The product area sees research focused on the verification of how the distinctive name (Made in), thanks to the production tradition that the country of origin extols, can strengthen the competitive edge of domestic enterprises. Customer perceptions of the product are not only related to the functional and performance characteristics but also to the information available on the country where it was designed and produced. The COO effect influences the attribution of a different value, whether positive or negative, to a product or service solely due to having been produced in a particular country or however associated to its traditions (Marino et al. 2009). The hypothesis advanced and confirmed by scholars is that in certain circumstances the image of the country of origin of goods represents part of a set of stereotypes that consumers incorporate in their decisions to choose and purchase foreign products (Mainolfi 2010). The COO of a product is therefore an indicator used by customers to make inferences about the product and the relative attributes that guide their final choice.

The third area in exploring the theme of brand considers this an element of the broader phenomenon of brand image, sustained not only by the brand name but also by the colours and expressions used (Graby 1980). In particular the brand is a type of mediator between COO and the consumer, able to modify the influence of place of origin on the perceptions of foreign demand (Marino et al. 2009). Examples are the espresso or cappuccino which are so inextricably associated with Italy as to induce non-Italian firms to use a brand in the Italian language to benefit from the country's reputation (Morris 2010).

Studies show that the brand name can influence evaluations in terms of quality to the point that an established and esteemed brand can overcome the negative effect of the country of production. Therefore the influence of country of origin is of greater relevance in the absence of strong brands that are able to reduce the COO effect. In addition, according to the results of a study by Aiello et al. (2009), the brand has different relevance in the minds of consumers depending on the product category. As concerns luxury goods the brand is the most important element, but in relation to consumer goods what matters most is price.

Ultimately the opening of markets in relation to the flow of goods, the movement of people and exposure to communication from the international media has led to changes in consumer evaluations of products from foreign countries.

Even in industrial markets, despite the fact that the technical language is universal and less subject to country-specific cultural influences, stereotyping linked to the COO of the party involved may create difficulties or lead to increased tension in the relationship between parties. The assessment of the product's COO is influenced by all the specific cultural elements of the countries involved in the relationship, starting from single partners as individuals, as agents of the firms in the relation and as parties of two-country systems. Verlegh and Steenkamp (1999) contradict the fact that the COO effect is more relevant for consumer goods than for industrial goods, although many researchers over time have argued the opposite, asserting that industrial customers that operate in a more informed way are less likely to be influenced by information on the COO of the good (Ahmed and D'Astous 1995). Many studies, for instance, have shown that German industrial products enjoy a favourable image in the US market, where buyers consider these products of a higher quality than their own (Jolibert 1979; Cattin et al. 1982). A similar situation is found for Japanese products that are considered by Korean importers as superior to American products.

3. THE CHARACTERISTICS OF THE BUSINESS-TO-BUSINESS MARKET

In BTB markets decisions within the firm are generally taken with the view of achieving business objectives. For this reason it would seem implausible that important decisions such as the procurement of intermediate products could be affected by personal considerations dictated by own national culture or by the historical past. In BTB personal considerations are constructive when they derive from experience and knowledge gained over time with the producers (Samiee 1994).

Nevertheless business markets are more complex and structured. They should contribute to providing solutions that bring value to the customer on an ongoing basis in order to develop the relationship over time and attain mutual benefits. In this approach traditional marketing tools are enhanced with additional levers[1] that allow the firm to identify and provide solutions for its client companies through the involvement of the network both within and outside the firm (Lagioni et al. 2001; Anderson et al. 2006). Different types of collaborative solutions are created this way, allowing companies and their nodes (the network) to evolve and to continue to exist (Hutt and Speh 1995; Hakansson et al. 2009).

In these situations the areas of contact between firms and their external stakeholders involve several components including interactivity, trust, references and know-how; areas that can be influenced by country reputation especially during the approach and establishment phases of the relationship between the parties (Battaglia and Cedrola 2010).

In addition in BTB a secondary and indirect influence of COO on industrial purchasers ensues in relation their perceptions of the supply firm. For example, products made in certain countries may be subject to a degree of categorization resulting from the supposed stereotypes of the manufacturing and technical skills attributed to these countries (Bradley 2001). COO also in BTB can be an extrinsic indicator in judging the quality of high technology products (Ahmed and d'Astous 1993).

The above considerations invite us to explore the theme of the COO effect in the BTB market in order to verify the relevance of country image in establishing and managing business relationships with foreign counterparts, especially in the presence of high cultural distance.

4. WORKING IN CHINA: MARKET CHARACTERISTICS

For nearly two decades China has occupied a significant position in the international arena. The isolation of the Middle Kingdom and the racial homogeneity of its people have helped create and maintain a widespread sense of national identity for centuries. Confucian ethics have undoubtedly contributed to standardizing the social behaviour of millions of people: according to Confucius social harmony can only be guaranteed if everyone accepts his role in society and identifies with it. This philosophy has resulted in some particularities of Chinese culture that remain intact to this day:

1. a strong sense of belonging to the family or, rather, adhesion to the extended clan of the family of origin;
2. widespread valorization of hierarchy in social coexistence;
3. an almost religious sense of social harmony with an ongoing search for compromise to satisfy the group as a whole rather than the individual.

Although with the establishment of the socialist republic in 1949 Confucian ethics was replaced by socialist ethics its centuries-old influence has remained, continuing to influence social behaviour within the lives of the Chinese. The family is central to all social life, the basis of the political and economic life of the country. Social hierarchy instead influences the behaviour of Chinese people in public life and is closely linked to the concept of saving face (*mianzi*). This concept is fundamental to the Chinese: indeed it is very important for these people to preserve their public image, their reputation with respect to the family, the company they operate in and society in general.

Closely related to the emphasis that the Chinese attach to social relations is the concept of *guanxi*, which means relationship and indicates long-term personal relationships established between two or more people. Personal relationships must be cultivated over time and are implemented through the exchange of gifts or favours: *guanxi* represents the mutual obligation that legitimates asking favours of others. *Guanxi* is also to be understood, especially for foreigners who decide to operate in China, as the right connections with local authorities, local customs and tax offices.

As concerns hierarchy instead, this forms the backbone of Chinese society since its observance determines the maintenance of social stability, which is reflected in language, in forms of greeting, in rituals and the behaviours of people in general. Hierarchical relationships therefore are the foundation upon which relationships are built within the family, the community, the government and business (Oschetti et al. 2008).

To operate in China requires understanding that Western and Eastern cultures have profoundly different traits to which a different approach to negotiations is also correlated. Westerners pursue more analytical methods based on efficiency criteria and a progressive cause-and-effect analysis. By contrast, in the East a consensual type of approach is privileged, characterized by harmony, a collective vision and shared decisions within the group. In this country negotiation cannot be considered completed even after the signing of the contract because the circular reasoning perspective of the Chinese forces them to periodically check the alignment of the contents of the contract with the demands of the moment.

Establishing a first contact with a Chinese partner is not simple: from their point of view, negotiation is not conducted with the individual intermediaries sent by the firm but with the firm itself that these negotiators represent. Therefore establishing good relations is imperative since not only the image of the individual but also the reliability and seriousness of the entire firm is at stake. For this reason from the very first contact a delegation should be dispatched consisting of members who hold different functions within the Western company. It is also essential to ensure the continuity of the group at the negotiating table since replacements could be interpreted as indicating a lack of earnestness. To this should be added the fact that for the Chinese it is very important to deal directly with the highest echelons of the Western company: which is why during negotiations the hierarchical relationships between people taking part in the negotiation must be made clear. The head of the delegation must be identified and should inspire authority and have decision-making power to conclude agreements without having to consult superiors.

The negotiation process is divided into distinct and consecutive phases. The first requires a considerable amount of energy from the Western party since the attitude of the Chinese operator is mostly one of reflection and studying the parties and the situations. Frequently this cognitive phase is attended by a trustee of the Chinese company who presents the counterparty and aims to create harmony within the negotiation group in order to reach an initial agreement, which generally contains the principles and purposes of the collaboration that will be established between the company and its Western partners in China. Subsequent phases are characterized by greater interaction between the stakeholders and more intense participation in the negotiation process to lead to a more detailed explanation of the programs and a clear definition of the particulars and technical aspects. For this reason negotiations in China take a considerable amount of time and a great deal of patience is required to manage them successfully.

5.   WORKING IN CHINA: BUSINESS MODELS AND MARKETING STRATEGIES FOR ITALIAN COMPANIES

The relational and cultural characteristics of the Chinese market require firms wanting to operate on a regular basis with China to rethink their business models. This section, which begins with a study of a sample of Italian companies, aims to highlight the operating characteristics and business models adopted in the Chinese market as well as the importance of the COO effect in activities carried out by Italian companies. We discuss COO effect, brand and firm reputation, while presenting case studies and the elements that come into play in evaluating the offer of Italian firms. Thereafter some conclusions are offered.

5.1   Methodology and Key Issues

To identify the operational characteristics and business models of Italian companies operating in China we referred to two studies conducted in 2009–2011 (Cedrola et al. 2011). A quantitative study included the administration of a closed-response e-mail questionnaire divided into two macro-areas. The first focused on the international marketing decision-making process, the second on understanding the operations of firms in the Chinese market as well as identifying the relevant relationships and partnerships throughout the supply chain.

The data is based on 338 valid questionnaires for the first section (redemption rate 9 per cent, Table 4.1) and 131 for the second. In the second research phase consisting of personal interviews with the CEOs, marketing managers and export managers of 14 BTB firms the following themes were analysed:

1.   firm characteristics and business models;
2.   strategies and decision-making processes for the Chinese market;
3.   collaborative relationships along the value chain;
4.   competencies required, or those to be developed, to operate success-fully in China;
5.   importance of brand, technology, business reputation;
6.   significance of Made in Italy in China;
7.   Made in Italy communications in China.

Table 4.1   Characteristics of responding firms

Italian regions	No.	Industry	No.	Number of employees	No.
Abruzzo	4	Food	8	1–15	66
Basilicata	2	Furnishing	22	15–50	103
Campania	6	Footwear	31	50–100	62
Emilia Romagna	49	Chemistry, Rubber and Plastic	18	100–250	63
Friuli	1	Mechanics	167	> 250	37
Lazio	2	Services	17	n.d.	7
Marche	38	Others	36		
Sardegna	1				
Sicilia	5				
Toscana	24				
Trentino	3				
Umbria	5				
Veneto	27				

Note: Firms in the sample = 338.

The main findings of the research are illustrated in the following sections.

5.2   Italian Firms in China

A first finding of this research indicated that the internationalization of Italian firms in China is not a recent phenomenon. In fact 86 per cent of firms surveyed declared their presence in the Asian market for over ten years. The Pearson's coefficient calculation shows a positive tendency (0.268) between the percentage of foreign sales to total sales and number of years of presence abroad. A positive correlation tendency was also found between the number of years of operation in the Chinese market and number of employees (0.118), indicating that mid-sized firms have a consolidated presence in China.

An important signal is derived from 39 per cent of the sample indicating the identification of strategic partners as an incentive to internationalization. This evolution in managerial behaviour is increasingly remote from individual behaviour or at least non-cooperative behaviour. It is interesting to note that this motivation was selected by 63 per cent of firms with over 250 employees and by around 52 per cent on average in the 100–249 range, demonstrating better understanding among larger firms of the importance of partnerships to succeed abroad in markets with

Table 4.2   Entry method into foreign markets (in %)

Export	93
National exporters	70
International exporters	14
Trading companies	9
Cooperative structures	14
Agents, distributors located in markets of interest	67
Own sales staff located abroad	17
Representative offices and branches	20
Direct contacts with firm	23
Licensing	4
Franchising	1
Production contracts	4
Service contracts	2
Joint venture	10
Acquisition of a foreign company	7
Greenfield	13
Internet	14

high geographical and cultural distance. Analysing the data by sector of belonging instead did not present any significant differences.

The reduction in production costs as a determinant of investments in Eastern markets is a priority for only 29.6 per cent of firms while confirming (Cedrola et al. 2009) that government, regional and community incentives are not taken into consideration. This may depend on the identification of strategic partners or on the fact that this market is difficult to penetrate especially for firms that have not yet developed a vocation towards relationships and cooperation (Chee and West 2005; Weber 2005).

In terms of mode of entry into international markets (Table 4.2) almost all interviewees undertake exporting activities (93 per cent). Using own sales staff or representative offices, notwithstanding limited size or requiring significant investments, is a common entry mode which confirms that many entrepreneurs understand the market characteristics.

Direct contact with the customer is crucial for all types of firms (23 per cent). However the way of interfacing varies: while midsize firms actually maintain direct and constant communications with the customer for micro and small enterprises this is often a result of their participation in international fairs.

With regard to company size, medium-sized and more structured firms indicate they use different market entry channels in combination as well as

Table 4.3   Collaborations along the supply chain (in %)

Logistics	31
Production	21
Promotion	26
Sales	40
Customer services	18
Purchasing	16
Human resources	7
R&D	3
Accounting and risk management	5
Legal and contractual consulting	20
Others	5

more innovative forms of collaboration. Smaller firms instead concentrate on indirect channels.

The second section of the questionnaire explored the activities that firms most involved in China (131) undertake in this market and the use of collaborations with local actors, institutions and organizations. In continuing the analysis of managerial behaviours, the majority of firms choosing to develop in China (86 per cent) establish partnerships with organizations working *in loco*, recognizing that in this extensively high-context, geographically and culturally distant market, direct or indirect marketing relationships in the territory cannot be neglected. The main collaborations focus on sales activities (Table 4.3), although some first significant signs are evident of collaborations aimed at covering other stages of the business chain.

Finally with regard to stakeholders that are essential to undertaking activities in China only 14 per cent of firms have no significant relations. Collaborations with suppliers and distributors play an important role in performing information functions, especially in the traditional Made in Italy sectors. Local institutions and governments also increasingly play a key role (Table 4.4).

It is not uncommon to find a municipality directly interfacing with potential foreign investors, thus contributing to the development of their area of expertise and providing services in support of the new enterprise (Child and Tse 2001; Chen et al. 2004).

5.3   COO Effect on Business Relations Between Italy and China

Reflecting on the internationalization strategy of Italian firms in China, while the Made in Italy concept, together with flexibility and customization

Table 4.4   Determinant collaborations in China (in %)

Public institutions and banks	40
Municipalities/local goverment	14
Central goverment	5
Banks/merchant banks	11
Italian Institute for Commerce and Trade (ICE)	15
Italian Chamber of Commerce	8
Others	5
Private institutions	31
Trade associations	16
Fair organization	18
Others	2
Suppliers	22
Clients	42
Traders and distributors	29
Others	15

Table 4.5   The 'Made in Italy' factor as a point of strength of Italian firms (in %)

	Definitely yes	Relatively	Not at all
Food	50	50	
Furnishing	55	45	
Footwear and Leather	61	35	3
Chemistry, Rubber, Plastic	17	56	28
Mechanics	24	55	14
Services	24	41	35
Textile and Clothing	46	54	
Others	44	50	6
Average	35	5	11

of the offer, are considered important the findings highlight different priorities. In fact to the question 'is being an Italian company considered a strength?' firms responded 'definitely yes' for 35 per cent and 'fairly' for 53 per cent. The differences by sector are given in Table 4.5 demonstrating the high significance of COO for traditional Italian export sectors such as leather and footwear.

Instead product quality, product innovation and customer pre/post-sales services are elements in which firms invest to penetrate a new market. Table 4.6 illustrates the characteristics of each sector: for example, furniture,

Table 4.6   Key investment factors for internationalization (in %)

	Flexibility	Product innovation	Quality	Design	Price	Services
Food	38	25	100	38	63	38
Furnishing	45	64	82	86	36	45
Footwear, Leather	23	61	87	68	26	26
Chemical, Rubber, Plastic	33	67	72	22	61	44
Mechanics	38	54	78	19	43	50
Services	29	24	65	18	47	24
Textile, Clothing	46	62	85	77	33	31
Others	36	54	79	41	13	36
Average	37	55	80	38	38	42

textile and footwear firms consider quality and design as priorities, likewise the engineering sector aims primarily at quality and innovation combined with a focus on price and service. In this case Made in Italy has little significance. The decisions of Chinese operators are driven by firm reputation which is built through the combination of relationships and product quality.

6.   COO EFFECT, BRAND AND FIRM REPUTATION

The results of the quantitative research highlighted some divisive situations in terms of the importance of COO in the internationalization of Italian firms. In the qualitative research stage the information and analyses of the 14 Italian firms operating in the Chinese market were edifying (Table 4.7). These firms use different strategies in the Chinese market thus making a more extensive case study possible.

In the following, we present details of three companies, Nuova Simonelli, FAAM and iGuzzini, to highlight the main themes explored in all 14 companies.

The Nuova Simonelli case study

Nuova Simonelli has produced professional espresso and cappuccino machines since 1936. Its products are positioned at the high end of the market for performance, quality and price. After an initial growth phase where sales were extended from Marche (the region where the company has its head office) to the national market, in 1980 Nuova Simonelli took its first steps outside national borders. It currently exports 82 per cent of its production made entirely in Italy.

Table 4.7 The 14 Italian firms analysed

Firms	Industry	Turnover mil €	Number of employees	Years in China	Production site for the Chinese market	Chinese plants produce for other markets	Marketing mix localization
Cobra	Electronics (security systems)	116	700	15	China–Asia	Yes	Product–Distribution
Manas	Shoe manufacturing	57	100	4	Italy	No	Distribution–Training salesforce
FAAM Group	Ecological batteries and cars	60	300	15	China	Yes	Product–Distribution–Training distributors
Caleffi	Hydro-thermo sanitary (valves and components)	260	950	17	Italy	No	Product–Distribution–Training salesforce and technicians
Riso Gallo	Food (rice production)	110	137	12	Italy	No	–
iGuzzini	Lighting engineering	168	1217	6	China	Yes	Product–Service
Ivars	Rubber chemical	44	170	7	China	Yes	Design
Lucchini RS	Engineering	240	969	8	Italy	No	Assembling
Mesdan	Textile engineering	25.6	78	30	Italy–China	No	Customer service–Distribution
Molemab	Metallurgical	16	76	30	China	Yes	–
Gerard's	Chemical cosmetic	3.6	23	2	Italy	No	Product–Distribution and Training
Gefran	Electronic	97	581	9	Italy–China	No	Product–Distribution
Cavagna	Engineering (valves)	132	700	5	Italy–China	Yes	Product
Nuova Simonelli	Espresso Coffee Machines	24.5	60	12	Italy	No	Distribution–Training salesforce

The first markets in their internationalization process were Canada and the United States together with other European markets sharing a common culture in espresso and cappuccino consumption. The company subsequently turned to Asia adopting a progressive penetration strategy characterized by two phases. First, having identified a potentially interesting market, direct visits were scheduled by the company's sales force. After establishing initial relations investments were made to ensure Nuova Simonelli's presence at national and international fairs aimed at identifying new customers and building partnerships with coffee roasters and distributors. Partnerships with distributors for pre- and post-sales services are essential in markets with high geographical distance. In fact downtime or machine maintenance in bars, coffee shops, hotel chains and corporations has to be limited to just a few hours.

In the traditional professional coffee machine sector (as opposed to the super-automatic sector) 90 per cent of the market is controlled by companies of Italian origin. This is because Italy is the expression of an espresso culture that has allowed manufacturers of espresso machines to establish themselves first in the Italian market and thereafter in international markets. In this area COO is therefore an important factor. When foreign customers have to make a choice they trust in Italian producers. However in markets where customers understand the coffee product and have enriched their store of knowledge on the world of espresso the COO factor is only attributed significance at the outset in purchasing decisions. According to the CEO and chief marketing officer of Nuova Simonelli, in this type of situation specific brand image and corporate reputation are increasingly important. Great value is attributed to the brand when perceptions on the seriousness and reliability of a company are associated with it. In this specific case customers trust Nuova Simonelli because they trust the brand, having been able to verify that this company in addition to offering a quality product offers a network of reliable and timely services. In the Chinese market COO allows initiating a phase of knowledge acquisition which is a prelude to building a business relationship beyond, as in other markets, identifying the characteristics that the manufacturer must meet if entering that specific area (certification). Italian production is recognized as superior in terms of image quality. Some firms (Expobar and Casavilo for example) have chosen to decentralize their production. In fact these companies were recognized as producing brands of inferior quality even before relocating production to China.

Ultimately, with reference to this case study, COO proves to be a prerequisite, a type of entry barrier, while brand image and corporate reputation become important factors in actual purchasing decisions. The brand image is supported with communication activities on different product lines (Nuova Simonelli and Victoria Arduino) and sponsorship of the World Barista Championship (Nuova Simonelli machines are used in the competitions). Corporate reputation is embodied not only in the design and implementation of innovative and high performance products but also in customer orientation. Customer proximity is reflected in sales force training, in training technicians, in the presence at fairs and in relationships. Sales managers maintain direct relations with customers through regular visits. In many cases this approach has determined market preference over products of competing Italian companies such as La Cimbali, Faema and Rancilio.

The FAAM Group case study

FAAM (Fabbrica Accumulatori e Autoveicoli Monterubbiano), an accumulator and automotive manufacturing firm, was founded in 1974 on the entrepreneurial initiative of two friends who had set themselves the goal of developing both the territory and employment in the region where the company's headquarters are located. Since its legal establishment FAAM changed from sole proprietorship to an international group with over 300 employees and over 100 units linked to the industrial sector. In addition to the three plants in Italy (dedicated to the production of starter, traction and stationary batteries as well as environmentally friendly electric, natural gas and hydrogen vehicles) the company operates with ownership structures in China and Uruguay.

From a meeting with the company president it emerged that the perception of the FAAM product is correlated with the European dimension (Made in Europe). Nevertheless quality of products and related services are not sufficient to build a corporate reputation in China. The firm must also work on relationships at all levels of the supply chain as well as with local stakeholders such as government agencies, universities, customs organizations and partners. 'The main reason to which we can attribute the success of FAAM is the trust that the company was able to create with all its key stakeholders.' Trust for the Chinese is essential in conducting good business and must be built by both parties along a lengthy pathway. Trust enables creating a network of interpersonal relationships (*guanxi*) *in loco*, acting as catalysts and business facilitators and unblocking access to resources. 'Relationships allow bypassing the bureaucratic system: when you have the right guanxi, there are few rules that cannot be broken or turned in your favour: someone described it as a tool to achieve the impossible.'

Trust as a resource is an expression of the reputational capital that this firm has been able to create in the Chinese market thanks to the interaction of four factors: the group's innate vocation to building relationships, respect for the environment, an intercultural approach to the market and achieving excellent financial results corresponding to the financial stability of the group first and thereafter to that of YIBF (Yixing Industrial Batteries FAAM – a Chinese wholly foreign-owned enterprise (WFOE)).

The group's ability to build relationships derives from the creation of strong relations with local government and the municipal and provincial authorities of the city of Yixing enabling it to obtain a production license. This results from the attention that FAAM devotes to the environment. Although Chinese laws in this sphere are far from being defined in line with European and international standards FAAM decided to adopt a policy to control the pollution of its plants with careful waste management policies. This has attracted the attention of the government to the extent that FAAM is considered a point of reference.

Regarding the introduction of intercultural management the reason for this organizational decision is the belief that understanding language and culture is essential in recognizing and seizing the opportunities offered. Showing interest in studying Chinese, combined with the integration of indigenous personnel in key roles in YIBF, has fostered mutual esteem and trust, essential for building a solid and profitable business relationship between the company and all its stakeholders.

Finally satisfactory financial results have brought the company visibility and credibility. To understand this aspect, we must bear in mind an important concept in business relationships in China explained to the president of FAAM by one of the first Chinese co-workers, 'they will ask you to sign agreements, letters of intent and so forth, to create joint ventures. The real thing you need to do is to bring work. Make the Chinese work, giving them the money they deserve and you'll see'. The company in the pre- and post-crisis period has steadily grown in turnover from €300 000 in 2006 to almost €11 million in 2011.

In conclusion we can affirm that for FAAM the COO effect intended from Made in Italy has no influence in the Chinese market. When instead assuming Europe as the designation of origin, then this guarantees Chinese industrial buyers the standards and technical specifications that are difficult to find in the local market. However although Made in Europe is a necessary condition for the acceptance of the company in China it is also insufficient on its own. Building reputational capital is essential to enable building trust, a fundamental resource both in conducting business and in the Chinese culture. This, together with professional customer service in close proximity as well as product reliability, has allowed the Group's offer to stand out in the large and complex Chinese market.

The iGuzzini Lighting case study

iGuzzini has been active in the field of interior and exterior architectural lighting since the late 1950s. Currently it is the first Italian company in the lighting industry and among the top five in the European landscape. Its mission is not simply to manufacture lighting fixtures at the highest level of quality but also to study, understand and make lighting understood, together with integrating with architecture through industrial design.

The company's strong expansion in domestic and international markets was supported by the consolidation of three factors of competitive advantage: innovation, design and attention to product quality. Since the early 1970s the company has linked export activities with the activation of production and sales units capable of permanently presiding over target markets. First a joint venture in Yugoslavia was implemented, and thereafter one in the United States.

In the late 1970s the company decided to change its market approach focusing on building its own commercial facilities, branches and companies with foreign distributors with a majority shareholding in Germany, France, Spain and the United Kingdom. In the 1990s penetration of other European markets was completed through the establishment of trading companies in Norway, Denmark, Sweden, Benelux and Switzerland.

The moderate growth registered in 2000 in the European markets led iGuzzini to seek new markets. The internationalization phase outside Europe saw the birth of three trading companies in Hong Kong, Russia, Singapore and the start of a production plant in Shanghai, China.

iGuzzini in China is positioned, as is the case at the international level, in the middle–upper market. The production plant in China is for the local market although a significant proportion of products are imported directly from Italy. The company does not have the same organizational structure in China as in Italy: in fact it does not have a network of specialized local distributors (monomandatory agents) but interfaces with professionals (architects, lighting designers and so on) who bring it into contact with either public and private buyers of projects to be undertaken (financiers).

From the interview with China's iGuzzini president it emerged that the source of supply (COO) 'brings with it both the positive and negative aspects of the stereotypes attributed to Italy'. To the Chinese, Made in Italy is evocative of Italy and its inhabitants. They perceive Italians as open people and very close to them from a historic–cultural point of view. Without doubt the history and tradition of the Land of the Dragon is as ancient as Italy's. This has great relevance along with other common elements such as the central role of the family, of relationships and friendships. China highly appreciates the creativity and lifestyle of the Italian people, and attributes added value to Made in Italy products considered high in style and design. Unfortunately Italy also inherits and projects to foreign countries the negative connotations of its country image such as the lack of behavioural continuity and reliability resulting from a centuries-old historical legacy.

For iGuzzini the foreign origin of the company in the first instance induces an amplification of the prism effect on the offer, giving a perception of higher quality especially compared to local competition and thus justifying a price gap. However this effect is increasingly eroding in part because of ongoing changes in the market. More and more Chinese enterprises have grown by imitating Italian products in which Italy is a leader by applying very aggressive pricing policies. It follows that the designation of origin of the offer should be combined with other elements, such as the relocation of production and a policy that aims to strengthen the brand identity in order to develop a long-term presidium in the industry to which they belong within the Chinese market.

The firm's reputational capital is a very decisive factor in the Chinese market. Trust develops through a well-established and positive company reputation over time.

The reputational capital that iGuzzini was able to build derives from the combination of four elements: brand awareness, direct presence in the market, its relations and its references.

Of fundamental importance is the presence of a direct member of the entrepreneurial family in the Chinese headquarters, namely the president, since in Oriental culture the concept of taking responsibility, committing one's own resources to the project (as confirmed by the manager himself), is a matter of great added value especially in business behaviours that allow the company to build references and relationships in the market over time.

These elements are combined with awareness of the iGuzzini Lighting brand in the sector of belonging and with professionals who recognize the high innovation, design and performance content.

6.1 Elements that Come Into Play in Evaluating the Offer of Italian Firms

Italy is known worldwide for a number of sectors and production specializations generating products or services that are distinguished for their quality, innovation and design. Italy is leader in many of these for exported products (Fortis 2009). The sample of 14 companies investigated (Table 4.7) include firms that belong to the above mentioned Made in Italy sectors and production specializations.

Based on the evidence presented above the companies were investigated with particular reference to the Chinese market in relation to the three following areas:

1. importance of COO, firm reputation and brand image;
2. distinctive features of the offer on which firms base their competitiveness;
3. the use of Made in and its communication.

The main findings in these areas are illustrated below (summary in Table 4.8).

COO, firm reputation and brand image: predominant effect
The importance of COO varies according to sector of belonging and market positioning as shown in Table 4.8. Companies belonging to the Made in Italy sectors assign high importance to the COO effect. They have been present in China for many years and due to the market characteristics have had to develop corporate reputation and at times specific brand policies (Nuova Simonelli, Mesdan). Some of the most recent entrants through intermediaries leverage exclusively on COO (Riso Gallo, Gerard's). Other companies not specialized in traditional Made in Italy production have characterized and distinguished themselves with specific technologies and products. These have been active in the Chinese market for some time, are well known and have developed corporate reputation and in some cases a brand image – so much so that some have the same product reputation whether these are made in Italy or in China (FAAM).

Firm reputation is created over time and is rooted in reliability, continuity of the relationship, innovation and local presence (FAAM). Some companies have approached the market to follow their customers. Subsequently they have also dedicated themselves to the development of the local market and penetration of the territory (Cobra). It is noteworthy that in the business market firm reputation and brand image almost overlap. Both the company name and brand are a guarantee of performance, whereas more traditional Made in Italy markets are accustomed to working extensively on the brand and on direct communication with end customers. Reputation and brand image are clearly articulated and distinguished in this case in the firm's corporate policies.

From our findings it emerged that only a few companies work with distinctive brands or product lines, deriving from the acquisition of companies with brand reputation as in the case of Nuova Simonelli with Victoria Arduino or Caleffi with RDZ.

It is interesting to note that at times Italian firms use their brand alongside the brand of the Chinese company in joint ventures whereby the use of two brands side by side adds value to the product manufactured in China. This is the case for Lucchini where 'COO is not important but instead the company name, which evokes Italianness, adds value'.

Distinctive elements of the offer

Among the elements that distinguish the Italian offer the interviews confirm that quality is of great importance in all sectors. However the emphasis on quality varies among sectors. The different connotations depend on the type of industry or segment. In some, products or processes combine with technology, in some with design, while in others with pre- or post-sales service thereby confirming the Fortis data in relation to the connotations of Made in Italy firms (Fortis 2005).

Service and pre- and post-sales assistance also take on different connotations depending on the industry. This entails listening to and understanding the local market together with willingness and flexibility in transferring operating practices to the local market including technical training for local operators, whether distributors or applicators, assistance in the design phase and in supporting customers, users and distributors.

Price is also among the elements of the offer and is a strong decisional factor in China. Numerous companies claim that given the same price Chinese firms buy Italian products. However other firms whose offer is less price sensitive declare that the Chinese customer is willing to pay a larger amount for Made in Italy or Europe products (Mesdan, Gerard's). In other cases the Chinese customer is willing to pay more for a Made in China product if it is produced by an Italian company, acquiring added value as a result of the company's origin (FAAM).

The perception that Chinese companies have of Italian and German products is very similar from a quality perspective (FAAM) while Italian industrial products are appreciated because of their competitiveness when compared to corresponding German and Japanese products (Molemab).

Made in communication

Companies use different approaches in COO communication. Some companies use the words Made in Italy, others Made in Europe, in relation to the greater importance of the country or region of belonging. In some cases the words Made in are used as an addendum to strengthen the brand name. In other cases the words Made in are not used, but the brand name or company name is used also in intermediate products which are then incorporated into other products or machines (Molemab) to guarantee the origin of the product. The Made in communication or origin of the

Table 4.8 Investigated areas in the qualitative research

Firm	Industry	Foremost Effect			Distinctive elements of the offer					Communication of the Made in Italy
		Made in	Firm Reputation	Brand image	Quality	Technology Process	Design	Pre and after sales service	Price	
Cavagna	Engineering (valves)	M	H	H	M	M	L	M	H	Europe
Caleffi	Hydro-thermo sanitary (valves and components)	H	H	H	H	H	L	H	L	Yes — Brand acquisition and brand support
Gefran	Electronic	H	H	L	H	H	L	H	H	Yes — Manufacture in China
Mesdan	Textile engineering	H	H	H	H	H	L	H	L	Yes
Nuova Simonelli	Espresso coffee and machines	H	H	H	H	H	H	H	L	No — Company reputation and Brand Reputation (Best award)
Manas	Shoes production	H	M	L	H	M	H	M	M	Yes — I love Italian shoes campaign
Gerard's	Chemical cosmetic	H	L	L	H	M	L	H	M	Yes — The brand name is adapted to the market by the distributor

Company	Sector											Notes
Riso Gallo	Food (rice production)	H	L	L	M	M	L	L	L	Yes	Europe	Use of various brand names
Ivars	Rubber chemical	L	H	M	H	M	H	M	H	M		
iGuzzini	Lighting engineering	M	H	H	H	M	M	H	M	Yes		
Lucchini	Engineering	L	H	H	H	H	H	H	L	No		Lucchini Brand along with the name of the Chinese JV
Molemab	Metallurgical	L	H	H	H	H	L	M	H	Yes		Made in is used to open negotiations
FAAM	Ecological batteries and cars	M	H	H	H	H	L	H	M	No		The brand communicates the high value of the product
Cobra	Electronics (security systems)	L	H	M	H	H	L	H	M	No		The name of the company transfers the values of the company (reputation) and brand values

Legend: H = High; L = Low; M = Medium

product is emphasized differently in relation to customer type, namely Chinese customers or international customers.

In particular the destination of the finished product is relevant depending on whether it remains in China or is exported beyond its borders. In the case of exports the words Made in Italy on the component constitutes a guarantee over time and space, hence also beyond China's borders (Molemab). Finally also highlighted is the use of the product name adapted to the Chinese market to recall Italianness, in this case usually managed by local distributors leveraging on COO.

7. CONCLUSIONS

Although the literature on COO is largely focused on consumer sectors it has just as much relevance in the industrial sphere. The empirical evidence presented in this work clearly demonstrates the importance of the COO effect in BTB markets too, although with a different emphasis in relation to industrial sectors and within these the segments in which firms operate. Sectors more associated with the traditional Made in Italy benefit most from the COO effect while COO greatly influences customer segments that are approaching specific technologies or products for the first time, confirming Han (1989).

The COO effect, regardless of whether or not it is used by the company, brings with it values linked to internationally recognized Italianness such as quality, craftsmanship, innovation, design and creativity (Fortis 2005). In the sectors identified by Fortis as characteristic of Italian enterprises recognized abroad the COO effect is always significant, constituting a reputational differential at least at the outset. It is also confirmed for other sectors that COO is relevant at the time of entry into a market when the industrial customer has no experience of the product or sector. Product or industry experience is recognized in purchasing decisions and adds value to the company's reputation or brand. The company's reputation is even more important in operations in the Chinese market where building a reputation entails product quality (as in other markets), technology and innovation (as in some other markets), trust and long-term relationships (more so than in other markets).

A transition from country reputation (COO) to corporate reputation seems to ensue. In China, where relationships and trust are critical to creating long-term business relationships, corporate reputation calls attention to country reputation, intended not so much as the capacity to make or create but as relational capabilities that are typical of Italians and thus culture-specific.

This concept includes flexibility, listening and adaptability which, according to the companies interviewed, are considered emblematic of Italian firms, particularly the small and medium-sized. This feature of Italianness is so distinctive as to constitute a stronger competitive differential to build on, so much so that some Italian companies have started manufacturing processes in China, at times in joint ventures producing products recognized as Italian despite being manufactured in China (COD effect).

These considerations are especially valid for sectors where semi-finished products are components of other finished products. For other more typical Made in Italy products relational capacity leads to a competitive advantage in relation to the creation of partnerships with distribution channels (Manas).

Among the aforementioned elements that come into play in the evaluation of Italian offers we would add the theme of price. Price is a matter of great consideration in the Chinese market, an element that has always been part of the purchasing decision and will assume increasing importance in view of the evolution underway entailing the production and technological upgrading of manufacturing firms in China.

NOTE

1. Intangible resources, internal resources, non-buyer external resources.

REFERENCES

Agrawal, J. and W.A. Kamakura (1999), 'Country of origin: a competitive advantage?', *International Journal of Research in Marketing*, **16** (4), 255–267.

Ahmed, S.A. and A. d'Astous (1993), 'Cross-national evaluation of made-in concept using multiple cues', *European Journal of Marketing*, **27**, 39–52.

Ahmed, A. and A. d'Astous (1995), 'Comparison of country of origin effects on household and organizational buyers' product perceptions', *European Journal of Marketing*, **29**, 35–51.

Aiello, G., R. Donvito, B. Godey, D. Pederzoli, K.P. Wiedmann, N. Hennigs, A. Siebels, P. Chan, J. Tsuchiya, S. Rabino, S.I. Ivanovna, B. Weitz, H. Oh and R. Singh (2009), 'An international perspective on luxury brand and country-of-origin effect', *Journal of Brand Management*, **16**, 323–337.

Anderson, J.C., J.A. Narus and W. Van Rossum (2006), 'Customer value propositions in business markets', *Harvard Business Review*, March, 91–99.

Battaglia, L. and E. Cedrola (2010), 'Interazione culturale e processi di negoziazione', in S. Guercini (ed.), *Marketing e management interculturale. Attori, politiche e organizzazione*, Bologna: Il Mulino, pp. 93–133.

Bilkey, W.J. and E. Nes (1982), 'Country-of-origin effects on product evaluations', *Journal of International Business Studies*, Spring–Summer, 89–99.

Bradley, F. (2001), 'Country–company interaction effects and supplier preferences among industrial buyers', *Industrial Marketing Management*, **30**, 511–524.

Cattin, P., A. Jolibert and C. Lohnes (1982), 'A cross cultural study of "made in" concepts', *Journal of International Business Studies*, Winter, 131–141.

Cedrola, E., L. Battaglia and C. Cantù (2011), 'Le imprese italiane in Cina: modelli di business emergenti', in T. Vescovi (ed.), *Libellule sul Drago*, Padova: Cedam, pp. 165–200.

Cedrola, E., L. Battaglia and A. Tzannis (2009), 'The Italian SMEs in the international context: a model to succeed in the global arena', *Collana Quaderni del Dipartimento di Istituzioni Economiche e Finanziarie*, **52**, Università di Macerata.

Chee, H. and C. West (eds) (2005), *Fare affari in Cina tra miti e realtà*, Milano: Etas.

Chen, T.-J., H. Chen and Y.H. Ku (2004), 'Foreign direct investment and local linkages', *Journal of International Business Studies*, **35** (4), 320–333.

Child, J. and D.K. Tse (2001), 'China's transition and its implications for international business', *Journal of International Business Studies*, **32** (1), 5–21.

Fortis, M. (ed.) (2005), *Le due sfide del Made in Italy: globalizzazione e innovazione*, Bologna: Il Mulino.

Fortis, M. (2009), 'Competitiveness and export performance of Italy', *Fondazione Edison, Università Cattolica*, Dipartimento del Tesoro.

Giraldi, A. (2009), 'Country of origin: una rassegna analitica dei principali lavori dal 1962 al 2008', *Paper from the International Congress of Marketing Trends*, 16–17 January, Paris.

Graby, F. (1980), 'Consumérisme et produits étrangers', *Coopération–Distribution–Consommation*, **5**, 17–23.

Hakansson, H., D. Ford, L.E. Gadde, I. Snehota and A. Waluszewski (eds) (2009), *Business in Networks*, Chichester: Wiley.

Han, C.M. (1989), 'Country image: halo or summary construct?' *Journal of Marketing Research*, **XXVI**, May, 222–229.

Hsieh, M. (2004), 'An investigation of country-of-origin effect using correspondence analysis: a cross-national context', *International Journal of Market Research*, **46** (3), 267–295.

Hutt, M.D. and T.W. Speh (eds) (1995), *Business Marketing Management*, Orlando, FL: The Dryden Press, fifth edition.

Jolibert, A. (1979), 'Quand les directeurs d'approvisionnement français et américains évaluent l'image des produits fabriqués dans cinq pays industriels', *Revue Française de Gestion*, Jan–Feb, 94–111.

Lagioni, I., L. Battaglia and T. Savorgnani (eds) (2001), *Business Marketing. Il progetto cliente nell'era del web*, Milano: Tecniche Nuove.

Mainolfi, G. (ed.) (2010), *Il modello della country reputation. Evidenze empiriche e implicazioni strategiche per le imprese del Made in Italy nel mercato cinese*, Turin: Giappichelli Editore.

Marino, V., C. Gallucci and G. Mainolfi (2009), 'L'interpretazione multidimensionale della Country reputation. Implicazioni strategiche per le imprese del made in Italy', in C. Pepe and A. Zucchella (eds), *L'internazionalizzazione delle imprese italiane*, Bologna: Il Mulino, pp. 93–97.

Morris, J. (2010), 'Making Italian espresso, making espresso', *Italian, Food & History*, **8** (2), 155–184.

Nebenzahl, I.D., E.D. Jaffé and J.C. Usunier (2003), 'Personifying country-of-origin research', *Management International Review*, **43** (4), 383–406.

Oschetti, A., A. Paparelli and M. Pira (2008), *La nuova rivoluzione cinese. Etica, business e cultura*, Milan: Hoepli.

Papadopoulos, N. and L.A. Heslop (eds) (1993), *Product and Country Images: Research and Strategy*, New York: The Haworth Press.

Peterson, R.A. and A. Jolibert (1995), 'A meta-analysis of country-of-origin effects', *Journal of International Business Studies*, **26** (4), 883–900.

Samiee, S. (1994), 'Customer evaluation of products in a global market', *Journal of International Business Studies*, **25** (3), 579–604.

Schaefer, A. (1997), 'Consumer knowledge and country of origin effects', *European Journal of Marketing*, **31** (1), 56–72.

Sharma, S. and T.A. Shimp (1987), 'Consumer ethnocentrism: construction and validation of the CETSCALE', *Journal of Marketing Research*, **23**, 280–289.

Usunier, J.C. and J.A. Lee (eds) (2009), *Marketing Across Cultures*, Harlow, UK: Person Education Limited, fifth edition.

Valdani, E. and G. Bertoli (eds) (2003), *Marketing e Mercati Internazionali*, Milan: Egea.

Verlegh, P.W.J. and J.B.E.M. Steenkamp (1999), 'A review and meta-analysis of country of origin research', *Journal of Economic Psychology*, **20** (5), 521–546.

Weber, M. (ed.) (2005), *La Cina non è per tutti. Rischi e opportunità del più grande mercato del mondo*, Milan: Edizioni Olivares.

# 5.	What is the link between 'Made in' and corporate social responsibility in SMEs? The value of socially oriented behavior in 'hostile' territories

Alessandra De Chiara

INTRODUCTION

The image of the area is undoubtedly an important determinant in its prosperity, attracting capital and foreign investors, but at the same time it conveys the image of companies located there.

In recent times, the Italian territory has not enjoyed a good reputation. The economic and political crisis, and the not exactly inspiring personal stories of the primary institutional partners, have all deeply undermined its image. If the land is not attractive all businesses are affected, but particularly those who have used the territory from which they come, and the value of 'Made in', to open up business opportunities in foreign markets.

In this chapter the author analyses the relationship between corporate social responsibility (CSR) and 'Made in' in small and medium-sized enterprises (SMEs), adding depth to a topic already addressed from other angles by this author (De Chiara 2009, 2012), with a view to recording the importance of the territorial factor and of its image for the international competitiveness of SMEs, while at the same time identifying the need for CSR in the event of a loss of value of 'Made in'. In fact, in these cases, which are unfortunately no longer isolated, there has been a decline in the international competitiveness of SMEs that have used this factor, exclusively or not, to open up opportunities in foreign markets. Companies have been forced to undertake a path of upgrading their resources and skills, which is characterized as socially responsible behavior.

The social responsibility of SMEs is a subject far removed from the time when these companies played a key role in the European economic system, and even more so in Italy, which is significantly characterized by the presence of SMEs.[1]

Among other things, the objectives of the European Union, sanctioned in the Lisbon Strategy (March 2000), have been explicitly to set a goal to 'become the most competitive knowledge-based economy in the world, capable of sustainable economic growth accompanied by an improvement and better jobs and greater social cohesion' (European Commission 2001, p. 3). Therefore, the European Union has suggested that SMEs cannot be kept out of the processes of knowledge relating to CSR, given the influence they have on society (European Commission 2002). The central role played by SMEs has also been stressed by the UN Global Compact (UNIDO 2002): in the developed world, SMEs, which tend to be specialized and knowledge-intensive, can influence the course of conduct of business; in developing countries, SMEs are the engine for the spread of market relations.

In the economic literature there is unanimous support for the need to adapt the specifics of SMEs towards social responsibility. If for large companies the study of CSR should be based on stakeholder theory, for SMEs it should be based on the concept of 'social capital' (Perrini 2006). Several theoretical contributions have emphasized that the need for SMEs to adopt responsible behavior arises from the strong ties that they have with the local system (Harvey et al. 1991; Perrini and Tencati 2008).

This issue was also addressed in the studies on the internationalization of companies. It is often pointed out that an area represents an important source of expertise and resources (Cavusgil 1980; Czinkota and Tesar 1982), and studies have also indicated how important it is for SMEs to exploit their geographic origin (Morace 2001; Guerini 2004). In fact, for many SMEs, their territory becomes the true differential against foreign competition, the resource on which to focus to succeed and flourish in international markets: the 'Made in' factor is an important determinant of the international competitiveness of SMEs. So, in SMEs, the need to adopt behavior patterns inspired by CSR may occur with greater emphasis, by virtue of the strong bond that these companies have with the local system.

The ultimate aim of this chapter may be summarized as the description of a positive relationship among CSR, 'Made in' and the international performance of SMEs.

The chapter first analyses the different theoretical perspectives of CSR in SMEs and of the country of origin effect ('Made in'), then presents the conceptual framework made up of the results of research and empirical evidence, followed by the conclusions.

CSR IN SMEs

The distinct features of CSR in small and medium-sized enterprises have been highlighted by several European research projects and in the literature of management. First, the strong influence exercised by the ethical and social values of the owner or manager are stressed. They are described as important factors that explain the small business involvement in social responsibility practices (European Commission – Observatory of European SMEs 2004). In Italy, the study of Molteni and Todisco (2008) provides a broader overview of the issues that affect CSR in SMEs by giving a classification into: (a) individual factors, belonging to the sphere of the individual and that most influence his decisions (related to birth and experience), and (b) contingent factors, affecting elements of context that can lead the individual to make more or less ethical decisions (e.g., the working environment). To these are added further categories: the intensity of the moral problem, personal characteristics, context and organization.

Further studies have identified some characteristics of SMEs that are compatible with the adoption of socially-oriented behavior: the influence of the subjective sphere, the importance of internal and external relations, the social roots of the company and the entrepreneur (Spence 1999; Spence et al. 2003; Del Baldo 2009).

In relation to the objective aspects of the sensitivity of SMEs in CSR, some European research has emphasized that the adoption of the tools of CSR seems to depend on the age of the firm, so the end of the fifth year of life defines the period in which the likelihood of small business involvement in the CSR emerges (European Commission – Observatory of European SMEs 2004). In other research conducted by CERFE Group (2001) and by the European Commission (2002), there was evidence that the involvement in the practice of CSR is positively related to firm size, and therefore increases with the move from micro businesses to small and medium-sized businesses. These same studies also show some of the traits of those European SMEs that engage in interventions of social responsibility: (a) their participation in networks of relations with an interest in quality; (b) their openness to foreign markets; (c) their involvement in products with a high environmental impact; and (c) their strong use of intellectual capital.

In relation to the areas of application, the research points out that the internal dimension is the most interesting. The adoption of socially responsible behavior seems to be directly related to the daily demand for improved effectiveness and efficiency in business activities and the creation of value, therefore actions taken by firms are mainly directed at staff and resources used (UNIDO 2002).[2] The research has also shown a higher sensitivity in SMEs towards the environmental and social problems of the territory in which they operate.[3] These companies have a strong sense of identity and local roots as 'land companies' connected to local contexts (Del Baldo 2009). The same conclusion comes from the work of Molteni and Todisco (2008) that identifies the relationships with employees, the local community and the environment; the areas most manned by SMEs.

All theoretical and empirical studies share the essential characteristics of CSR in SMEs. We talk increasingly implicitly (Matten and Moon 2004), informally (Perrini 2006) and silently (Jenkins 2004) of socially responsible behavior which is sometimes adopted by the entrepreneur without him being aware of the meaning of social responsibility, but that occurs in a strongly globalized context which becomes a reliable factor of differentiation, a generator of competitive advantage that brings companies a high visibility and an increase in profit (Molteni and Todisco 2008).

For these authors, beyond the typical aspects of CSR in SMEs, it is interesting to dwell on the theoretical perspective that should be of interest in the study of social responsibility in these companies. Indeed, if the stakeholder theory is the most appropriate theoretical approach to study CSR in large businesses, for SMEs the study should be based on the concept of 'social capital' (Perrini 2006). The relational aspect is a distinctive feature of SMEs (Birley 1985), it is a driver for developing strategic paths that rest on the ability to weave informal relations, internal and external, through participation in networks (Marchini 1995). Moreover, the relational aspect is a distinctive aspect of the socially oriented SMEs (Chirieleison 2002). Some studies emphasize the importance of CSR in SMEs because of the bond they have with the local system (Harvey et al. 1991; Perrini and Tencati 2008). These companies, in fact, are usually tightly integrated with the local community from which they draw resources that are often unavailable or difficult to reproduce within the structure. So there exists a relationship of mutual interdependence between businesses and the communities in which they operate and, consequently, the competitiveness of the area depends on the prosperity and competitiveness of SMEs with strong local roots. The ability to build consensus and confidence around the business plan is an essential element for these companies, along with the ability to make relationships by virtue of the presence of many small firms in industrial districts, where the link between businesses and the area is emphasized and the role of relationships emerges as a strategic asset. These elements suggest a clear direction for the spread of CSR in SMEs, suggesting these companies should develop processes and policies of social responsibility based on the richness of their own 'social capital'.

THE DIFFERENT PERSPECTIVES IN THE STUDY OF 'MADE IN'

The product's origin, or the country-of-origin effect, is located in the literature between the extrinsic characteristics of goods and can play a different role depending on the social context, the products being chosen and the individual characteristics of the consumer (Bertoli et al. 2005).

The literature has studied this issue from different angles. The significance of geographical origin is the first and most important issue, as today companies tend to articulate more and more the value chain at the supranational level. On this point, starting from an initial position which identifies the country of origin of a product as that in which the manufacture or assembly takes place (Han and Terpstra 1988a), or one in which the registered office of the company is located (Johansson et al. 1985), the literature has come to distinguish between the 'origin country', namely the country that consumers associate with a specific product independently of the knowledge of where the product was manufactured; the 'designed-in country' in which a conception, design or product design is made; and the 'Made in country' where production takes place (or the assembly of components) (Nebenzahl et al. 1997).

Another aspect investigated in the literature is the role of country-of-origin effect, namely the fact that the country of origin of the good has an effect on consumer choice (Schooler 1965). The basic assumption is that the image of the country of origin of the product is used by the consumer as 'substitute information', and therefore is an element in the evaluation process of the consumer which can exert a 'halo effect' (halo construct), where the consumer has no direct experience of products from a given country, and a 'summary effect' in the case of previous experiences of purchase (summary construct) (Bertoli et al. 2005).

The literature has also studied the conditions for information on the country of manufacture of the product, as it may exert some influence on the consumers' buying process (Usunier 2002). Among the variables introduced in the analysis we found[4] aspects that qualify the consumer, such as socio-demographic characteristics (Shimp and Sharma 1987), ethnocentric and patriotic propensity (Balabanis and Diamantopoulos 2004) and traditionalist and nationalist sentiments (Han and Terpstra 1998b), and aspects of the product and/or country with which it is associated. The literature has analysed how the name of 'Made in', thanks to a production tradition that boasts the country of origin, can boost the competitive advantage of domestic offers (Roth and Romeo 1992) – aspects related to the economic environment (Johansson and Nebenzahl 1986) and aspects related to the brand (Kotabe and Helsen 2003).

There is no doubt now that it is necessary to adopt an approach known as multi-cue in order to assess the impact of the factor 'Made in' relative to other variables that are typically involved in the processes of choice of individuals, thus moderating the effect exerted by the country of origin (Peterson and Jolibert 1995).

Another perspective of this chapter is the analysis of the attractiveness of 'Made in', where the planning and the management of the relationship between the country's image and the products realized is a real challenge for companies intending to assign a strategic value to the geographical origin of the product. The contribution of Roth and Romeo (2002) provides interesting insights on how to manage the country of origin effects. But beyond this remarkable work, it is difficult to find a useful instrument for the realization of a strategy based on image.

A particular focus of the studies in this direction comes from some Italian authors. The literature on the internationalization of firms has often made reference to the difficulty SMEs have in implementing the marketing investment necessary to become truly visible on an international level (Cafferata and Genco 1997). Among the possible solutions listed, along with the use of partnerships and alliances (Becattini and Meninghello 1988), is the possibility of recourse to the enhancement of geographic origin (Morace 2001; Guerini 2004). The territory can become the key resource against foreign competition, the resource on which to invest to succeed, and consolidate the presence of SMEs in international markets.[5] While other research has highlighted, even in the presence of a positive value of 'Made in', the difficulties related to the need to translate the image of a country in a promotion and marketing program (Dobni and Zinkham 1990).

Finally, with regard to the analysis of the hallmarks of Made in Italy – beauty, functionality and taste (Corbellini 2004); craftsmanship, understood as creativity and imagination; culture, social and relational qualities;[6] and the parameter of variety and multiplicity – all are considered important aspects (Eurisko 2007) together with the ability to balance opposing elements, apparently difficult to reconcile: tradition and modernity, craftsmanship and technology, aesthetics and functionality.

It has been said that the Made in Italy industries of food, fashion, footwear and furniture (Corbellini 2004; Fraschini 2008; Massi 2009) identify Italy for its creativity and manufacturing capacity. It is a heritage of quality which must be not only recognized but also promoted, protected and enhanced in order to improve the competitiveness of small and medium-sized Italian companies (Cianetti 2007).

But in relation to the identification and protection of the brand Made in Italy, the process has not had an easy life: the Decree-Law No. 135 of

September 25, 2009, relating to 'Urgent provisions for the implementation of Community obligations and enforcement of judgments of the Court of Justice of the European Communities' (the so-called 'Ronchi Decree') sets out clearly and unequivocally that 'the product or goods may be classified as "Made in Italy" only if the design, planning, processing and packaging are made exclusively in the Italian territory'. Recently, law 55/2010, which entered into force with the decision of 06/05/2010, modified its decision, stating that for footwear, clothing, textiles and furniture businesses, at least two phases of work must be carried out in Italy in order for the words Made in Italy to be used on the products sold.

THE CONCEPTUAL FRAMEWORK

The Italian economy is significantly characterized by the presence of SMEs, often involved with local districts and parts of the community. Their success is often correlated with the degree of legitimacy and approval by the local stakeholders, as well as by the image that the Italian country enjoys abroad: to promote their products outside their national territory, SMEs point to the connection of their company with the territory of origin from which they draw their resources and skills, often failing to build a relationship of mutual interdependence with the communities in which they operate.

But what happens when the country's image has a negative impact on competitiveness, thus affecting the process of the international development of companies? If a once highly thought of area becomes subject to negative publicity, the various economic actors present in that territory can no longer enjoy the advantage of the differential allocation of resources at the international level and make use of any comparative advantage in that area, they will also suffer from the negative exposure of the territory that will affect the competitive advantage of their companies and raise the costs that they will incur to curb the inefficiencies produced by the local system.

This chapter argues that the companies which sustain their competitiveness in foreign markets, where there is a reduction of the positive value of 'Made in', can apply CSR strategies or at least CSR initiatives (code of ethics, social balance, SA8000 certification, EMAS certification, and so on). CSR is then considered as a viable strategic alternative that allows the company to stem the negative impact produced by the local system and to regain competitiveness in domestic and foreign markets, through the revaluation of assets and of business skills.

Therefore, companies need to implement integrated management of these two factors of competitiveness, 'Made in' and CSR, and this rela-

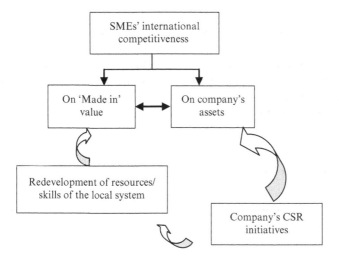

Figure 5.1   Relationships among 'Made in', CSR and international performance of SMEs

tionship can be articulated in multiple ways. In fact, depending on their needs, companies can simultaneously handle the two factors, investing in the product's link with the territory, but at the same time investing in the product (quality, safety, visibility, and so on) and in the information to be imparted to consumers. It could also happen that CSR intervenes in support of a loss of value of 'Made in', and can be used as a possible lever for differentiation: enrichment of the social and environmental characteristics of products or directing the production process to comply with a greater respect for the environment (Molteni and Todisco 2008).

From this comes the belief that CSR initiatives, although still not structured in a broader strategic plan,[7] lead to a strengthening of corporate assets consolidating the competitiveness that is based on the distinctive resources/competencies of the company (see Figure 5.1).

The ultimate aim of this chapter may be summarized as emphasizing the importance of integrated management of these two factors and the description of a positive relationship among 'Made in', CSR and the international performance of SMEs. In order to achieve these goals, the specific aspects of research that have been analysed are:

1. the importance that the factor 'Made in' holds for the international development of SMEs, its relevance to the decisions of firms to internationalize and the perception of the value attributed by foreign customers;

2. the relationship between CSR and characteristics of the property, as well as the external dimension of CSR in relation to: consumers, the local community and the environment;
3. the relationship between the factor 'Made in' and CSR tools such as alternative or complementary factors in the management of international development of SMEs;
4. the presence of a positive relationship among 'Made in', CSR and the international performance of the company.

METHODOLOGY

The empirical research was conducted using the case method (Dubois and Gadde 2002; Yin 2002), with the help of a questionnaire administered to owners/managers of selected enterprises in the period from February to April 2011.

The criteria to select firms focused on four aspects:

1. the firms to be interviewed to come under the category of SMEs, as set forth in the latest indication of the EU;
2. the firms to demonstrate a significant level of internationalization, expressed in the sale of products in foreign markets in reasonable percentages and not on an occasional basis;
3. the presence in the firms of at least one of the tools of CSR (code of ethics, social balance, ISO, and so on);
4. the firms to be in an area where there is the added value of Made in Italy, but who at the same time are experiencing a loss in value.

Starting from the latter, it was decided to select the food industry and, specifically, the sectors of oil, wine and dairy products, in relation to companies operating in the Campania region in Italy (see Table 5.1).

The characteristics of the food industry, such as tradition, quality and authenticity of the product, powered by a popular culture of know-how, make it inextricably linked to the territory. With particular attention to the Campania region, the territory was unfortunately the scenario of a succession of crises (the question of waste, the excessive presence of dioxin, various frauds and contamination). This situation has undermined the image of those sectors of the food industry that are strongly rooted in the territory, some of them selected in the empirical investigation, and has caused the loss of the positive connotation of the brand Made in Italy and encouraged companies to seek new factors for international competitiveness.

Table 5.1 Interviewed firms' characteristics

Firms	Size (no. employees)						Level of internationalization						CSR tools (*)
	Micro <10		Small <50		Medium <250		Up to 10%		From 10 to 30%		Over 30%		
	n.	%	n.	%	n.	%	n.	%	n.	%	n.	%	
Wine	9	75	3	25	–	–	8	67	4	33	–	–	Code of Ethics (7), environmental labeling (7), quality and environmental certifications (8).
Oil	3	75	1	25	–	–	2	50	1	25	1	25	System Certification: ISO 14001 (2), BRC (1), IFS (1), Environmental labels (2).
Cheese	1	33	1	33	1	33	2	67	1	33	–	–	Code of Ethics (1), Social Report (1); system certifications: ISO 9001 (2), ISO 14001 (1) ISO 22005 (1), OHSAS 18001 (1), environmental labeling (1), laboratory analysis of CHELAB SINAL accredited (1).

Note: (*) The numbers of cases detected are reported in parentheses.

The CSR is analysed in this work as one of the alternatives to restore the international competitiveness of enterprises, where the factor 'Made in' as a means of entry into foreign markets is less meaningful in the buying processes of international consumers.

The indicators used to evaluate companies in respect of the external dimension of CSR in relation to certain categories of stakeholders (customers, the local community and the environment), are selected from those put forward as suitable by the Project CSR–SC (Corporate Social Responsibility–Social Commitment) of the Ministry of Labour and Social Policy (2005).

RESULTS OF SURVEY

Characteristics of Enterprise and Awareness of CSR

The level of awareness of the tools of CSR does not seem to depend on either the size of the company nor the type of legal form. Neither does the education level of members affect the level of awareness. In fact, there are no significant differences in the number of instruments adopted between companies with shareholders who hold high school qualifications and those in which the proprietor is in possession of a university degree. However, the latter element seems to have a weight in the reasons for the adoption of CSR tools. In fact, in the companies that have a corporate structure with members who hold degrees, there is evidence of use of the tools of CSR to penetrate new markets for reasons of image and corporate values, compared to the primary reason in all firms – a request by the client.

Specifically, this motivation prevails in the wine business, while for the oil mills an increased preference is recorded, albeit a slight one, for reasons of penetration into new markets and for the effect of image. Finally, in the dairy business a desire to respect the rules is recorded, together with motivations indicated by the other companies (see Table 5.2).

The analysis also shows that the higher the education level, the greater the propensity for the participation of members in non-profit areas in general and to social engagement, including with regard to environmental issues.

Depending on the type of instruments used, the survey shows a greater preference of companies for various forms of certification of product quality and environmental certifications (18 preferences); for environmental labeling (10); and for the code of ethics (8).

Regarding the external dimension of CSR, the analysis reveals that the

Table 5.2   Level of education and motivations of members to the adoption of CSR

Motivations	Number of preferences				Level of education of members	
	All	Wineries	Oil mills	Cheese factories	University degree	High school qualifications
Buyer's request	13	9	2	2	5	8
Penetration into new markets	6	2	3	1	4	2
Relapse image	6	2	2	2	3	3
Business legislation (specify whether domestic or foreign)	–	–	–	2	1	1
General regulatory obligations (specify whether domestic or foreign)	–	–	–	–	–	–
Values and corporate culture	6	2	3	1	4	2
Other (specify)						

highest number of preferences expressed by the companies interviewed is at the level of consumer interventions, in particular with initiatives for customer satisfaction (79 per cent of all firms), and the information on and labeling of products and services (84 per cent). In relation to individual sectors, the survey shows that 100 per cent of wineries have wine tastings, and in some cases carry out special initiatives such as the 'tales of wine night' (in three cases). All of these companies have developed the product labeling Destination of Origin (DOC). Even oil production companies have invested in developing a label and organic certification (67 per cent), as well as in customer satisfaction initiatives (67 per cent), while dairy companies have set up call centers to respond to requests and manage complaints, and have invested in a policy of transparency of communication of quality and product safety, using information labels (100 per cent).

With regard to the actions of CSR in the community, a small number of cases show businesses being involved in organizing cultural events through the preparation of culinary courses to foster knowledge of the product, open factory initiatives to prove the genuineness of the different stages of processing, and sponsorship of sporting events and fairs in the area. In one case, which concerns a dairy farm, the presence of initiatives targeted at foreign communities was found, promoting the product through information courses to Cairo (Egypt).

Finally, interventions in the environment are really small in number (only three cases) and relate to actions to reduce energy consumption and waste production. The dairy companies surveyed appear to be more aware of the importance of social responsibility towards the environment, constantly adopting solutions to reduce fuel consumption and pollutant emissions (that is, using internal analysts to monitor consumption, and investment in a natural gas boiler).

The Value of Made in Italy for International Competitiveness

The survey results confirm that the factor Made in Italy is of great importance in the internationalization strategies of firms (100 per cent of the oil mills and dairies, 83 per cent of wineries), although there are some differences: in wineries that have higher percentages of sales abroad, and in the dairy business, with a high concentration in the overseas market, the factor Made in Italy is seen as an additional element, since in these cases the companies base their strategy for foreign market penetration on the quality of the products offered, on the investment in Protected Destination of Origin (DOP) products and on brand policy.

Quality, culture and craftsmanship, seen as know-how, are the hallmarks of Made in Italy with foreign clients, as indicated by the companies interviewed and those which are investing in promoting the product abroad. The dairy companies also note that participation in international food fairs, as well as local ones, is a very useful tool for research and the selection of foreign markets, as well as the use of certificates to prove the quality and authenticity of the product. The companies that produce oil have referred to the traceability of extra virgin olive oil, to the organoleptic analysis attached to the invoice, and to the labeling and packaging care, among the initiatives to support the quality of the product.

The survey then asked for an opinion on the possible changes produced on Made in Italy by Law No. 135/2009. In this regard, the analysis showed

Table 5.3 *Damage arising from environmental emergencies and fraud in the food sector (number of cases)*

	Decline in sales		Loss of foreign markets
	Italy	Abroad	
Up to 10%	3	2	
From 10% to 20%	2	2	Japan, USA
From 20% to 50%	2	1	

that the impact in the segments analysed is not relevant, because some adjustments had already been required by legislation on DOP and DOC (63 per cent of preferences).

Regarding the phenomenon of the value of Made in Italy, in the sectors investigated the companies said that as a result of the various frauds that have affected the food industry and the environmental crisis that is affecting the Campania region, first with regard to the matter of waste and second the dioxin levels, the value of Made in Italy has decreased (Table 5.3). In particular, it seems that oil mills and the dairy businesses have mainly been affected. The first reported a decline in sales in Italy up to 20 per cent, as well as a reduction in foreign sales (up to 15 per cent), where there is both a loss of an export market (Japan) and a failure to enter into the US market. Similarly, the entire sector of buffalo farming was deeply shocked by these events, which led to a significant drop in sales of buffalo mozzarella with consequent repercussions on all farms. As pointed out by companies, such events have steered the customer away from the product significantly, producing a drop in sales both in Italy and abroad (up to 50 per cent) and the loss of the US as a market (in one case). The companies have stated unanimously that the crisis in the dairy sector has affected all firms in Campania, as in the overseas market a tendency has emerged to generalize the origin of the product without distinguishing between the territorial divisions of the various provinces of Campania.

It would appear that the wineries have defended themselves better, with only one case showing a decline in sales, while in other cases there has been no change in the choices made by consumers. Notably, in three cases companies have provided certificates of product quality on request.

Relations among 'Made in', CSR and International Performance

The analysis of firms' international performance must consider the following elements:

1.   the relationship between performance and area of origin;
2.   the relationship between 'Made in' and CSR;
3.   the role of local authorities to improve the competitiveness of sectors.

On the first point, the survey found that the area appears to have greater importance for the dairy companies and oil mills. The first two out of three have argued that the DOC product is so typical that it would be impossible to reproduce elsewhere and therefore the link with the territory is inseparable. This typicality is recognized and appreciated worldwide, so the area of origin of the product assumes a great importance for the firms' international success. It should, however, be recorded that an important aspect has been noted in one case, namely that the lack of knowledge of regional differences with regard to the different provinces of the Campania region that are more or less involved in the crisis has resulted in damaging the international performance of the company, which has lost its US market.

In contrast, in 75 per cent of cases, wineries have declared that the territory assumes an average importance.

With regard to the relationship between CSR and 'Made in', the survey showed that in all the companies, the tools of CSR are judged positively in improving the international competitiveness of businesses: in particular benefits creating a greater customer loyalty and improvement of social consensus and image (15 preferences), and are considered an important advantage in the increase in market share (11 preferences) and entry into new markets (9 preferences).

Regarding the relationship between CSR and 'Made in', a distinction needs to be made between the different sectors analysed. In the dairy companies the use of the instruments of CSR has been motivated mainly by

Table 5.4   CSR and impact on business competitiveness (number of preferences)

Type of impact	Wineries	Oil mills	Dairies	All firms
Increased market share	9	1	1	11
Reduced costs	–	1	–	1
Entering new markets	7	2	1	10
Customer loyalty	11	2	2	15
Positive externalities on the community	–	–	–	–
Social consensus and image	11	2	2	15
Other (specify)	–	–	–	–
ND	1	2	–	3

the need to cope with the crisis in the sector and in the image of Made in Italy. In fact, the tools of CSR were considered a valuable support in overcoming the crisis in the sector. Although the initiatives of call centers as a tool for the customer already existed in the company before the crisis, the tools of information and labeling were used to increase the transparency of information and quality certificates were also introduced to gain more credibility on international markets. In addition, for these companies, the presence of CSR tools before the crisis was considered a positive element. The coexistence of the two factors, Made in Italy and CSR, compensated for when the Made in Italy label lost value, by allowing the companies to significantly enhance their CSR initiatives.

Companies that produce oil demonstrate a significant relationship between the use of CSR initiatives and the crisis of Made in Italy, although they also show the link between product and territory to be an important element. They choose to invest in product quality and its communication through explanatory labels and organic labels, thus focusing more on a political brand.

Wineries in the sector have adopted CSR tools irrespective of the crisis of Made in Italy. In fact 91 per cent of companies said they had not suffered any damage in sales both in Italy and abroad, although for more than 75 per cent of businesses, Made in Italy is an important factor. These companies are investing in product labeling, and therefore most are pursuing a policy of brand.

Finally, in relation to the role of local institutions, companies have unanimously declared that the dialogue between institutional and private operators is crucial for the image and credibility of their branches, especially outside of the regional market. Some companies have also stated that, next to the moral contribution, it would be desirable to have a system of tax and economic incentives and, as well as for some wineries, local institutions should assume the role of real local development planners. A more specific analysis is merited for the dairy companies who have stated the following demands: more targeted investments[8] and greater control of the destination and uses of funds, bureaucratic simplification and greater coordination between the various bodies responsible for monitoring and surveillance. The overlapping of authority creates, in fact, wasted time and costs for both institutions and for the company.

MANAGERIAL IMPLICATIONS

The information obtained from empirical research leads to an initial reflection on the need for integrated management of the two international competitiveness factors investigated in this work: 'Made in' and CSR. If the local territory holds a high importance for companies' international success and the factor 'Made in' is a key factor for international competitiveness, if it loses its value CSR initiatives can be implemented by companies primarily to regain competitiveness with foreign clients. Conversely, where the area of origin is not a decisive influence on the choices of foreign customers and the 'Made in' is an additional factor in the decision-making process of consumers, CSR initiatives should further strengthen the competitiveness that is based on corporate assets.

This situation describes different models of behavior in relation to internationalization strategies that can be pursued by the companies through integrated management of these two factors (see Table 5.5).

The first category may be contained in those situations where foreign customers do not attach a certain value to 'Made in' in their purchasing decisions and, therefore, for the enterprise 'Made in' does not ensure competitive advantage in international markets. The international marketing, in these cases, should be directed at bringing out the distinct character of a product, through a careful marketing policy that aims at enhancing the brand, investing in the quality and authenticity of the product and timely communication to customers (eco-brand, environmental labeling). Therefore the strategy of internationalization should not be based on the exaltation of the 'Made in' factor, which is intended as an additional factor of competitiveness. The policy of international expansion should be selective and take place through a careful management of foreign clients. The quality of the product and the confidence gained from the foreign customers should become competitive factors.

Under this strategy, the loss of value of 'Made in' does not damage a company's competitiveness, or only to a minor degree, and therefore CSR initiatives are seen as tools to further enhance competitiveness, which is based on corporate assets. So they are not designed to compensate for the loss of value of 'Made in'.

The second category describes a model of corporate behavior that considered extremely important the positive perception that foreign consumers have of the product with 'Made in'. Consequently, for decisions regarding international development, these firms should base their policies on the marketing value of this factor. The choice of markets should reflect this view, as countries of destination are different (in the cases analysed they are mainly European countries – France, the UK, Holland, Germany and Switzerland, but also Japan and the US).

The strong identification of the product with the value given to 'Made in', and the internationalization strategy focused on the presentation of a healthy territory and on a quality product, has led to the crisis in the sector

Table 5.5 Matrix of prevailing models of SMEs' behavior in international markets

'Made in' perception by the consumer	'Made in' value for the company	Internationalization strategies	Markets	International competitiveness factors	Firm's CSR initiatives
High	'Made in' is a competitiveness factor.	Enhancing the relationship with the territory.	Extensive policy.	Belonging to the land.	Tools to recover the competitiveness valuing the business assets.
Low	'Made in' is not a guarantee of competitive advantage.	Enhancement of company offer. Brand-oriented policy.	Selected policy.	Company assets: quality product, trust of the foreign client.	Tools to strengthen the international competitiveness of the company based on company assets.

followed by crisis in the companies. In response to this situation, companies have been forced to rethink their strategy and have enhanced their use of CSR instruments to a greater extent some of which had already been introduced in companies before the crisis. In this model, CSR initiatives have become indispensable tools for the revaluation of corporate assets and the recovery of competitiveness on foreign markets.

CONCLUSIONS

Two main conclusions can be made regarding this work. The first concerns the danger of an internationalization strategy that relies solely on the factor 'Made in' and the need for integrated management of the two factors, 'Made in' and CSR, to sustain the competitive advantage of SMEs operating abroad. For many SMEs until a few years ago, the label Made in Italy enhanced and supported their presence in international markets. Now, unfortunately, given the frequent environmental crises, as well as the fraud that has affected many Italian manufacturing industry sectors, companies are aware of the need to invest more on their product, brand visibility, customer information, and pursuing ways and means of demonstrating social responsibility.

The second conclusion concerns the importance of concerted action with local institutions to defend a territory and to promote the 'Made in'. In both literature and European research the importance of adopting an approach based on local networks has been emphasized, where SMEs can take advantage of the opportunity to operate as a meta-organization, and institutions play a key role in brokering to promote strategies inspired by CSR, acting as intermediaries between businesses and the local context in which they operate (Antoldi et al. 2008; De Chiara 2012). However, research reveals how far we are from this model, although the companies surveyed in all sectors have highlighted the importance of strategic leadership in synergy with the local system and the importance of a wider involvement of the institutions, together with the initiatives of individual companies, to spread the adoption of CSR and to support industries.

The limitations of this research, that at the same time represent stimuli for future development, can be detected in the absence of a parallel investigation with foreign clients in order to assess the actual weight that CSR initiatives have on the restoration of the competitiveness of manufacturers.

NOTES

1. In Europe 99 per cent of enterprises are SMEs which provide 67.4 per cent of total jobs and produce approximately 58 per cent of total value added (Eurostat, estimates 2008). In addition, in the European economic system Italian firms are smaller (3.9 is the average of workers employed compared to 6 in the 15 EU states) (Eurostat 2005).
2. For further reading on drivers and barriers to the development of CSR practices in SMEs, see Alastair (2009).
3. See European Expert Group on CSR and SMEs (2007).
4. For analysis and references see Bertoli et al. (2005).
5. Many of the references are found in the theory of industrial districts and in studies on the processes of international development of SMEs. Among others, see Cavusgil (1980) and Czinkota and Tesar (1982).
6. Italians have a strong sense of family and community, and this is perceived as an important element of strength from the point of view of economics and productivity (just think of the company–family districts).
7. Some studies have shown that in order to speak of a CSR strategy two conditions must occur: an explicit statement of social/environmental objectives in the mission and in the strategic choices; and the formalization of organizational solutions for the implementation of the strategy (Smith 2003; Porter 2008; Contri and Maccarone 2009).
8. One of the most immediate problems to be resolved concerns the difficulties in terms of time and cost for the rapid transport anywhere in the world of easily perishable dairy products, such as buffalo mozzarella from Campania DOP. Some time ago, the National Council of Research (CNR) decided to solve the problem by studying a plant product that was able to stop the fermentation of cheese, but because of the excessive cost of the patent the project has not been developed.

REFERENCES

Alastair A. (2009), 'Literature review and conceptual framework for the drivers and barriers to imparting free environmental knowledge and training to SMEs', in A. Mumba and Tarja Ketola (eds), *Responsible Leadership: Proceedings of the Corporate Responsibility Research (CRR) 2009*, Vaasa, Finland: Conference Proceedings of the University of Vaasa, Reports 157, pp. 731–748.

Antoldi F., D. Cerrato and Alessandra Todisco (2008), 'La responsabilità sociale delle PMI distrettuali', in Molteni Mario and Alessandra Todisco (eds), *Responsabilità sociale d'impresa. Come le PMI possono migliorare le performance aziendali mediante politiche di CSR. Logiche, strumenti, benefici*, Milano: Guida del Sole 24 Ore, pp. 115–142.

Balabanis, G. and A. Diamantopoulos (2004), 'Domestic country bias, country-of-origin effects and consumer ethnocentrism: a multidimensional unfolding approach', *Journal of the Academy of Marketing Science*, 32(1), 80–95.

Becattini, G. and S. Meninghello (1998), 'Il Made in Italy distrettuale', *Sviluppo locale*, 5(9).

Bertoli, G., B. Busacca and L. Molteni (2005), 'Consumatore, marca ed "Effetto Made in". Evidenze dall'Italia e dagli Stati Uniti', *Finanza, Marketing e Produzione*, 47, 5–32.

Birley, S. (1985), 'The role of networks in the entrepreneurial process', *Journal of Business Venturing*, 3(1), 107–117.

Cafferata, Roberto and Pietro Genco (1997), *Competitività e internazionalizzazione delle piccole medie imprese*, Bologna: Il Mulino.

Cavusgil, T.S. (1980), 'On the internationalization process of firms', *European Research*, 8(6), 273–280.

CERFE Group (2001), *Action Research on Corporate Citizenship among European Small and Medium Enterprises*, CERFE Laboratory.

Chirieleison, Cecilia (2002), *Le strategie sociali nel governo dell'azienda*, Milano: Giuffrè.

Cianetti, E. (2007), 'Made in Italy', *De Qualitate*, 3, 56–63.

Contri, A. and P. Maccarone (2009), 'The integration of CSR into business strategy: an empirical analysis of large Italian firms', in A. Mumba and Tarja Ketola (eds), *Responsible Leadership: Proceedings of the Corporate Responsibility Research (CRR) 2009 Conference*, Vaasa, Finland: Conference Proceedings of the University of Vaasa, Reports 157.

Corbellini, E. (2004), 'Comunicare il Made in Italy', *Economia & Management*, 5, 48–49.

Czinkota, Michael R. and George Tesar (eds) (1982), *Export Policy: A Global Assessment*, New York: Praeger.

De Chiara, Alessandra (2009), 'When an area becames an enemy: the role of CSR in SME's development strategies', in A. Mumba and Tarja Ketola (eds), *Responsible Leadership: Proceedings of the Corporate Responsibility Research (CRR) 2009 Conference*, Vaasa, Finland: Conference Proceedings of the University of Vaasa, Reports 157, pp. 749–765.

De Chiara, A. (2012), 'La competitività responsabile nelle PMI: strategia vincente nei territori "nemici"', *Piccola Impresa/Small Business*, 1, 29–52.

Del Baldo, M. (2009), 'Corporate social responsibility e corporate governance: quale nesso nelle PMI?', *Rivista Piccola Impresa/Small Business*, 3, 61–102.

Dobni, D. and G.M. Zinkham (1990), 'In search of brand image: a foundation analysis', *Advances in Consumer Research*, 17, 100–119.

Dubois, A. and L.E. Gadde (2002), 'Systematic combining – an abductive approach to case research', *Journal of Business Research*, 55, 553–560.

Eurisko (2007), 'Sei modi per dire qualità', rapporto di ricerca sul 'Made in Italy', http://www.symbola.net/html/press/pressrelease/Seimodiperdirequalita.

European Commission (2001), 'Promuovere un quadro europeo per la responsabilità sociale delle imprese', Libro Verde, http://eur-lex.europa.eu.

European Commission (2002), 'Corporate social responsibility: a business contribution to sustainable development', http://trade.ec.

European Commission – Observatory of European SMEs (2004), 'Final results and recommendations', http://ec.europa.eu.

European Expert Group on CSR and SMEs (2007), 'Responsabilità nuove prospettive. Come aiutare le piccole imprese ad agire in modo socialmente e ambientalmente responsabile', http//.europa.eu.

Eurostat (2005), 'Small and medium-sized enterprises (SMEs)', http://epp.eurostat.ec.europa.eu/portal/page/portal/european_business/special_sbs_topics/small_medium_sized_enterprises_SMEs.

Fraschini, A. (2008), 'Tutti frutti del Made in Italy', *Largo Consumo*, 10, 37–39.

Guerini, Carolina (2004), *Made in Italy e mercati internazionali. La valorizzazione dell'origine geografica nelle strategie di marketing delle imprese italiane*, Milano: Egea.

Han, C.M. and V. Terpstra (1998a), 'Country of origin effects for uni-national and bi-national products', *Journal of International Business Studies*, 16, 235–255.

Han, C.M. and V. Terpstra (1998b), 'The role of consumer patriotism in the choice of domestic vs foreign products', *Journal of Advertising Research*, June–July, 25–32, Cambridge Journals.

Harvey, Brian, Henk Van Luijk and Guido Corbetta (1991), *Market Morality and Company Size*, London: Kluwer.

Jenkins, H.M. (2004), 'A critique of conventional CSR theory: an SME perspective', *Journal of General Management*, Summer 29(4), 37–57.

Johansson, J.K. and I.D. Nebenzahl (1986), 'Multinational production: effects on brand value', *Journal of International Business Studies*, 17(3), 101–126.

Johansson, J.K., S.P. Douglas and I. Nonaka (1985), 'Assessing the impact of country of origin on product evaluations: a new methodological perspective', *Journal of Marketing Research*, 22, 388–396.

Kotabe, Masaaki and Kristiaan Helsen (2003), *Global Marketing Management*, New York: John Wiley & Sons.

Marchini, Isa (1995), *Il governo della piccolo impresa*, Vol.II, *La gestione strategica*, 1st edn, Genova: ASPI/InsEdit.

Massi, F. (2009), 'Il sostegno all'abitare Made in Italy', *Largo Consumo*, 3, 22–23.

Matten, D. and J. Moon (2004), 'Corporate social responsibility education in Europe', *Journal of Business Ethics*, 54(4), 323–337.

Ministry of Labour and Social Policy (2005), 'Project CSR-SC', www.welfare.gov.it/CSR.

Molteni, Mario and Alessandra Todisco (eds) (2008), *Responsabilità sociale d'impresa. Come le PMI possono migliorare le performance aziendali mediante politiche di CSR. Logiche, strumenti, benefici*, Milano: Guida del Sole 24 Ore.

Morace, Francesco (2001), *La strategia del colibrì. La globalizzazione e il suo antidoto*, Milano: Sperling & Kupfer.

Nebenzahl, I.D., E.D. Jaffé and S.I. Lampert (1997), 'Towards a theory of country image effect on product evaluation', *Management International Review*, 37(1), 27–49.

Perrini, F. (2006), 'SMEs and CSR theory: evidence and implications from an Italian perspective', *Journal of Business Ethics*, September, 67 (3) 305–316.

Perrini, Francesco and Antonio Tencati (2008), *Corporate Social Responsibility*, Milano: Egea.

Peterson, R.A. and A.J.P Jolibert (1995), 'A meta analysis of country of origin effects', *International Journal of Business Studies*, 26(4), 883–900.

Porter, T.B. (2008), 'Managerial applications of corporate social responsibility and systems thinking for achieving sustainability outcomes', *Systems Research and Behavioral Science*, 25(3).

Roth, M.S. and G.B Romeo (1992), 'Matching product category and country image perceptions: a framework for managing country of origin effects', *Journal of International Business Studies*, 3, 447–497.

Schooler, R.D. (1965), 'Product bias in Central American common market', *Journal of Marketing Research*, 2, 394–397.

Shimp, T.A. and S. Sharma (1987), 'Consumer ethnocentrism: construction and validation of the CETSCAL', *Journal of Marketing Research*, 26, 280–289.

Smith, N.C. (2003), 'Corporate social responsibility: whether or how?', *California Management Review*, 45(4), 52–76.

Spence, L., R. Schimidpeter and A. Habisch (2003), 'Assessing social capital: small and medium size enterprises in Germany and UK', *Journal of Business Ethics*, 47(1), 17–29.

Spence, L. (1999), 'Does size matter? The state of art in small business ethics', *Business Ethics: A European Review*, 8(3), 163–174.

UNIDO (2002), *Corporate Social Responsibility: Implications for Small and Medium Enterprises in Developing Countries*, Vienna, www.unido.com.

Usunier, J.C. (2002), 'Le pays d'origine du bien influence-t-il encore les évaluations des consommateur?', *Revue Francaise du Marketing*, 189–190, 49–65.

Yin, Robert (2002), *Case Study Research, Applied Social Research Methods Series*, Vol. 5, Newbury Park, CA: Sage.

PART III

The tools to exploit the country of origin
effect

6. Distribution channel governance and value of 'Made in Italy' products in the Chinese market

Donata Vianelli, Patrizia de Luca and Guido Bortoluzzi[1]

The country of origin advantage is not sufficient for success in foreign markets if the governance of distribution channels is weak. A company's strategy to leverage the country of origin of a product (or company) in international markets must take into consideration the role of distributors in order to deliver part of the value that is embedded in the given product or brand to final consumers.

The present research aims to analyse the degree of control exerted on distribution channels by small and medium-sized Italian companies entering the Chinese market. All selected companies (a total of 71) considered belong to the furniture, food and fashion industries: sectors in which Italian companies typically leverage the Made in Italy effect and where the role of the foreign distributor is significant to strengthen the positive value of the country of origin effect. An online self-administered questionnaire was used to collect results.

The main results show the need for improvement in the governance of distribution channels for Italian companies operating in China. The current use of indirect entry modes and problematic relationships with Chinese distribution partners make it difficult to convey the value of Made in Italy to the final consumer, limiting the future growth of Italian companies in the Chinese market.

1. INTRODUCTION

Valorization of country of origin is strongly linked not only to branding and communication strategies but also to management and control of distribution channels. In company internationalization strategies, this control is intrinsically linked to the choice of mode of entry and to the definition of channel structure in the foreign target country. Distribution, connecting supply and demand and representing the place where the brand meets the client, is crucial in influencing visibility and the symbolic perception of the brand by foreign consumers. This is especially true when considering Made in Italy, which is facing hard times in a context of crises and increasing globalization. Italian companies, mainly SMEs, are encountering serious difficulties in differentiating their products from other European competitors. In most cases the reason for this is that they are not able to strengthen and convey to final consumers the symbolic value of their brand, due to a lack of capacity to control distribution channels.

In the context described above, this chapter aims to show the results of an exploratory analysis related to control of distribution channels for Made in Italy products in the Chinese market. While, in recent years, China has offered enormous business opportunities, management of distribution channels is extremely complex.

The literature review, carried out in the preliminary stage of the study, is focused on the role of governance in the internationalization process of company sales, and on the relationship between modes of entry, channel structure and control. The term 'governance' indicates those activities, such as the definition of the distribution channel structure and the choice of the distribution partner, which are related to channel management and are developed for the entry strategy in a foreign market. More specifically, we investigated the main difficulties that indicate a gap of control in strategic and operative marketing decisions, limiting opportunities for success in the Chinese market.

In the second part of the study, after depicting the role of Made in Italy in China, we present results of an empirical research study on a sample of 71 Italian companies. Companies considered in the analysis operate in the food, fashion and furniture market, where the governance of Made in Italy is an essential element of differentiation, especially in the Chinese market. Findings reveal the factors that weaken the channel governance and create a serious risk for the value of Made in Italy.

2.   DOES ENTRY IN THE CHINESE MARKET FIT TRADITIONAL THEORIES AND MODELS?

Interest in the Chinese market by foreign companies is increasing dramatically. According to the World Bank, over the last five years the amount of inward foreign direct investment (FDI) directed to China have risen by roughly 50 percent, from $124 bn in 2006 to $185 bn in 2010 (Balance of Payments database, data in current US$). Scientific interest has gone hand-in-hand with the FDI trend, as noticed by Fetscherin et al. (2010).

If we look back at the last 20 years of Chinese history, two main events can help to explain this upsurge. The first dates back to 1993. In November, the third plenary session of the XIV Central Committee of the Chinese Communist Party set the introduction of market mechanisms within the former socialist system as definitive and irrevocable. The success obtained by Jiang Zemin followed positive results showed by the Special Economic Zones (SEZ) that were strongly supported by Deng Xiaoping from the end of the 1970s. The second event was in December, 2001, when China officially entered the World Trade Organization (WTO). The entry came after several months of tough negotiations over former restrictions imposed by the Chinese Government to foreign investors.[2] Five years later, the levels of incoming FDI nearly doubled.

The greatness of China, and of emerging markets in general, has only recently become more and more apparent as there is an increasing polarization of global market performance. There are, on the one hand, advanced economies such as Europe and the US, which are characterized by a faint and unstable recovery from the worst economic crisis of the last 80 years, and also threatened by the sustainability of their national debts. At the same time there are emerging markets – primarily China and India – who are experiencing an impetuous and seemingly never-ending growth (Table 6.1).

In this upturned economic scenario, where emerging economies attract more developed ones, it is becoming mandatory rather than merely an opportunity for Western companies to enter emerging markets.

Table 6.1   GDP's growth (%) in selected areas and countries

	2008	2009	2010
World	1.4	–2.3	4.2
Euro Area	0.4	–4.3	1.9
USA	0.0	–3.5	3.0
Italy	–1.2	–5.1	1.5
China	9.6	9.2	10.4
Russian Federation	5.2	–7.8	4.0
Turkey	0.7	–4.8	9.0
Brazil	5.2	–0.6	7.5
India	4.9	9.1	8.8
South Africa	3.6	–1.7	2.8

Source: Our elaboration on World Bank website (last accessed: June 2012)

On the scientific side, the growing interest of Western companies for emerging markets has revived the debate over entry strategies for companies. This debate has developed in three main directions:

- the transaction costs economic (TCE) perspective;
- the stage models;
- the holistic perspectives.

According to the TCE perspective, company make-or-buy decisions in foreign markets (typically, FDIs vs. export) are mainly affected by the transactional uncertainty of business relationships. The higher the uncertainty, the higher the degree of control that companies will maintain over foreign activities (Buckley and Casson, 1976, 1981).

Stage models put market knowledge and accumulated experience at the grounding of company decisions in foreign markets. These models are particularly useful for explaining why companies tend to expand gradually (from one market to many markets, from simple export to FDIs) in international markets (Johansson and Vahlne, 1977, 1990).

The holistic perspectives try to explain the company entry decision using multidimensional frameworks. In the case of the OLI paradigm, the entry mode is driven by ownership, localization and internalization advantages (Dunning, 1980, 1988).

Adoption of those lenses to the case of emerging markets has shown incompatibilities from the beginning. It seems that decisions made by companies entering emerging markets are not significantly affected by aspects related to transactional uncertainty as suggested by the TCE perspective. On the contrary, it seems that institutional factors count more when explaining choices by companies (Luo, 2001; Peng, 2003; Wright et al., 2005; Meyer et al., 2009). Those institutional factors – such as cultural differences or the effectiveness of IP rights safeguard mechanisms – remained in the background in past studies since their impact on a company's entry decisions was considered limited.

It also seems that foreign companies entering emerging markets are less 'gradual' in their entry process, as to be expected. They tend to shoot ahead and enter directly, from the real beginning through 'heavy' modes such as FDI and JV, rather than using less risky and resource-committing strategies, such as export (Child and Tse, 2001; Cavusgil et al., 2002).

Even holistic perspectives risk not being holistic enough when applied to emerging markets since the explanatory power of not-in-the-model variables (cultural factors, for example) tend to be significantly higher than in traditional markets. In general, it is difficult to apply pre-defined theoretical frameworks to explain internationalization strategies of companies in emerging markets. Hence, deeper explanations are needed.

By limiting our discussion to the internationalization processes for sales, it is necessary for the company entering the Chinese market to take into account not only the entry mode, but also the marketing strategy so as to ensure long-term sustainable growth. For this reason, managing international distribution channels becomes crucial in order to successfully transmit brand image and create a continuous stream of business transactions (Stern et al., 1996; Jaffe and Yi, 2007).

3. ENTRY MODES, DISTRIBUTION STRATEGIES AND GOVERNANCE IN THE CHINESE MARKET

3.1 Entry Modes

For this contribution, we rely on two research streams: that of International Business which is interested in entry modes of companies, and that of International Marketing, which deals with the management of distribution channels in international markets.

In general terms, company entry mode selection is influenced by both external (to the company) and internal factors (Andersen, 1997; Shenkar and Luo, 2008; Hill, 2009; Hollensen, 2011). Regarding external factors, many have proved relevant, for example: cost of labor, fiscal advantages, intensity of rivalry, existence of government incentives to foreign investors (Cavusgil et al., 2007).

Management scholars tend to be more interested in internal factors, however. The literature agrees on the fact that size matters, since bigger companies prefer capital-intensive modes to lighter ones when entering foreign markets. Also, the degree of complexity of products influences company entry decisions. In fact, by pursuing FDI, companies are more able to control business relationships with their clients and distributors. Managing distribution channels is crucial for selling complex products that need both pre- and post-sale services (Andersen and Kheam, 1998).

Strategy also matters. For example, a company can decide to enter an unprofitable market driven by future expectations. The same can apply to the entrepreneurial level where a company moves are driven by entrepreneurs' feelings and perceptions (McDougall and Oviatt, 2000). Risk aversion and the desire to maintain flexibility act in opposite directions, encouraging entrepreneurs to enter less aggressively in foreign markets by using exports or strategic alliances.

When applied to the Chinese market, all of the above can be brought into the discussion. Deng (2001) claims that companies prefer WOFEs (wholly owned foreign enterprises, a form of FDI) to joint ventures, not only because of the higher control they will be able to maintain over foreign activities, but also because of former failures experienced when allying with Chinese partners. Luo (2001) finds that WOFE are preferred by companies that fear for their intellectual capital. In general, institutional factors are particularly critical in China and sometimes not well understood, even by global leading companies[3] (Aulakh and Kotabe, 1997; Wright et al., 2005; Peng et al., 2008; Meyer et al., 2009; Vianelli and de Luca, 2011).

Vice versa, JVs tend to be preferred by companies that perceive a high degree of environmental uncertainty (Luo, 2001). This result is intriguing since, according to the TCE perspective, companies perceiving a high degree of uncertainty should enter a market through safer modes. In the case of China, the expectations of companies amply counterbalance their uncertainty levels. In other words, companies are willing to accept a higher degree of uncertainty when entering the Chinese market because of the expectations they have for the future growth of that market.

Regarding contractual entry modes, franchising could also be an interesting opportunity for foreign companies entering the Chinese market (Alon and Welsh, 2005; Alon, 2010). However, the fact that franchising has only been fully authorized since 2007 has limited its spread among foreign companies (Zeidman, 2011).

3.2   Governance of Distribution Channels in Made in Italy Products

Considering the Italian export portfolio, based on a model that continues to be Eurocentric, the Chinese market is marginal. Within the category of manufactured products, in 2010 the value of Italian exports to China was only 2.5 percent of the total, with a value of about 8.2 billion Euros (Table 6.2).

Performance in the Chinese market is particularly challenging when it comes to the industry of Made in Italy, i.e. those products that convey the image of design, fashion and quality typical of Italian production. In 2010, the apparel–fashion sector reached an export sales value of 862 million Euros (10.5 percent of total Italian export to China), followed by food and furniture with 190 (2.3 percent) and 120 million Euros (1.5 percent) respectively (Pegan, 2011). If it is true that these data are the result of an extremely positive five-year trend (+45.0 percent), despite world economic crises, the need for a radical move by Italian companies and institutions to promote and facilitate internationalization is evident.

Entering the Chinese market is an option that cannot be postponed if

Table 6.2   Italian exports of transformed and manufactured* products in the 15 main foreign target countries (values in millions of Euros)

Countries	2006	2007	2008	2009	2010	VAR %
Germany	41,461	44,759	44,638	34,348	41,300	−0.4
France	37,415	40,440	39,880	31,922	37,393	−0.1
US	24,368	24,062	22,864	16,915	19,997	−17.9
Spain	23,419	26,239	22,753	15,540	18,631	−20.4
UK	19,359	20,445	18,560	14,063	16,928	−12.6
Switzerland	12,264	12,911	13,862	12,967	15,365	25.3
Belgium	9,186	10,364	9,556	7,695	8,329	−9.3
Poland	6,784	8,580	9,386	7,575	8,236	21.4
China	**5,635**	**6,236**	**6,372**	**6,280**	**8,171**	**45.0**
Netherlands	7,507	8,113	8,242	6,598	7,890	5.1
Turkey	6,701	7,011	7,232	5,550	7,885	17.7
Russia	7,536	9,450	10,365	6,344	7,769	3.1
Austria	7,762	8,326	8,272	6,330	7,325	−5.6
Greece	6,395	7,270	7,315	5,682	5,105	−20.2
Romania	5,489	5,525	5,733	3,807	4,899	−10.7
World	319,771	350,946	353,297	276,421	322,262	0.8

Note: * Section D Ateco 2002 for 2006–2009 and section C Ateco 2007 for 2010

Source: Our elaboration on ISTAT database

Italian companies want to benefit from a large and growing market. A recent study (Confindustria, 2011) reports that in 2015 affluent Chinese (i.e. with a per-capita GDP of at least $30,000 A/N) will number 201 million (14.5 percent of the total population), equal to the population of France, Germany and Italy put together. Forecasts indicate that this trend is likely to grow consistently over the next decade.

However, challenges will be not easy to deal with. In particular, the Chinese market is firmly controlled by national companies, and there is a coexistence of modern and archaic distribution formats, the latter being unsuitable to convey the symbolic value of Made in Italy products (Luk, 1998; Goldman, 2001; Dong et al., 2008). Hence, control of the distribution channel becomes a weapon, not only in terms of more appropriation of added value, but also of the increased efficacy required to reach specific target segments and manage correct strategic positioning of their own products and brands.

The academic debate about the governance of foreign distribution channels was originally developed within the transaction costs economics theory (Anderson and Coughlan, 1987; Klein et al., 1990). However, when considering emerging markets, the literature highlights belated and fragmented development (Burgess and Steenkamp, 2006). As for China, the first author to study distributive issues was Wortzel (1985), who provided a list of consumer goods and their distribution channels in the Chinese market. Since then, interest in this topic has rapidly increased, but not in proportion to the economic development of the Chinese market. Without pretending to be exhaustive, we have identified three main areas of research:

1. Studies describing (including an evolutionary perspective) distribution channels existing in the Chinese market and company choices (Luk, 1998; Jiang and Prater, 2002; Jaffe and Yi, 2007) varying from using foreign distributors (Hollensen, 2011) to franchising (Alon, 2010);
2. Studies reporting retail strategies developed by companies entering the Chinese market (Goldman, 2001; Chaney and Gamble, 2008; Uncles, 2010), with a particular focus on the choice of distribution format;
3. Studies on the selection of foreign distribution partners and on relational dynamics within sales channels (Luo, 1997; Liu and Wang, 1999; Dong et al., 2008).

Transversal to the three areas reported above, it is important to also consider the '*guanxi*' issue and its influence on strategic and operative distribution and marketing decisions (Ambler et al., 1999; Wong and Chan, 1999).

Regarding the typology of distribution channels and alternative strategies, the picture is articulated and strongly dependent on industry dynamics. Referring to governance, the channel's length represents a transversal problem. In the case of long channels, the company can hardly exert attentive control on activities of brand valorization, with the risk of weakening product image (Keegan and Green, 2008) or modify price positioning as a consequence of price escalation (Hollensen, 2011). Each alternative channel is associated with a different degree of control: lower if using foreign distributors, and increasingly higher in distribution through agents, franchising, or directly-owned stores where vertical integration guarantees strong control up to the final consumer.

Focusing our attention on industries – food, apparel and fashion, and furniture – which incorporate values of Made in Italy, China appears to be highly complex in terms of distribution channel governance. Since the 1990s, the food industry has undergone lengthy development, with the introduction of State or foreign-owned supermarkets. With a market share of 35 percent of the total retail distributive formats (about 60,000 units) supermarkets are the most important form of distribution. Their growth has been challenged recently by the hypermarkets, which act as point-of-sale for final consumers as well as cash and carry for small retailers. China has also seen the recent introduction of convenience stores: in the last few years 6,000 have opened in Shanghai alone. Mainly run by Chinese small entrepreneurs, they can be considered the evolution of small stores and local kiosks. They spread through branches and franchising, with self-service sales and integrated services (laundry, telephony, etc.), and offer a broad assortment of local food (New Zealand Trade and Enterprise, 2007; Musso, 2008; ICE Shanghai, 2009; Vianelli and de Luca, 2011).

In the apparel industry, French foreign retailers and also Italians have made a positive contribution to development of the industry, with specialized stores inside large shopping malls. These stores are primarily 'shop windows' for the creation of brand value and, starting from Hong Kong, are also spreading into second-tier cities (Vianelli and de Luca, 2011).

Finally, regarding furniture, the most important centers are Shanghai and Beijing, where not only foreign, but also domestic companies operate. The latter work as suppliers to foreign companies and also maintain their commercial presence through subsidiaries, stores and showrooms to facilitate sales in the local market. In the furniture industry, big buyers – professionals and retailers – mainly buy from manufacturers or, alternatively, from agents and distributors. As far as retail is concerned, specialized stores represent the most widespread distribution format. They are normally located in large shopping malls (typically for luxury products) or, for medium to low products, in shopping malls dedicated to home furnishing (ICE, 2009; Vianelli and de Luca, 2011).

After illustrating channels and distributive strategies, an important issue for channel governance is quality of the partner relationship. The literature highlights many attributes that can influence the relationship with the distributive partner. They can be identified as the partner's financial stability, product knowledge, marketing and managerial capabilities and degree of commitment (Geringer, 1991). The company's financial characteristics (Shah and Swaminathan, 2008; Roy and Oliver, 2009) are an indicator of partner strength and provide a guarantee of reliability in offering a long-term relationship with final clients. Furthermore, they reveal if the company is able to financially support marketing and sales activities (Cavusgil et al., 1995), and, hence, investing in the valorization of Made in Italy in the Chinese market. Financial criteria are often correlated to the evaluation of partner reputation, which is not always easy to evaluate, due to subjectivity, but it is extremely relevant in relation to the security of the brand (Al-Khalifa and Peterson, 1999; Shah and Swaminathan, 2008; Roy and Oliver, 2009). Finally, the willingness to invest in the business may also be an indicator of the degree of involvement and motivation of the partner (Salavrakos and Stewart, 2006).

Consistency with the potential partner in terms of image, positioning and strategy, is another important element to verify, especially when the company must manage, as happens in many cases, not only a product but also a brand. Various authors (Cavusgil et al., 1995; Doherty, 2009) highlight that the best distributors are those that manage product lines positioned close to those of the company and target the same segments and, therefore, have the capacity and the experience necessary to serve the final customers.

Coverage of the distribution network, the ability to manage a marketing plan and the various operational activities related to product marketing, such as logistics, assortment management, etc. (Cavusgil et al., 1995; Al-Khalifa and Peterson,1999; Salavrakos and Stewart, 2006; Dong and Glaister, 2006) are all aspects that identify marketing and sales ability. These skills can be put into a broader assessment of managerial skills considered essential for the management of the business in an emerging economy like China's (Hitt et al., 2000).

As a conclusion of this literature review, it is possible to say that to analyse the governance of distribution channels for Made in Italy products, the following research questions must be addressed:

1. What are the distribution channels used by companies offering Made in Italy products in the Chinese market?
2. What are the prevalent formats in the various sectors?
3. What are the main difficulties that can weaken the strength of the value of Made in Italy in the Chinese market?

4. THE RESEARCH

4.1 Methodology

In order to identify the statistical universe for the present research study,[4] a database of 1183 companies was created using secondary data: trade journals, internet, and trade associations in the relevant sectors of Made in Italy: food and beverage, fashion, and furniture.

After a pre-test phase, an e-mail with an introductory letter and a link to a self-administered questionnaire (surveymonkey.com©) was sent to the manager in charge of the Chinese market of roughly 900 companies

Table 6.3   Composition of the sample

Size (turnover, millions €)	Sectors			Total
	Food and Beverage	Fashion	Furniture	
Small companies (2–10)	6	15	6	27
Medium–small companies (11–260)	9	12	12	33
Medium–large companies (>260)	5	4	2	11
Total	20	31	20	71
% within sectors	28	44	28	100

who were contacted previously and had agreed to cooperate. We col-
lected data in the period of November 2009–July 2010. At the end of the
survey, 71 complete questionnaires were obtained from companies of the
sectors considered:[5] 20 from companies in food and beverage (28 percent),
31 from companies in fashion (44 percent), and 20 from companies in
furniture (28 percent), with SMEs prevailing over large sized companies
(Table 6.3). The data were processed for a prevalently descriptive purpose.
The sample is not statistically representative. The interviewed companies
gave explorative considerations regarding the questions of this study.

4.2   Results

4.2.1   The choice of entry mode
In order to evaluate the level of control exercisable in the Chinese market,
the modes of entry of the Made in Italy companies were considered first,
as indicated in the literature.

Table 6.4 shows that the level of control exercised by the companies of the
sample is low. Only 17 percent of the modes of entry is connected to IDE,
while over 50 percent regards export modes. The majority of exports derive
from distributors or importers that, after obtaining ownership of the goods,
do not always share the marketing strategies of the company. The collaborations have a weight of 26 percent. This result is only partially positive as
it derives from a prevalently production point of view (as in the case of joint
ventures) rather than from a commercial perspective (as for franchising).

It is interesting to note that, while in the case of direct investment there
are not significant differences between the sectors, collaborations show
a lack of homogeneity. In food and furniture, exports prevail over collaborations (66 percent vs 17 percent and 61 percent vs 22 percent). In the
case of fashion, even if exports prevail, collaborations play a bigger role
(35 percent).

Table 6.4   Modes of entry and sectors of Made in Italy

Mode of entry	Food and Beverage		Fashion		Furniture		Total	
	N	%	N	%	N	%	N	%
Export	20	66	26	47	22	61	68	56
Distributor (in China)	8		7		9		24	
Importer (in China)	7		9		3		19	
Independent agent (in China)	4		5		3		12	
Dealer (in China)	0		3		6		9	
Italian exporter	1		2		1		4	
Collaborations and Strategic Alliances	5	17	19	35	8	22	32	27
Joint venture	3		9		4		16	
Franchising	2		4		3		9	
Licencing	0		6		1		7	
Foreign Direct Investment (FDI)	5	17	10	18	6	17	21	17
WOFE (wholly owned foreign enterprise)	2		3		2		7	
Commercial subsidiary	2		6		0		8	
Subsidiary (manufacturing and commercial)	1		1		3		5	
FICE (foreign invested commercial enterprise)	0		0		0		0	
Manufacturing subsidiary	0		0		1		1	
Total	30	100	55	100	36	100	121	100

4.2.2   The choice of distribution channel

Along with the choice of entry mode, the prevailing channel is made up of independent foreign distributors (Table 6.5). It is also interesting to note the growing role of franchising that, even if it is used in only nine cases as an entry mode, it is used more as a distribution channel (16 cases). The mentioned cases are companies from the fashion sector working on franchising networks managed by independent foreign distributors. Also, directly-owned stores are not numerous, which highlights how limited direct investments are.

Considering the prevailing distribution formats in the relevant sectors, where department stores (30 percent) and specialized stores (29 percent) prevail, the framework is coherent with what the literature shows (Table 6.6). Overall, this is true for fashion, where these forms weigh 43 percent and 36 percent. Supermarkets count for 12 percent of the total

Table 6.5   The distribution channel in the Made in Italy sectors

Distribution channel	Food and Beverage	Fashion	Furniture	Total	
	N	N	N	N	%
Foreign independent distributors (importers, wholesalers, etc.)	12	10	13	35	31
Franchising	3	9	4	16	14
Chinese agents, sale representatives or brokers (working on commission)	5	5	3	13	11
Foreign direct investments (own structures in the foreign country, as branches, subsidiaries, etc.)	3	7	3	13	11
Directly owned stores	1	5	1	7	6
Direct selling	1	2	3	6	5
Foreign intermediaries in Italy (buying office of a foreign chain)	2	4	0	6	5
Italian intermediaries managing the sale of the Italian products in China (trading companies, export houses, etc.)	2	2	0	4	4
Italian agents or brokers (with commission on sales)	1	3	0	4	4
Internet	0	2	1	3	3
Commercial company in Italy (totally owned or in joint venture)	1	0	1	2	2
Export consortia	1	1	0	2	2
Others	1	0	2	3	3
Total	33	50	31	114	100

and are one of the prevailing channels overall for the food sector (25 percent). In spite of widespread presence on the market, convenience stores, kiosks and open-air markets are rarely considered. This result is consistent with the high positioning of Made in Italy and with the main organizational difficulties of contact with this fragmented typology of channels.

Table 6.6   Types of points of sale for Made in Italy in China

Distribution formats	Food and Beverage		Fashion		Furniture		Total	
	N	%	N	%	N	%	N	%
Department stores	9	19	18	43	3	23	30	30
Small specialized shops	7	14	15	36	7	54	29	29
Supermarkets	12	25	0	0	0	0	12	12
Others	6	12	3	7	2	15	11	11
Small traditional shops	3	6	5	12	0	0	8	8
Hypermarkets	5	10	0	0	1	8	6	6
Discounts	3	6	0	0	0	0	3	3
Convenience stores	2	4	1	2	0	0	3	3
Kiosks/Bazaars/Open air markets	2	4	0	0	0	0	2	2
Total choices	49		42		13		104	

4.2.3   The relationship with the commercial partner

Analyzing the governance of the distribution channel, the difficulties of controlling marketing strategies which are relevant for Made in Italy also came from problems that companies in the sample recognized in the Chinese market (Table 6.7).

The reliability of the partner is the main problem in all sectors considered. The companies agree that it is very difficult to find partners able to provide convenient information and operational support and recognize a high difficulty of control. This aspect is evident overall for fashion, where the problem of reliability and governance assume a higher critical state. Overall, it is important to study the aspects that can weaken improvement of Made in Italy. Table 6.8 shows that almost all of the dimensions studied present a high or medium–high degree of critical state.

5.   CONCLUSIONS

The empirical research clearly shows how long and complex the road for Italian companies wanting to grow in the Chinese market continues to be. The governance of the distribution channel is weak, determining a risk for the valorization of the intangible resource of Made in Italy in an emerging market like China's, which offers big opportunities.

In the most recent report of 'Multinational Italy' (Mariotti and Mutinelli, 2010) it was stated that initiatives started by Italian companies

Table 6.7   *Difficulties perceived by Italian companies in selection and management of the distribution channel*

According to your experience, which are the difficulties that can be met when entering the Chinese market as a seller? (1 = no difficulties . . . 7 = very high difficulties)

Made in Italy: aggregated data			
Difficulties . . .	N	Mean	SD.
. . . in establishing reliable partnerships in the Chinese market	66	4.94	1.663
. . . in the identification of institutions and potential business partners that could provide suitable information and operational support	67	4.66	1.620
. . . in monitoring the intermediaries activity	65	4.69	1.629

Food and Beverage			
Difficulties . . .	N	Mean	SD.
. . . in establishing reliable partnerships in the Chinese market	17	4.53	1.908
. . . in the identification of institutions and potential business partners that could provide suitable information and operational support	19	4.47	1.744
. . . in monitoring the intermediaries activity	17	4.24	1.921

Fashion			
Difficulties . . .	N	Mean	SD.
. . . in establishing reliable partnerships in the Chinese market	31	5.19	1.424
. . . in monitoring the intermediaries activity	30	5.13	1.306
. . . in the identification of institutions and potential business partners that could provide suitable information and operational support	29	4.69	1.671

Furniture			
Difficulties . . .	N	Mean	SD.
. . . in establishing reliable partnerships in the Chinese market	18	4.89	1.811
. . . in the identification of institutions and potential business partners that could provide suitable information and operational support	19	4.79	1.475
. . . in monitoring the intermediaries activity	18	4.39	1.720

Table 6.8   Relationship with commercial partner and governance of distribution channel

When a company has to select an intermediary in the Chinese market it is difficult to find a partner that . . . (1 = completely disagree (it is very easy) . . . 7 = fully agree (it is very difficult)

	Aggregated data Mean	Food and beverage Mean	Fashion Mean	Furniture Mean
Is able to financially support the marketing and sales activity in the Chinese market	5.22	5.29	5.11	5.31
Is available to eliminate from his portfolio the competitors' products	5.08	4.56	4.96	5.72
Is available to invest in the development of sales networks	4.93	4.94	4.96	4.88
Is available to invest in your product's communication	4.91	4.94	4.80	5.05
Guarantees a good service before and after sales	4.72	4.47	4.57	5.15
Has a good product knowledge	4.68	4.70	4.40	5.05
Is able to implement a marketing plan	4.67	4.70	4.57	4.78
Has an efficient sales network	4.60	4.52	4.42	4.94
Sells product lines of similar quality/brand	4.53	4.76	3.88	5.20
Has experience in the target market	4.51	4.62	4.37	4.63
Is on time with deliveries	4.37	4.17	4.37	4.58

in major emerging countries such as China and India have grown not only in quantity but also in quality, with constant development of greenfield investments. This fact is the result of a growing consciousness and strategic commitment by Italian companies in these markets. This tendency is not seen in the representative industries of Made in Italy considered in our study. It is also not found in export sales data, which are still marginal if compared to other countries of export in Europe or in the United States for Italian food, fashion and furniture.

More specifically, direct investments have limited relevance: they are mainly found for production purposes while they are very limited when considering the commercial presence of our companies. Multiples are the elements highlighted in the research, which show how critical the issue of channel governance and, as a consequence, control over the Made in Italy value are.

Considering modes of entry and distribution channels, the prevalent use of distributors and importers can seldom guarantee the valorization of Made in Italy symbols. These choices are certainly justified, as pointed out in the literature, by the limited size of our companies, which are mainly small and medium. They frequently face scarce financial resources and weak managerial and organizational capabilities that lead them to undertake less risky internationalization strategies, which are highly externalized but, by their own nature, unable to guarantee the control of the distribution channel and the final market.

Penetration into the Chinese market and the necessary differentiation from competitive products require a stronger effort. If the investment is not affordable, the possible alternative is intermediate modes of entry which involve the company more without requiring complete internalization of activities, with high risk, low flexibility and a large commitment. In the apparel-fashion industry this transformation seems to be underway, but the delay is surprising in the furniture industry. Companies in this sector, incarnating the values of beauty and design and Italian style which are appreciated worldwide, exercise moderate use of franchising and directly-owned stores, yet stress large difficulties in convincing distributive partners to eliminate competitive products from their portfolio.

Control difficulties emerge when considering the relationship with the distributive partner, which is the main weak link of the distribution channel. Finding a good partner is complex since companies must face the problem of low reliability, lack of trust and limited marketing capabilities. Standing at the partner's side to increase the possibility for success of their own products is not an easy task: partners evade the company's control, do not want to invest, and show a lack of sales and marketing experience, especially in relation to sales of high image and quality products, which is the case with Made in Italy.

To conclude, our results show clear suggestions for Italian companies for growth in the food, fashion and furniture industry in the Chinese market. The distributive channel must be more controlled, and all the financial and managerial resources a company can provide must be put in place. This implies the existence of a strong entrepreneurial spirit that is certainly part of the Italian company culture. Nevertheless, the entrepreneurial effort must be accompanied by significant investments in order to guarantee commercial control of the company and, consequently, the continuing defense and valorization of a brand which reflects the values of Made in Italy.

NOTES

1. Although reflecting the joint effort of the three authors, the major responsibilities for writing this chapter were divided among them. Donata Vianelli wrote sections 3.1 and 4.2.3, Patrizia de Luca wrote sections 3.2 and 4.2.2, and Guido Bortoluzzi wrote sections 2 and 4.2.1. The other sections were written together.
2. For example, a limit to the spread of single brand producers shops owned by foreign brands.
3. The Nike–Chinese Government case is, in this sense, significant. In 2004 Nike produced an advert for the Chinese market depicting James LeBron, the famous basketball player, defeating a martial arts master, some women in Chinese traditional dresses and some dragons. The Chinese Government banned the ad after claiming blasphemy.
4. From a methodological point of view, a problem is that there is no complete list of Italian companies present in China. We only know that there are roughly 2,000 (Vianelli et al., 2012).
5. 'Response rates for primary research studies range from as low as five percent to approximately 95 percent' (Mullen et al., 2009).

REFERENCES

Al-Khalifa, A.K. and S.E. Peterson (1999), 'The partner selection process in international joint ventures', *European Journal of Marketing*, **33** (11/12), 1064–1073.

Alon, I. (2010), *Franchising Globally: Innovation, Learning and Imitation*, New York: Palgrave Macmillan.

Alon, I. and D. Welsh (2005), *International Franchising in Emerging Markets: China and Other Asian Countries*, CCH, Inc., Washington DC: CCH Inc. Publishing.

Ambler, T., C. Styles and W. Xiucun (1999), 'The effect of channel relationships and guanxi on the performance of inter-province export ventures in the People's Republic of China', *International Journal of Research in Marketing*, **16**, 75–87.

Andersen, O. (1997), 'Internationalization and market entry mode: a review of theories and conceptual framework', *Management International Review*, **37** (2), 27–42.

Andersen, O. and S.L. Kheam (1998), 'Resource-based theory and international growth strategies: an exploratory study', *International Business Review*, **7** (2), 163–184.

Anderson, E. and A. Coughlan (1987), 'International market entry and expansion via independent or integrated channels of distribution', *Journal of Marketing*, **51**, January, 71–82.

Aulakh, P.S. and M. Kotabe (1997), 'Antecedents and performance implications of channel integration in foreign markets', *Journal of International Business Studies*, **28** (1), 145–175.

Buckley, P.J. and M. Casson (1976), *The Future of the Multinational Enterprise*, London: Macmillan.

Buckley, P.J. and M. Casson (1981), 'The optimal timing of a foreign direct investment', *Economic Journal*, **92**, 75–87.

Burgess, S.M. and J.-B. Steenkamp (2006), 'Marketing renaissance: how research in emerging markets advances marketing science and practice', *International Journal of Research in Marketing*, **23**, 337–356.

Cavusgil, S.T., P. Yeoh and M. Mitri (1995), 'Selecting foreign distributors: an expert systems approach', *Industrial Marketing Management*, **24**, 297–304.

Cavusgil, S.T., P.N. Ghauri and M.R. Agarwal (2002), *Doing Business in Emerging Markets: Entry and Negotiation Strategies*, Thousand Oaks, CA: Sage.

Cavusgil, S.T., G. Knight and J. Riesenberger (2007), *International Business: Strategy, Management and the New Realities*, Upper Saddle River, NJ: Prentice Hall.

Chaney, I. and J. Gamble (2008), 'Retail store ownership influences on Chinese consumers', *International Business Review*, **17**, 170–183.

Child, J. and D.K. Tse (2001), 'China's transition and the impacts on international business', *Journal of International Business Studies*, **32** (1), 8–21.

Confindustria (2011), *Cina: nuovi ricchi concentrati nelle aree urbane costiere*, No. 11-1, http://www.confindustria.it, accessed 20 August 2011.

Deng, P. (2001), 'WFOEs: the most popular entry mode into china', *Business Horizons*, July–August, 63–72.

Doherty, A.M. (2009), 'Market and partner selection processes in international retail franchising', *Journal of Business Research*, **62**, 528–534.

Dong, L. and K.W. Glaister (2006), 'Motives and partner selection criteria in international strategic alliances: perspectives of Chinese firms', *International Business Review*, **15**, 577–600.

Dong, M.C., D.K. Tse and S.T. Cavusgil (2008), 'Efficiency of governance mechanisms in China's distribution channels', *International Business Review*, **17**, 509–519.

Dunning, J.H. (1980), 'Toward an eclectic theory of international production: some empirical tests', *Journal of International Business Studies*, **11**, First Quarter, 9–31.

Dunning, J.H. (1988), 'The eclectic paradigm of international production: a restatement and some possible extensions', *Journal of International Business Studies*, **19**, Spring, 1–31.

Fetscherin, M., H. Voss and P. Gugler (2010), '30 years of foreign direct investment to China: an interdisciplinary literature review', *International Business Review*, **19**, 235–246.

Geringer, J.M. (1991), 'Strategic determinants of partner selection criteria in international joint ventures', *Journal of International Business Studies*, **22** (1), 41–62.

Goldman, A. (2001), 'The transfer of retail formats into developing economies: the example of China', *Journal of Retailing*, **77**, 221–242.

Hill, J.S. (2009), *International Business*, Thousand Oaks, CA: Sage Publications.

Hitt, M.A., M.T. Dacin, E. Levitas, J.L. Arregle and A. Borza (2000), 'Partner selection in emerging and developed market context: resource-based and organizational learning perspectives', *Academy of Management Journal*, **43** (3), 449–471.

Hollensen, S. (2011), *Global Marketing: A Decision Oriented Approach*, Harlow, England: Pearson Education Ltd.

ICE (2009), *Furniture Market in China*, Market Report http://www.ice.gov.it/paesi/

asia/cina/upload/174/FURNITURE%20MARKET%20REPORT%202009.9.
pdf, accessed 20 August 2011.

ICE Shanghai (2009), *Il mercato cinese dei prodotti agroalimentari e del vino*, http://
www.ccio.it, accessed 20 August 2011.

Jaffe, E.D. and L. Yi (2007), 'What are the drivers of channel length? Distribution
reform in the People's Republic of China', *International Business Review*, **16**,
474–493.

Jiang, B. and E. Prater (2002), 'Distribution and logistics development in China:
the revolution has begun', *International Journal of Physical Distribution &
Logistics Management*, **32** (9), 783–798.

Johanson, J. and J.E. Vahlne, (1977), 'The internationalization process of the firm
– a model of knowledge development and increasing foreign market commitment', *Journal of International Business Studies*, **8** (1), 23–32.

Johanson, J. and J.E. Vahlne (1990), 'The mechanism of internationalization',
International Marketing Review, **7** (4), 11–24.

Keegan, W.J. and M. Green (2008), *Global Marketing*, Upper Saddle River, NJ:
Prentice Hall.

Klein, S., G.L. Frazier and V.J. Roth (1990), 'A transaction cost analysis model
of channel integration in international markets', *Journal of Marketing Research*,
27 (2), 196–208.

Liu, H. and Y.P. Wang (1999), 'Co-ordination of international channel relationships: four case studies in the food industry in China', *Journal of Business &
Industrial Marketing*, **14** (2), 130–150.

Luk, S. (1998), 'Structural changes in China's distribution system', *International
Journal of Physical Distribution & Logistics Management*, **28** (1), 44–67.

Luo, Y. (1997), 'Partner selection and venturing success: the case of joint ventures with firms in the People's Republic of China', *Organization Science*, **8** (6),
648–662.

Luo, Y. (2001), 'Determinants of entry in an emerging economy: a multilevel
approach', *Journal of Management Studies*, **38** (3), 443–472.

Mariotti, S. and M. Mutinelli (2010), *Italia multinazionale 2010. Le partecipazioni
italiane all'estero ed estere in Italia*, Soveria Mannelli: Il Corbettino.

McDougall, P.P. and B.M. Oviatt (2000), 'International entrepreneurship:
the intersection of research paths', *Academy of Management Journal*, **43**,
902–908.

Meyer, K.E., S. Estrin, S.K. Bhaumik and M.W. Peng (2009), 'Institutions,
resources, and entry strategies in emerging economics', *Strategic Management
Journal*, **30**, 61–80.

Mullen, M.R., D.G. Budeva and P.M. Doney (2009), 'Research methods in the
leading small business-entrepreneurship journals: a critical review with recommendations for future research', *Journal of Small Business Management*, **47** (3),
287–307.

Musso, F. (2008), La Cina come mercato: prospettive, vincoli, illusioni. Relazione
presentata al convegno 'Cina e oltre. Piccola e media impresa fra innovazione e
internazionalizzazione', Lodi, 10 October 2008.

New Zealand Trade and Enterprise (2007), *Market Profile for Food and Beverage
Retail in China*, http://www.ntze.gov.nz, accessed 14 July 2011.

Pegan, G. (2011), 'Il Made in Italy in Cina: un quadro di sintesi', in T. Vescovi,
*Libellule sul Drago. Modelli di business e strategie di marketing per le imprese
italiane in Cina*, Padova: Cedam, pp. 1–16.

Peng, M.W. (2003), 'Institutional transitions and strategic choices', *Academy of Management Review*, **28**, 275–296.

Peng, M.W., D. Wang and Y. Jiang (2008), 'An institution-based view of international business strategy: a focus on emerging economies', *Journal of International Business Studies*, **39**, 920–936.

Roy, J.P. and C. Oliver (2009), 'International joint venture partner selection: the role of the host-country legal environment', *Journal of International Business Studies*, **40**, 779–801.

Salavrakos, I.-D. and C. Stewart (2006), 'Partner selection criteria and determinants of firm performance in joint ventures', *Eastern European Economics*, **44** (3), 60–78.

Shah, R.H. and V. Swaminathan (2008), 'Factors influencing partner selection in strategic alliances: the moderating role of alliance context', *Strategic Management Journal*, **29**, 471–494.

Shenkar, O. and Y. Luo (2008), *International Business*, Thousand Oaks, CA: Sage Publications.

Stern, L.W., A.I. El-Ansary and A.T. Coughlan (1996), *Marketing Channels* (5th edn), Upper Saddle River, NJ: Prentice-Hall.

Uncles, M.D. (2010), 'Retail change in China: retrospect and prospects', *The International Review of Retail, Distribution and Consumer Research*, **20** (1), 69–84.

Vianelli, D. and P. de Luca (2011), 'Scelte di marketing delle imprese italiane in Cina. La Distribuzione', in Vescovi, *Libellule sul Drago. Modelli di business e strategie di marketing per le imprese italiane in Cina*, Padova: Cedam, pp. 89–114.

Vianelli, D., P. de Luca and G. Pegan (2012), *Modalità d'entrata e scelte distributive del made in Italy in Cina*, Milano: Franco Angeli.

Wong, Y.H. and R. Chan (1999), 'Relationship marketing in China: guanxi, favouritism and adaptation', *Journal of Business Ethics*, **22**, 107–118.

Wortzel, H.V. (1985), 'The logistics of distribution in China', *International Journal of Physical Distribution & Materials Management*, **15** (5), 51–60.

Wright, M., I. Filatotchev, R.E. Hoskisson and M.W. Peng (2005), 'Strategy research in emerging economies: challenging the conventional wisdom', *Journal of Management Studies*, **26**, 1–34.

Zeidman, P.F. (2011), 'Franchise legislation'. *Franchise Times*, June 29, http://www.franchisetimes.com/content/story.php?article= 00346, accessed 10 July 2011.

7. Country of origin effect, brand image and retail management for the exploitation of 'Made in Italy' in China[1]

Tommaso Pucci, Christian Simoni and Lorenzo Zanni

1. INTRODUCTION

Increasing globalization has characterized the world economy development since the end of the Second World War. Despite this, until the 1980s many goods were sold in the same country in which they had been produced (Srinivasan and Jain, 2003). The adoption of internationalization strategies, the development of new technologies that facilitate long distance communication, the agreements on trade liberalization, and the development of more modern infrastructures have thus allowed the development of global brands and the possibility for companies to design new products in a certain country and then manufacture them elsewhere.

The first scholar to introduce the concept of country of origin (COO) was Ernest Dichter. In his article 'The world customer' (1962), he highlighted the importance of 'made in' as an essential information cue in the consumers' product evaluation process (Bloemer et al., 2009). The studies on country of origin have been increasing since the 1970s, but it is only from the mid-80s that they coagulated into a solid body of literature (Papadopoulos and Heslop, 2002).

Although the issue has been addressed by several disciplines, including agricultural economics, marketing and management, in the literature one can identify some relationships that are common to several contributions (Figure 7.1).

A first stream of literature focuses on measuring the effects COO has on consumer evaluation of one or more product categories or one or more brands. More in detail, the first relationship can be typically found in articles published in the 1980s and early 1990s (Bilkey and Nes, 1982;

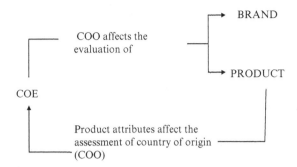

*Figure 7.1   A summary of the relationships among country of origin
(COO), country of origin effect (COE), brands and products*

Li and Wyer, 1994). The second starts from the middle 1990s in parallel to the emerging literature on brand management (Tse and Gorn, 1993; Pappu et al., 2006). The second stream of research concentrates on how product attributes affect the evaluation of the country of origin (Aiello et al., 2009).

With few exceptions (Wang and Yang, 2008; Baldauf et al., 2009), the research conducted in this area investigated the combined effects of country of origin and components of brand equity on consumer purchase intentions (Ashill and Sinha, 2004). This chapter focuses on the influence of Italy, as country of origin, on the evaluation of product and brand in China. We place our study in the first stream of studies discussed above, with the aim of investigating the importance of the various declinations of the concepts 'origin' and 'brand', the way they interact in influencing the purchasing preferences of Chinese consumers and how the store management policies can enhance the country of origin effect.

We decided to test our hypotheses in the children's clothing market in China for two main reasons: the children's clothing industry is part of the fashion industry, where brand enhancing policies play a strategic role in the competitive success of firms (Pucci et al., 2011); therefore the excellence of Made in Italy clothing products and related brands is a globally recognized stereotype (Roth and Romeo, 1992).

In summary, the research aims to answer three main questions:

1. What are the main factors that influence consumer preferences when buying garments in China?
2. How does the image of Italy affect the assessment of children's clothing brands in China?

3. What store management policies can more effectively convey the specific attributes of an Italian brand in the fashion products market in China?

2. THEORETICAL BACKGROUND AND RESEARCH HYPOTHESIS

2.1 Factors that Influence Childrenswear Consumer Preferences

Our first research question is aimed at understanding the factors that influence consumer preferences of children's clothing in China and the features that are common to the buying behaviour in the broader field of luxury and fashion market.

The distinctive features of Italian competitive advantage have long been known in the international literature. Since the early 1960s, a combination of different elements related to craftsmanship, quality of production, and creativity led to Made in Italy excellence in typical industries (fashion, mechanics, food, home furnishing). The expression 'Made in Italy' gradually assumed a more important meaning than that of a simple label of origin (Fortis, 2005) to become a byword for excellence in design, quality and reliability that are globally recognized in the products and technologies of Italian firms.

Italian fashion especially has been able to contribute to the definition of a unique meaning of Made in Italy that allows it to stand out in international competition in terms of (Corbellini and Saviolo, 2004, p. 28): social values attributable to firms in general (passion, craftsmanship, functionality); stylistic identity of products (design, elegance, linearity); and image identity attributed to the communication of fashion (beauty, sensuality, romance). For these reasons, it is expected that customers are willing to pay a premium price for Made in Italy fashion products. For at least a decade, the new challenges of globalization as well as the emergence of new countries that compete in manufacturing products in which Italy is specialized, have put the traditional strengths of Made in Italy into question, thus forcing different actors (individual firms, industrial districts, institutions, governments) to review corporate strategies and policies. The diffusion of relocation and outsourcing processes have contributed to an extension of the concept of 'Made in' from a merely physical manufacturing location. As a result, some companies have opted to pay less attention to the place of production and more in general to enhance the corporate brand that has an increasingly great importance in the consumer buying process (Corbellini and Saviolo, 2004, p. 25). At the same time, the extension of the concept of 'origin' has sometimes made a 'misappropriation' of the Italian cultural heritage by foreign brands possible, especially in new emerging markets.

Italian SMEs show the difficulty in responding to this rapidly changing competitive landscape which requires more advanced approaches than the simple indirect export formulas to non-episodically enter in foreign markets (Rabino et al., 2008). Succeeding in distant markets with a high level of competition, such as China, requires strengthening and enhancing already strong marketing resources, especially brands, and to more closely and aggressively manage distribution activities (Bertoli, 2004).

Recent research on the Italian fashion system (Aiello and Guercini, 2010) showed how strengthening the role of a direct distribution channel is key in supporting a brand and directly managing its presence on international markets. Some emerging countries are therefore at the centre of the attention of Italian fashion firms not only as a place of production, but also as a market for their final products through the implementation of foreign direct investments in retail.

Despite the importance in the Italian literature, there are not many empirical studies that have examined the issue of country of origin with reference to Made in Italy products and brands (Bertoli et al., 2005), as well as studies that investigate the effects in a comparative international study (Aiello et al., 2009) or still more extensive surveys to gauge the role of the so-called country reputation on perceptions and consumption behaviour abroad (Marino et al., 2009).

We therefore decided to test empirically our hypotheses in the childrenswear industry, which is part of the wider fashion industry where previous research has shown that the strategies adopted to build and maintain a successful brand are among the main keys to the firm's competitive success (Carpenter and Fairhurst, 2005). The excellence of Made in Italy apparel products is an internationally recognized stereotype (Roth and Romeo, 1992), although its value has yet to find further confirmation in new emerging countries like China, India, Brazil, etc. China in particular, despite being the first country in the world for exports of children clothing with a share that exceeds 51 per cent, in recent years is one of the main markets for Italian companies, especially those that are positioned in the medium–high segment of the market, for the most part still to be exploited (Databank, 2010).

2.2 Country of Origin Image, Product Image and Brand Image

To answer the second research question we have made some assumptions based on the prevailing literature as discussed herein.

Several studies indicate that consumers may have different assessments of products or brands from different countries, thereby significantly influencing their intention to purchase (Papadopoulos and Heslop, 1993). One of the first theories on country of origin was proposed by Nagashima (1970). He defines the image that a consumer associates to a given country of origin as 'the picture, the reputation, the stereotype that businessmen and consumers attach to products of a specific country. This image is created by such variables as representative products, national character-istics, economic and political background, history, and traditions'. More recently, Roth and Romeo (1992) define the COO image as the under-standing that a consumer has of a country based on the earlier perception of a product compared to the strength or weakness of the production and marketing of that country.

In literature, several explanations have been put forward as to how consumers react to COO information. Among these, one of the most cited is surely Han (1989). The author identifies two specific roles of the COO: the halo effect and the summary effect. With regard to the first, the COO serves as a signal to the consumer for the cognitive evaluation process in all those situations in which one is not familiar with the product or the brand. The summary effect arises rather as an abstraction process when the image of a country is based on previous experiences and consumer per-ception of the attributes that characterize the products from that country. Both effects show that the COO image serves as an indication to infer the quality of the products or brands of a certain country (Yasin et al., 2007).

Many consumers use COO stereotypes to evaluate products by relying on the fact that a label 'Made in' would indicate the superiority or otherwise of a product or a brand based on their perception of that country (Bilkey and Nes, 1982). Other studies show that the impact of the geographic origin would seem to be stronger for those categories of products (and related brands) the realization of which is associated with a country renowned for its tradition of production such as Brazilian coffee, Swiss chocolate, American jeans, Italian fashion, French perfumes, etc. (Roth and Romeo, 1992).

In the literature, however, there are also papers that minimize the effect of COO (Rahman et al., 2008). Usunier (2006) in particular suggests that for the production of knowledge about the country to have some influence on consumer buying, it is vital that they consider the information on the origin of the product as appropriate with respect to their choice and that the importance of this information is such to induce them to invest time and resources in research and comparison of alternative backgrounds.

Creating successful brands has now become a priority for many compa-nies because of the many benefits that this entails in terms of competitive advantage (Aaker, 1991 and 1996). This has prompted researchers and marketing professionals to question the nature and size of the brand equity that is the differential effect that brand knowledge has on consumer response (Keller, 1998). There are many factors that influence the assessment and several research programmes focused on the relevant variables of marketing mix (Yoo, Donthu and Lee, 2000). Papers that investigate the relationship between brand equity and other variables besides marketing mix, such as the country of origin, are more scarce (Wang and Yang, 2008; Baldauf et al., 2009).

There are two main components of brand equity: brand awareness and brand image (Ashill and Sinha, 2004). The first refers to the ability of a consumer to identify a brand under different conditions (Aaker, 1996). The second refers to that set of cognitive and affective associations that consumers have of a brand (Feldwick, 1996). The brand image therefore consists of a set of complex and interrelated associations (Yoo et al., 2000) in the minds of consumers due to personal beliefs, targeted marketing, direct experiences with the product or inferences based on existing associations (Aaker, 1991). The combination of these tangible and intangible attributes thus contributes to the brand image that companies strive to strengthen and maintain (Aaker, 1996).

All this suggests our first and second research hypotheses:

H1: Italy image exerts a significant positive influence on children-wear's Chinese consumer preferences.

H2: The associations of a) brand image and b) product image have a significantly positive impact on purchasing preferences.

As already mentioned, there are not many papers that investigate the relationship between country of origin and brand equity (Yasin et al., 2007). Although the literature shows a direct positive impact of the latter on the buying behaviour of consumers, the relative importance of brand image can also be caused by the image of the country of origin (Roth and Romeo, 1992). Thakor and Katsanis (1997), for example, suggest that the COO affects the perception of the quality of a product either directly or indirectly through the effect of the brand. More recently, the results of Pappu et al. (2006) show that the impact of COO on brand equity occurs when consumers perceive a difference between countries with respect to the associations of their products–countries. Even Yasin et al. (2007) show that COO image positively influences the dimensions of brand equity and Wang and Yang (2008) come to similar conclusions, however focusing solely on brand personality. Zeugner-Roth et al. (2008) then show how brand equity is influenced by perceptions of the image of the country of origin and impact positively on consumer buying preferences.

Our third research hypothesis is therefore:

H3:   The image of the country of origin tends to positively moderate: (a) the relationship between brand image and consumer preferences, and (b) the relationship between product image and consumer preferences.

2.3   Store Management Policies for the Exploitation of 'Made in Italy'

Retail image and store positioning are two factors that could influence consumer loyalty and retail success; in the fashion business the store image could deeply affect store choice and customers' perception (Birtwistle et al., 1999). In the last two decades in the fashion apparel industry, competition on price and quality have not been enough to reach a sustainable success, while brand image, product styling and direct control of distribution have assumed greater importance; more integrated firms that control the retail chain could link a quick and flexible manufacturing response with a deeper knowledge on demand and customer satisfaction (Richardson, 1996).

The retail internationalization process could also be considered an entry mode choice in newly emerging markets that in recent years have become critical in the fashion business; the entry mode could be different over time and emerges as the result of a combination of historical, experiential, financial, opportunistic, strategic and company-specific factors (Doherty, 2000). Failure in international retailing is not uncommon (Burt et al., 2003), so it is important to find the right partners, to study carefully the strategy to adopt in the foreign markets (foreign direct investments, joint ventures, franchising, etc.) and to give a qualified operational support (Doherty, 2007). Intense competition and a fast product innovation create different challenges in fashion retail policies and require developing and leveraging core marketing capabilities (Moore and Fairhurst, 2003); in particular, some marketing capabilities (image differentiation, promotions, external-market knowledge, customer service) could have a positive impact on firm level performance. Brand management and product development are extremely important in the differentiation of international fashion retailers (Wigley et al., 2005).

Italian fashion firms have realized in recent years the growing importance of direct control of the point of sales in the foreign markets, above all in some emerging countries such as China (Aiello and Guercini, 2010); the new opening of stores in foreign countries confirms a process of substitution from multibrand to monobrand stores, a strategy that could enforce brand image and awareness. This strategy is followed by both well-known brands of large international companies in the luxury markets and less-known Italian brands positioned in the middle-high segment of the fashion market.

Our fourth and fifth research hypotheses are therefore the following:

H4:   An Italian store sign and effective store policies enforce the Italian brand image and exert a positive influence on Chinese consumer preferences for childrenswear.

H5:   A monobrand retail strategy enforces the Italian brand image measured in terms of premium price effect.

3.   METHODOLOGY

3.1   Questionnaire and Measures

Our research was supported by 'Bimbo Italia' Consortium[2] and by a medium-size Italian enterprise in the industry that already has its own stores in the Chinese market (we refer to it as company X for confidentiality reasons). We designed two questionnaires to be submitted to a sample of Chinese consumers. The first questionnaire was submitted to consumers right in front of multibrand stores whereas the second in front of company X monobrand stores.[3]

The common structure of the two questionnaires consists of two parts. The first part measures the influence of certain factors on the choice of buying children's clothing, the product attributes that are considered in the evaluation of its quality and the attributes of the image of Italy as a country of origin. The second part investigates the demographic information and the purchasing behaviour of the respondents. In the questionnaires used in front of monobrand retail outlets[4] the consumers were also asked to: evaluate the attributes of company X brand and product image, and specify the degree to which they associate with Italy a series of elements related to store management, including signs in Italian, store window, catalogues, interior design, posters and videos, music.

The Italy image was initially operationalized using four items: innovation, design, prestige and workmanship (Roth and Romeo, 1992; Aiello et al., 2008). The product attributes selected are reliability, quality and trust (Chen et al., 2004; Fionda and Moore, 2009). The associations

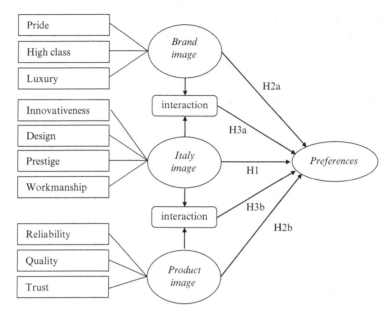

Figure 7.2   Structural model and research hypotheses

for the brand image are pride, high class and luxury image (Yasin et al., 2007; Fionda and Moore, 2009). All the items for the three constructs are measured through a Likert scale ranging from 1 'minor' to 5 'extremely important'. Finally, the preference of purchase is measured by a scale on the price differential (premium price) that customers would be willing to pay for an item of Italian clothing for children (Dodds et al., 1991; Feldwick, 1996) that varies between 1 '0 per cent' and 4 '20 per cent or more'. The structural model and hypotheses are shown in Figure 7.2.

A pilot study of the questionnaires was conducted to assess the constructs and their measurement scales. The content validity was assessed by 12 managers of a few Italian exporting firms operating in the field of children's clothing. The questionnaires were first translated to Chinese and then translated again into Italian in order to verify the accuracy of the translation. We then tested the questionnaires with 50 local consumers that were asked not only to answer the questions but also to possibly criticize them. All 50 respondents answered completely and no observation or feedback made it necessary to review the setting of the questionnaire.

The questionnaire was then submitted during the period May–June 2011. The total sample consists of 1110 respondents. The distribution of

Table 7.1   Geographical distribution of the sample of respondents

City	Store type	n.
Shangai	Multibrand	212
Ningbo	Multibrand	209
Suzhou	Multibrand	200
Total interviews in front of multibrand stores		621
Shenzhen	Monobrand	148
Guangzhou	Monobrand	96
Shenyang	Monobrand	76
Tianjin	Monobrand	57
Guilin	Monobrand	50
Jinan	Monobrand	32
Liaoning	Monobrand	30
Total interviews in front of monobrand stores		489
Total interviews		1110

the respondents by city and by type of store in front of which the interview was conducted is shown in Table 7.1.

3.2   Sample and Descriptive Statistics

The socio-demographic profile of the respondents is shown in Table 7.2.

As can be noticed, the buyer is in most cases a mother aged between 25 and 40 years. The mothers are not very young. This can reveal that in Chinese social upper classes the average age at which women have children is getting higher, as in many other Western countries. Yet the education level is medium–high and a share of non-marginal consumers have a medium–high income level.

Table 7.3 shows the data on buying behaviour.

The data shows the presence of repeat purchases during the year for Chinese consumers, like in most industrialized countries (see Xiao and Kim, 2009). It also denotes the strong centrality of mothers in the purchasing process (see Sin and Yau, 2004), which is a result that differentiates China from other countries of the so-called 'Old World', where the role of the family (especially grandparents) has a greater economic and social value. The data also points out the prevalence of functional reasons (change of season, change of size) than purely hedonistic reasons for purchase. This is reflected in the literature (Rahman et al., 2008) although one third of respondents considers fashion as a major motivation in the purchasing process by highlighting the presence of a market segment most exquisitely 'fashion-oriented'.

Table 7.2   Socio-demographic segmentation of respondents

Variables	Proportion %
Gender	
Male	26.4
Female	73.6
Age	
< 25 years	20.5
25–40 years	68.1
> 40 years	11.4
Shopper	
Mother	70.9
Father	15.9
Grandmother/Grandfather	4.9
Other family member	6.6
Others	1.7
Personal income/month	
< 5000 Yuan	28.8
5000–8000 Yuan	32.5
8000–10,000 Yuan	15.0
10,000–15,000 Yuan	12.9
> 15,000 Yuan	10.8
Education	
Lower than university	30.3
University or above	69.7
Children's age	
0–3 years	31.2
4–6 years	45.1
7–14 years	23.7

3.3   Reliability and Validity

With regard to the second research question, the reliability of the constructs was tested using Cronbach's alpha coefficient, which varies, in our case, between 0.746 and 0.888 (Table 7.4). The result is larger than the standard generally accepted 0.7.

To determine the effectiveness of the constructs, the scales relating to Italy image, product image and brand image were tested for both convergent and discriminant validity. The convergent validity is the degree of agreement between two or more measures within the same construct. We used bivariate correlation analysis to provide evidence of their validity. All the correlation coefficients related to the components of each construct are statistically significant at $p < 0.01$ and ranging from 0.436 to

Table 7.3   Buying behaviour

Variables	Proportion %
Average annual purchases	
1–2 times	21.0
3–8 times	48.3
> 8 times	30.7
Person that influences the choice*	
Child	27.9
Mother	66.9
Father	10.7
Grandmother/Grandfather	7.3
Reason for purchase*	
Change of season	52.3
Festive holiday	31.8
Outgrown clothes	50.8
Fashion	28.8
Replacement	25.0

Note: * The sum is not 100% because the answer may be multiple.

0.766. Each component is also strongly correlated with its overall scale of measurement.

Discriminant validity refers to the extent by which different measures of conceptually distinct constructs differ. To test the discriminant validity we run a factor analysis on the components of Italy image, brand image, product image and purchase intent (Table 7.5).

The results show that the four factors explain more than 78 per cent of the total variance. The factors weighing more than 0.5 are all in their corresponding constructs, showing that respondents discriminate between measures of COO image, product image, brand image and purchase intent, thus providing evidence of discriminant validity.

The different measures were then subjected to a confirmatory factor analysis (CFA). The indices of fit (χ^2/df = 1.57, goodness-of-fit index [GFI] = 0.90, adjusted goodness-of-fit index [AGFI] = 0.91, confirmatory fit index [CFI] = 0, 94, normed fit index [NFI] = 0.91, root mean squared error of approximation [RMSEA] = 0.042) suggesting a good fit of the measurement model and all items are significantly loaded (critical ratio [CR] = 1.94) on their corresponding constructs by providing valid measurements.

Table 7.4   Measures and reliability

Variables	Items	Cronbach's α
Italy Image (Likert scale, ranging from 1 'not important' to 5 'extremely important')	Innovativeness Design Prestige Workmanship	0.888
Product image (Likert scale, ranging from 1 'not important' to 5 'extremely important')	Reliability Quality Trust	0.847
X Brand image (Likert scale, ranging from 1 'not important' to 5 'extremely important')	Pride High class Luxury	0.746

Table 7.5   Factorial analysis results

Construct	Factor 1	Factor 2	Factor 3	Factor 4
Italy Image				
Innovativeness	0.728			
Design	0.812			
Prestige	0.826			
Workmanship	0.805			
Product image				
Reliability		0.816		
Quality		0.885		
Trust		0.799		
Brand image				
Pride			0.730	
High class			0.743	
Luxury			0.739	
Purchasing behaviour				0.873

Note: Total variance explained: 78.1%.

Table 7.6   Factors that influence childrenswear purchasing behaviour

	Mean	St. dev.	Proportions %				
			1	2	3	4	5
Quality	4.74	0.66	0.48	0.95	5.90	12.37	80.30
Conformity	4.45	0.86	0.93	2.57	11.51	24.56	60.43
Style	4.13	0.93	1.57	2.56	19.78	32.19	43.90
Easy care	4.10	1.02	1.85	6.64	17.41	30.69	43.41
Price	3.91	1.01	1.49	6.87	26.86	28.76	36.02
Trends	3.82	1.11	3.75	8.21	27.59	26.57	33.88
Brand	3.28	1.23	10.89	10.79	34.65	22.92	20.75
COO (China)	2.87	1.30	21.80	11.64	36.19	16.93	13.44
COO ($\neq$ China)	2.85	1.29	23.37	10.98	37.72	15.76	12.17
Tradition	2.73	1.28	26.47	11.42	37.03	14.94	10.14

4.   RESULTS

Our first research question is aimed at exploring the main factors that influence consumer preferences when buying children's clothes in China. To answer this question, the analysis was conducted on the entire sample of 1110 respondents.

In Table 7.6, the factors that influence childrenswear purchasing behaviour are listed in decreasing order of priority: the main factors are connected with technical elements of the products (quality, conformity), followed by design factors.

At a first glance, other factors such as tradition, country of origin or brand are less important in the childrenswear market when compared to other segments of the fashion system (for example, luxury products). This impression is confirmed if we focus our attention on the attributes that, for the Chinese consumers, explain the term 'quality' in the childrenswear market (Table 7.7): again manufacturing or technical aspect (comfort, safety, green fabric, workmanship) are more important than intangible attributes (design). Despite this, if we consider the key Italy image characteristics, a different ranking emerges (Table 7.8): in this case design and workmanship (an attribute strictly connected with the craftsmanship capabilities of the Italian artisans) assume greater importance, more than prestige (as in the case of luxury products) or innovativeness.

Italy image seems to exert a positive influence on Chinese consumer preferences for childrenswear. This is confirmed by the willingness to pay a higher price for a 'Made in Italy' product (Table 7.9). More than one

Table 7.7   The attributes that explain the term quality in the childrenswear market in China

	Mean	St. dev.	Proportions %				
			1	2	3	4	5
Comfort	4.75	0.67	0.47	1.90	4.38	8.85	84.40
Safety	4.59	0.81	1.10	2.69	6.37	15.54	74.30
Green fabric	4.30	0.93	0.90	4.46	13.79	25.00	55.85
Workmanship	3.91	1.12	3.80	8.43	19.22	29.91	38.64
Design of detail	3.84	1.10	3.90	6.46	26.97	26.98	35.69
Long life	3.48	1.26	8.91	12.33	27.77	23.32	27.67

Table 7.8   Key Italy image characteristics

	Mean	St. dev.	Proportions %				
			1	2	3	4	5
Design	3.99	1.12	4.05	7.19	17.51	27.53	43.72
Workmanship	3.96	1.49	5.71	7.85	16.72	26.91	42.81
Innovativeness	3.78	1.23	7.02	9.00	20.28	26.01	37.69
Prestige	3.68	1.25	7.85	10.42	20.33	28.48	32.92

Table 7.9   How the Chinese are willing to pay more for children's apparel 'Made in Italy'

Premium price	Sample		Multibrand		Monobrand	
	n	%	n	%	n	%
0%	84	7.64	34	3.14	50	4.50
1%–10%	261	23.52	89	8.02	172	15.50
11%–20%	354	31.85	204	18.34	150	13.51
≥ 21%	411	36.99	294	26.48	117	10.51
Total	1110	100.00	621	55.98	489	44.02

third of the Chinese consumers interviewed would pay more than 21 per cent on top of a standard price.

Contrary to what we originally expected, the retail strategy does not seem to significantly influence the image effect in terms of price difference (Table 7.10). We thought that a monobrand retail strategy could better support a premium price policy than a multibrand independent store's

Table 7.10   Likert scale 'premium price'

	Mean*	St. dev.
Entire sample	2.98	0.95
'Multibrand' sample	3.22	0.89
'Monobrand' sample	2.68	0.95

Note: * The Likert scale ranges from 1 to 4.

distribution strategy. This result may be due to different reasons: city/regional differences, store locations, store management policies, which, as previously pointed out, are designed and implemented by the general manager of the equity joint venture (EJV) who is a Chinese shareholder who seems to be more interested in implementing his own vision than in following the Italian firm brand and marketing guidelines. Further researches are needed on this specific issue.

The second objective of our study was to investigate the relationship between country of origin (Italy), brand image, product image and consumer preferences with specific reference to the field of children's clothing in China. To answer this question, the analysis was conducted on the sample of 489 respondents that were interviewed in front of monobrand stores.

To test the proposed hypotheses, we conducted a hierarchical regression analysis after controlling for the variables gender, age, education level and monthly personal income. The control variables are all categorical and have been included in the model in the form of dummy variables. The results show that none of the control variables is significant in influencing the purchase intent. Table 7.11 shows the five regression models we developed.

Our first hypothesis predicts that the country of origin (Italy) exerts a significant positive influence on the intention to purchase. In this case, consistently with models 2 and 5 the change in R^2 is 9.0 per cent and statistically significant at $p < 0.001$. The standardized regression coefficient is positive (0.215) on the COO image, which supports H1.

Our second hypothesis is that the associations of (a) brand image and (b) product image have a significant positive impact on purchasing preferences. In the first case, according to models 3 and 5 the change in R^2 is 1.9 per cent and statistically significant at $p < 0.001$. The positive standardized regression coefficient (0.124) on the brand image supports H2a. The result is, on the one hand, confirmed in the literature (Wang and Yang, 2008; Baldauf et al., 2009), although it contradicts the work of Chen et

Table 7.11   Hierarchical regression analysis results

Variables	Mod. 1	Mod. 2	Mod. 3	Mod. 4	Mod. 5
Gender	–	–	–	–	–
Age	–	–	–	–	–
Education	–	–	–	–	–
Personal income/month	–	–	–	–	–
Italy image		$(0.363)^1$	$(0.243)^1$	$(0.123)^1$	$(-0.253)^1$
		$(0.309)^2$	$(0.207)^2$	$(0.105)^2$	$(-0.215)^2$
Brand image			$(0.216)^1$	$(0.133)^1$	$(-0.156)^1$
			$(0.171)^2$	$(0.105)^2$	$(-0.124)^2$
Product image				$(0.543)^1$	$(0.528)^1$
				$(0.501)^2$	$(0.488)^2$
Italy image X brand image					$(0.099)^1$
					$(0.506)^2$
Constant	3.202	1.844	1.446	0.734	1.800
F	1.37	116.76	71.34	192.50	150.01
	–	$p<0.001$	$p<0.001$	$p<0.001$	$p<0.001$
R^2	0.005	0.095	0.114	0.343	0.452
R^2 change	0.005	0.090	0.019	0.229	0.109
Adj – R^2	0.001	0.094	0.113	0.341	0.447
Overall model p value	–	0.000	0.000	0.000	0.000

Notes:
1. Non-standardized regression coefficient;
2. Standardized regression coefficient.

al. (2004), for which the brand has little impact on the choice of clothing for children in China. A possible explanation may be related to the time lag between the two surveys. The contextual conditions in countries like China have changed a lot during the past five years. As already mentioned, more than one third of the respondents consider fashion as a significant motivator in the purchasing process. This suggests an evolution of consumption patterns towards market segments where consumers are more influenced by intangible variables, including brands. In the second case, according to models 4 and 5 the change in R^2 is 22.9 per cent and statistically significant at p <0.001. The standardized regression coefficient is positive (0.488) on the product image, thus supporting H2b. The results are confirmed in the literature (Roth and Romeo, 1992).

Our third hypothesis is that the image of Italy tends to positively moderate (a) the relationship between brand image and consumer preferences and (b) the relationship between product image and consumer preferences. In accordance with Model 5, the change in R^2 is 10.9 per cent and statistically significant at p <0.001 and the standardized regression coefficient is 0.506, thus indicating that the interaction has a positive impact on purchasing preferences other things being equal. Thus, the country of origin image acts as a moderator between positive brand image and consumer preferences, confirming H3a. In this case the result is confirmed in the literature (Wang and Yang, 2008).

According to our hypotheses, the country of origin has a direct influence that is exercised by its image and an indirect impact through the interaction with brand image on the consumer preferences. The results reveal that the three factors considered individually have a significant positive impact on the willingness of Chinese consumers to pay a premium price, which is consistent with the literature (e.g., Roth and Romeo, 1992). At the same time, we found evidence that the COO image represents a fair moderator in the relationship between image and brand preferences. To reach similar results Wang and Yang (2008), considering brand personality instead of brand image, suggest that such a moderating effect may play an important role not only in one dimension of brand equity, but in all its components (Yasin et al., 2007). Finally, we did not find significant interaction between Italy's image and product image.

With regard to our third research question, Tables 7.12 and 7.13 show, respectively, the consumers' association between the X brand and Italy, and the consumers' association among store elements of the X brand and Italy. The data reveals that an effective retail sign policy can have a positive association between Italy and the brand; this result is consistent with the competitive strategy observed in practice where we see some Chinese competitors in the fashion business that are adopting Italian names in their brand strategies.

With regards to store management policies, the results show that none of the elements of store layout has a greater importance in the association between the X brand and Italy when compared to the others, but they are all equally important. This suggests that to effectively exploit the

Table 7.12   The association between the X brand and Italy

	Mean	St. dev.	1	2	3	4	5
			Proportions %				
Association	3.46	1.31	11.61	11.94	22.90	26.45	27.10

Table 7.13   The association among store elements of the X brand and Italy

	Mean	St. dev.	Proportions %				
			1	2	3	4	5
Poster and video	3.36	1.41	14.76	14.21	20.33	21.73	28.97
Catalogue	3.29	1.34	13.75	14.28	25.88	21.56	24.53
Sign (in Italian)	3.21	1.42	17.23	14.14	25.19	16.45	26.99
Interior design	3.17	1.31	15.25	13.56	29.10	22.60	19.49
Store window	3.12	1.36	16.48	17.31	23.35	23.08	19.78
Music	2.86	1.47	25.64	17.66	22.22	13.68	20.80

advantage offered by the country of origin in the perception of the Chinese consumer evaluation, it is necessary to provide integrated communication policies that involve the entire management of the store.

5.   DISCUSSION, THEORETICAL AND MANAGERIAL IMPLICATIONS

The results reveal that the three constructs considered individually have a significant positive impact on the willingness of Chinese consumers to pay a price differential. This is in line with part of the literature (e.g., Roth and Romeo, 1992). At the same time, we found evidence that the COO image represents a fair moderator in the relationship between image and brand preferences. To reach similar results, Wang and Yang (2008), however, considering the brand personality and brand image, suggests that such a moderating effect may play an important role not only in one dimension of brand equity, but in all its components (Yasin et al., 2007).

The research also has interesting managerial implications. First, making the country of origin crucial in allowing differential pricing (premium price) may represent not only a lever to reach better economic and financial performance, but also a strategic factor when dealing with possible local partners (especially trade clients) as well as in the direct management of the store.

Second, the direct relationship between product attributes and consumer preferences suggests to the managers of companies operating in China that the expansion of the product range of features (notably the degree of novelty and quality) can be a discriminating factor for the consumer buying process.

Third, as COO image exerts a significant role in the relationship between brand image and consumer preferences, it may be an additional factor that can differentiate and enhance their brand in today's hypercompetitive market and mature as is the fashion.

Fourth, we expected the retail strategy (monobrand vs. multibrand stores) to have a stronger influence on brand image when measured in terms of premium price perception. Our hypothesis was not confirmed. This result may depend on differences in the cities or in the store locations. The reason for this unexpected result may also lie on the type of strategy adopted by the Italian firm to enter the Chinese market. The decision not to or the inability to directly control distribution and retail marketing in China may depend on differences in the interests and visions between the Italian firm and the local partners in terms of brand image and positioning. A follow-up interview with company X managers highlighted how the retail strategy in China has so far been different than in other countries as a result of having a minority stake in the EJV that has made it impossible to orient the development in China consistently with its global brand positioning. This may have been sustainable until the Chinese market was close and poorer. Nowadays it may seriously undermine company X's future development in what is becoming the largest market for luxury products in the world. The case stresses the importance of maintaining a strict control on brand and marketing strategies in a foreign market. It also suggests that being a minority in an EJV in a foreign market without proper corporate governance rules that can ensure the alignment of the EJV decision making with the brand image may jeopardize or reduce the positive impact of the COO effects and of brand and retail management on consumer preferences.

6.   LIMITATIONS AND FUTURE RESEARCH

We are conscious that our research has some limitations:

1. The study considered a single product category. The same analysis conducted in markets for different product categories may lead to different results. The problem is, however, endogenous to the country of origin concept itself: the impact of the geographic origin is known to be stronger for those categories of products the production of which is associated to countries known precisely for that specific production tradition.
2. We did not include in the model the degree of involvement with the product, although we believe that the purchase of children's clothing is not a high-involvement situation as the choice of an automobile or similar products.

3. Finally, we did not consider the possible level of uncertainty about the recognition of the origin of a particular brand that others have instead highlighted (e.g. Zhuang et al., 2007) with specific reference to China.

Further research could consider: The analysis could have possible future developments such as:

1. The opportunity to test the hypotheses in other countries such as India, Russia and Brazil that represent emerging markets not only for the main Italian large luxury firms, but also for many SMEs of the fashion system that are internationalizing their businesses.
2. The influence of retail strategy (monobrand versus multibrand stores) on brand image considering a wider number of variables.
3. Finally, a dynamic analysis by repeating the survey in the future to check if any changes in perceptions and purchase intentions of consumers have occurred with the increase of market maturity, which may be especially interesting when considering that the childrenswear market in China is currently in the early stages of its life cycle.

NOTES

1. The present work is the result of a joint effort. Nevertheless, Tommaso Pucci wrote sections 3 and 4, Christian Simoni wrote section 5 and Lorenzo Zanni wrote sections 1 and 2. The authors jointly wrote section 6.
2. Consorzio Bimbo Italia is an export consortium mostly specialized in the childrenswear industry.
3. The retail activities are managed through an equity joint venture (EJV) with a Chinese partner that decides and implements both product policies and stores layout. The store sign and brands are those of the Italian firm.
4. The X brand is not sold in multibrand stores in China.

REFERENCES

Aaker, David A. (1991), *Managing Brand Equity*, New York, NY: Macmillan.
Aaker, David A. (1996), *Building Strong Brands*, New York, NY: The Free Press.
Aiello, G. and S. Guercini (2010), 'Relazioni tra brand e punto vendita per lo sviluppo di nuovi mercati per le imprese italiane della moda', *Mercati e Competitività*, **4**, 15–49.
Aiello, G., R. Donvito, B. Godey, D. Pederzoli, K. Wiedmann, N. Hennigs, A. Siebels, P. Chan, J. Tsuchiya, S. Rabino, S.I. Ivanovna, B. Weitz, H. Oh and R. Singh (2009), 'An international perspective on luxury brand and country-of origin effect', *Brand Management*, **16** (5/6), 323–337.
Ashill, N.J. and A. Sinha (2004), 'An exploratory study into the impact of com-

ponents of brand equity and country of origin effects on purchase intention', *Journal of Asia-Pacific Business*, **5** (3), 27–43.

Baldauf, A., K.S. Cravens, A. Diamantopoulos and K.P. Zeugner-Roth (2009), 'The impact of product–country image and marketing efforts on retailer-perceived brand equity: an empirical analysis', *Journal of Retailing*, **85** (4), 437–452.

Bertoli G. (2004), 'Globalizzazione dei mercati e competitività delle imprese italiane', in G. Bertoli (ed.), *La competitività del sistema Italia: dal locale al globale*, Milano, IT: Franco Angeli, pp. 15–54.

Bertoli, G., B. Busacca and L. Molteni (2005), 'L'interazione tra "made in" e marca nel processo di scelta del consumatore: un'indagine empirica nel contesto italiano e statunitense', Conference Proceedings *Le tendenze del Marketing in Europa*, Paris.

Bilkey, W.J. and E. Nes (1982), 'Country-of-origin effects on product evaluations', *Journal of International Business Studies*, **13** (1), 89–99.

Birtwistle, G., I. Clarke and P. Freathy (1999), 'Store image in the UK fashion sector: consumer versus retailer perceptions', *The International Review of Retail, Distribution and Consumer Research*, **9** (1), 1–16.

Bloemer, J., K. Brijs and H. Kasper (2009), 'The CoO–ELM model: a theoretical framework for the cognitive processes underlying country of origin-effects', *European Journal of Marketing*, **43** (1/2), 62–89.

Burt, S., J. Dawson and L. Sparks (2003), 'Failure in international retailing: research propositions', *The International Review of Retail, Distribution and Consumer Research*, **13** (4), 355–373.

Carpenter, J.M. and A. Fairhurst (2005), 'Consumer shopping value, satisfaction, and loyalty for retail apparel brands', *Journal of Fashion Marketing and Management*, **9** (3), 256–269.

Chen, X., W.M. Au and K. Li (2004), 'Consumption of children's wear in a big city in Central China: Zhengzhou', *Journal of Fashion Marketing and Management*, **8** (2), 154–165.

Corbellini, E. and S. Saviolo (2004), *La scommessa del Made in Italy e il futuro della moda italiana*, Milano, IT: ETAS.

Databank (2010), *Competitors. Abbigliamento Infantile*, May.

Dichter, E. (1962), 'The world customer', *Harvard Business Review*, **40**, 113–122.

Dodds, B.K., K.B. Monroe and D. Grewal (1991), 'Effect of price, brands, and store information on buyers' product evaluation', *Journal of Marketing Research*, **28**, 307–319.

Doherty, A.M. (2000), 'Factors influencing international retailers' market entry mode strategy: qualitative evidence from the UK fashion sector', *Journal of Marketing Management*, **16** (1/3), 223–245.

Doherty, A.M. (2007), 'Support mechanisms in international retail franchise networks', *International Journal of Retail & Distribution Management*, **35** (10), 781–802.

Feldwick, P. (1996), 'What is brand equity and how do you measure it?', *Journal of Market Research Society*, **38** (2), 85–104.

Fionda A.M. and C.M. Moore (2009), 'The anatomy of the luxury fashion brand', *Journal of Brand Management*, 16, 347–363.

Fortis, M. (2005), *Le due sfide del Made in Italy: globalizzazione e innovazione*, Bologna, IT: Il Mulino.

Han, C.M. (1989), 'Country image: halo or summary construct?', *Journal of Marketing Research*, **26**, 222–229.

176   *International marketing and the country of origin effect*

Keller, K.L. (1998), *Strategic Brand Management: Building, Measuring and Managing Brand Equity*, Englewood Cliffs, NJ: Prentice Hall.

Li, W. and R.S. Wyer (2001), 'The role of country of origin in product evaluations: informational and standard-of-comparison effects', *Journal of Consumer Psychology*, 3 (2), 187–212.

Marino, V., C. Gallucci and G. Mainolfi (2009), 'L'interpretazione multidimensionale della country reputation. Implicazioni strategiche per le imprese del made in Italy', in C. Pepe and A. Zucchella (eds), *L'internazionalizzazione delle imprese italiane. Contributi di ricerca*, Bologna, IT: il Mulino, pp. 93–126.

Moore, M. and A. Fairhurst (2003), 'Marketing capabilities and firm performance in fashion retailing', *Journal of Fashion Marketing and Management*, 7 (4), 386–397.

Nagashima, A. (1970), 'A comparison of Japanese and US attitudes toward foreign products', *Journal of Marketing*, 34, 68–74.

Papadopoulos, N. and L. Heslop (1993), *Product–Country Image: Impact and Role in International Marketing*, London, UK: International Business Press.

Papadopoulos, N. and L. Heslop (2002), 'Country equity and country branding: problems and prospects', *Brand Management*, 9 (4/5), 294–314.

Pappu, R., P.G. Quester and R.W. Cooksey (2006), 'Consumer-based brand equity and country-of-origin relationships', *European Journal of Marketing*, 40 (5/6), 696–717.

Pucci, T., C. Simoni and L. Zanni (2011), 'Marketing imprenditoriale, gestione degli intangibles e competitività. Un'analisi nel settore dell'abbigliamento infantile', *Mercati e Competitività*, 1, 93–113.

Rabino, S., C. Simoni and L. Zanni (2008), 'Small and medium gold and fashion enterprises (SMEs) in Arezzo, Italy: competitive challenges and strategic implications', *Journal of Global Marketing*, 21 (2), 141–159.

Rahman, O., X. Zhu and W.S. Liu (2008), 'A study of the pyjamas purchasing behaviour of Chinese consumers in Hangzhou, China', *Journal of Fashion Marketing and Management*, 12 (2), 217–231.

Richardson, J. (1996), 'Vertical integration and rapid response in fashion apparel', *Organization Science*, 7 (4), 400–412.

Roth, M.S. and J.B. Romeo (1992), 'Matching product category and country image perceptions: a framework for managing country-of-origin effects', *Journal of International Business Studies*, 23 (3), 477–497.

Sin, L.Y.M., and O.H.M. Yau (2004), 'Female role orientation of chinese women: conceptualization and scale development', *Psychology & Marketing*, 21 (12), 1033–1058.

Srinivasan, N. and S.C. Jain (2003), 'Country of origin effect: synthesis and future direction', in S.C. Jain (ed.), *Handbook of Research in International Marketing*, Cheltenham, UK and Northampton, MA, USA: Edward Elgar, pp. 458–471.

Thakor, M.V. and L.P. Katsanis (1997), 'A model of brand and country effects on quality dimensions: issues and implications', *Journal of International Consumer Marketing*, 9 (3), 79–100.

Tse, D.K. and G.J. Gorn (1993), 'An experiment on the salience of country-of-origin in the era of global brands', *Journal of International Marketing*, 1 (1), 57–76.

Usunier, J.C. (2006), 'Relevance in business research: the case of country-of-origin research in marketing', *European Management Review*, 3, 60–73.

Wang, X. and Z. Yang (2008), 'Does country-of-origin matter in the relationship between brand personality and purchase intention in emerging economies? Evidence from China's auto industry', *International Marketing Review*, **25** (4), 458–474.

Wigley, S.W., C.M. Moore and G. Birtwistle (2005), 'Product and brand: critical success factors in the internationalisation of a fashion retailer', *International Journal of Retail & Distribution Management*, **33** (7), 531–544.

Xiao, G. and J.O. Kim (2009), 'The investigation of chinese consumer values, consumption values, life satisfaction, and consumption behaviors', *Psychology & Marketing*, **26** (7), 610–624.

Yasin, N.M., M.N. Noor and O. Mohamad (2007), 'Does image of country-of-origin matter to brand equity?', *Journal of Product & Brand Management*, **16** (1), 38–48.

Yoo, B., N. Donthu and S. Lee (2000), 'An examination of selected marketing mix elements and brand equity', *Journal of the Academy of Marketing Science*, **28** (2), 195–211.

Zeugner-Roth, P.K., A. Diamantopoulos and M.A. Montesinos (2008), 'Home country image, country brand equity and consumers' product preferences: an empirical study', *Management International Review*, **5**, 577–602.

Zhuang, G., X. Wang, L. Zhou and N. Zhou (2007), 'Asymmetric effects of brand origin confusion: evidence from the emerging market of China', *International Marketing Review*, **25** (4), 441–457.

8. The role of country of origin in supporting export consortia in emerging markets

Fabio Musso, Barbara Francioni and
Alessandro Pagano

1. INTRODUCTION

In the last few decades various contributions (Baldoni et al. 1998; Lanzara et al. 1990; Rabellotti 1998) have highlighted the diffusion of export consortia as a strategic option for penetrating foreign markets. In recent years international competition has strongly increased, pushing companies to tap into new resources and competences. As well, the development of emerging markets implies the adoption of more articulated and complex sales strategies due to the higher cultural, geographic and institutional distance compared to traditional Western markets. Within such a competitive scenario, companies falling short in specific competences might display a renowned interest in alliances and specifically on multilateral agreements as export consortia. This organizational tool might prove more effective in complex and new foreign markets if it demonstrated the ability to coordinate the individual behaviour of member companies and to manage collective resources such as the common country of origin (COO), whose effect could provide various benefits in terms of evaluation and perception of foreign commercial partners and final consumers (Agrawal and Kamakura 1999; Al-Sulaiti and Baker 1998; Papadopoulos et al. 1993).

This chapter investigates the role of COO effects in facilitating export consortia market penetration efforts in emerging markets. The analysis is focused on Italian companies active in the food industry attempting to enter the Indian market through an export consortium.

The reasons for this study are two-fold. On the theoretical side, export consortia have received limited attention in the academic literature, therefore they deserve further study to gain insights into their contribution as organizational tools in the new market scenario. Moreover, the role of

COO in export consortia has thus far been neglected. The theme of COO has been investigated widely with regard to its impact on customers, but only to a lesser extent has it been studied as a strategic option to be actively adopted and exploited by firms (Beverland and Lindgren 2002).

On the empirical side, the Italy–India combination allows for the examination of companies originating from two countries that have strong traditions in terms of cooking and food and are weak in terms of structural features. Italian food companies are active in foreign markets, however they need to overcome their high degree of fragmentation by setting up external partnerships. The Indian food market, on the other hand, is gradually opening up to foreign trade, however it still suffers from weak distribution channels and high trade and non-trade barriers.

The research methodology is qualitative and is based on the case-study analysis of an Italian export consortium active in the food market in India. The main focus is on the role of the COO effect on the strategies and behaviour at the consortium and individual companies level. The impact of this variable is assessed in combination with factors related to the setting up and the evolution over time of the consortium.

The chapter is structured in six sections. Section 2 provides the background of the chapter on the topics of strategic alliances, export consortia and the COO effect. In the final part of the section an overview of the Indian food market is outlined. The third section develops the research objectives and methodology in detail. Section 4 is concerned with the empirical research of the export consortium under examination. Section 5 is devoted to the discussion of empirical results, while the final section draws some conclusive remarks on the limitations of the research and suggests some directions for further investigation.

2. BACKGROUND OF THE CHAPTER

The Role of Export Consortia

It is well known that companies need to be active in global markets to face competition effectively. Therefore both large and small–medium businesses attempt to penetrate foreign markets using export strategies and setting up networks of subsidiaries and local units (Di Gregorio et al. 2008; Ruzzier et al. 2006). These efforts are highly demanding for small firms, which often do not have internal resources – in terms of organization, technology and products – to gain a stable position in foreign markets (Leonidou, 1995), which show high levels of complexity as in the case of emerging countries as China and India. Such obstacles have been defined as 'those gaps which need to be filled before the competitive producer becomes a successful exporter' (Lall 1991: 139).

Therefore, mainly small businesses pursue effective solutions to overcome their competitive gaps. Some studies highlight the growing attitude toward active development of flexible vertical and horizontal relationships with firms and other partner organizations (Coviello and Munro 1997). Networking capabilities are deemed a key factor in gaining access to foreign markets, by reducing the impact of high cultural and institutional differences between the home and the host markets (Johanson and Vahlne 2009). Relationships set up during the international expansion might represent a useful channel through which to acquire market knowledge, learning opportunities and relational assets such as trust (Zhou et al. 2007). This allows for a gradual and risk-controlled entry into a foreign market (Oviatt and McDougall 1994).

The export consortium is a traditional collective tool for facing foreign markets (Dollinger and Golden 1992). It can be defined a formal association of independent companies whose goal is to facilitate the export of products and all related promotional activities (Albaum and Duerr 2008; Valdani and Bertoli 2010). Thus the consortium represents a network-based option allowing member companies to invest financial and organizational resources to a limited and flexible extent. Moreover, in various countries export consortia might receive financial assistance by government authorities within their export promotion programmes.

Various types of export consortia have been described in the academic literature. The main distinction is between promotional and sales consortia. The former have the goal to provide services and assistance for the promotion of member companies' products in international markets. Companies alone could not access these resources while still controlling their costs. Services comprise consulting and marketing support, promotional services, public relations, assistance for trade missions and participations to trade fairs (Bertoli and Bertuzzi 2002). In the latter case, the consortium buys products from member companies and actively sells them to foreign intermediaries and customers.

Various studies highlight the main variables (Table 8.1) that impact on the functioning of export consortia (Bertoli and Bertuzzi 2002; Depperu 1996; Ghauri et al. 2003; Welch and Joynt 1987). One main factor is the degree of cohesion among members, whose alignment might represent a driver to achieve consortium objectives. The level of cohesion depends on various factors such as the number of members, their strategic convergence and cultural homogeneity. Firms might pursue different goals while joining an export consortium: commercial penetration in foreign markets, market and technological learning, brand promotion, and the

Table 8.1   Types of export consortia

Variable	Typology
Objective	Promotional and sales consortia
Number of sectors	Mono-sectoral and multi-sectoral consortia
Relationship between partners	Consortia between competitors and non-competitors
Partners' headquarter	Regional, multi-regional, national and international consortia
Number of partners	Simple and complex consortia
Target area	Area-specific and global consortia
Time	Short- and long-term consortia
Ownership structure	Public and private consortia

Source: UNIDO (2009).

set up and development of strategic relationships with key partners. In case of low degrees of cohesion, export consortia are more complex to manage and experience high levels of internal divergence and conflict. One relevant factor which could provide higher cohesion is the common COO. However, this aspect thus far has received very limited attention in the management literature on consortia (Beverland and Lindgren 2002; Bhaskaran and Sukumaran 2007).

A further critical dimension of export consortia is the organizational configuration and the type of competence. The effectiveness of projects and actions might depend on the organizational structure adopted and specifically on the internal flow of information and knowledge. Moreover, the export consortia's performance might be affected by the technical and managerial competences detained by the dedicated personnel acting on behalf of the consortium. All these factors might shape the behaviour of export consortia, also in terms of the effective involvement of all members in common projects and their organizational and financial investment.

Management literature has examined in depth most of the determinants impacting export consortia performance. Less attention has been devoted to the evolution of 'models' in the business practice. At the end of the 1990s various scholars highlighted the end of the 'traditional approach' based on limited services and limited financial involvement, low degree of participation and low satisfaction of participants. More emphasis was placed on new approaches emerging within export expansion plans. A new model was based on the setting up of a 'centre for strategic services for internationalization', pursuing specialization and customization in the offering of services. An alternative model was the 'centre for commercial operations' based on the planning and implementation of special projects on target markets (Bertoli and Bertuzzi 2002). In the last few years the topic of export consortia has received less attention, with the exception of some contributions on emerging markets companies choosing to set them up to promote their products in foreign markets (Ghauri et al. 2003; UNIDO 2009).

Country of Origin

The COO effect is a widely researched topic in the field of international business (Paterson and Jolibert 1995; Pharr 2005). It could be defined as 'the country with which the firm producing a brand is associated' (Agrawal and Kamakura 1999: 258). It seems that most of these contributions have agreed on placing emphasis on the effect of COO on product evaluations by foreign consumers (Agrawal and Kamakura 1999; Al-Sulaiti and Baker 1998; Papadopoulos et al. 1993). Various studies highlight the positive impact of COO of foreign brands on perceptions of consumers in emerging markets, such as India (Kinra 2006). However, recent work on this topic argues that the globalization of markets might change how COO is perceived and structurally composed. Existing contributions focus on a number of related concepts based on emerging business practices, such as 'country of manufacture' (Agrawal and Kamakura 1999), 'country of assembly', 'country of parts', 'country of design' (Pharr 2005).

Thus most of the literature is concerned with the analysis of the COO effect on perceptions and evaluations by foreign customers. A related topic still not explored in detail is the strategic use of COO by companies to promote their products and services in foreign consumer and business markets. Perceptions of COO among customers might change due to business and marketing programmes actively implemented by firms (Beverland and Lindgren 2002; Bhaskaran and Sukumaran 2007). Information processing might have an impact on COO evaluations. Thus an ability in setting up communication strategies could have positive results in terms of COO effects (Pharr 2005). This is more likely when COO and product category are not strongly linked, thus requiring specific promotion efforts. Products such as wine, fruit and vegetables are traditionally linked to countries or regions and often imply lower levels of investment in marketing (Beverland and Lindgren 2002).

The use and impact of COO could have a positive or negative effect on strategic aspects such as pricing decisions (Agrawal and Kamakura 1999). Therefore adequate market research is a prerequisite for effective COO-based communications strategies. Changing market conditions might push firms to a different strategic use of COO, which might evolve over time (Beverland and Lindgren 2002). Companies can adopt a wide variety of marketing and promotion techniques. For instance, promotion tools in the food industry might include courses in culinary institutes, demonstrations by professional chefs, and meeting and testing initiatives with distributors, journalists and local media. It should be noted that use of COO might imply a certain degree of risk: emphasis on category rather than specific company products might support competing firms selling the same product (Beverland and Lindgren 2002).

Specific variables that might influence the use of COO are the level of product complexity and the economic development of the country (Beverland and Lindgren 2002; Bhaskaran and Sukumaran 2007). It has been argued that use of COO might prove useful when entering new markets (Beverland and Lindgren 2002). Also the management of brand names might influence whether and how COO is strategically used. A strong brand name might reduce the attractiveness of placing emphasis on COO; in this case companies prefer to rely mainly on their own reputation (Beverland and Lindgren 2002). In other situations firms choose brand names which are closely linked to COO beliefs (Bhaskaran and Sukumaran 2007). Also past experiences in COO use might influence companies' strategic choices (Beverland and Lindgren 2002).

The Food Market in India

India is the second most populated country in the world, after China, and the population continues to increase (Ling et al. 2004; Promar International 2005). Thanks to improved infrastructure, economic reforms, rapid economic development and the subsequent market deregulation, this country is also emerging as a very important market for international companies (Choo et al. 2004).

With specific reference to the food market the potential is enormous, especially considering that most consumers are young and can influence consumption patterns (Ling et al. 2004). Indian imports of food and beverages (F&B) were valued at 7.76 billion euros in 2009, up from 3.62 billion euros in 2005 (Stanton, Emms & Sia 2010). With specific reference to Italy, total Indian imports of Italian F&B products reached 18.3 million euros in 2009 and 29.84 million euros in 2010, up from 13.8 million euros in 2005 (ISTAT-COEWEB 2012). Moreover, although the food business is still largely unorganized, India is characterized by a substantial change in the food retail system, in response not only to rapid urbanization but also to diet diversification. Consequently, Western style outlets are gaining a foothold in most Indian cities, and this expansion is supposed to lead to further diffusion of homogenous foods and of a global diet (Pingali and Khwaja 2004).

Nevertheless, the Indian market is not easy to penetrate for foreign exporters because besides geographical, religious, cultural, psychological and lifestyle diversity, tastes and preferences in food also diverge from place to place (Ali et al. 2010; Goyal and Singh 2007; Tripathi and Srivastava 2011). Indeed, food preferences vary on the basis of the region of origin and the locally practised religion. Even within a religious group food habits differ depending on the caste or sub-caste (Mahadevan and Blair 2009).

These diversities are closely correlated with Indian attitudes towards different products and they affect the purchase and consumption of food (Ahlgren et al. 2004). For example, the consumption of meat, milk and vegetables is particularly influenced by religious principles. The majority (80.5 per cent) of the population is Hindu, but also within this group there are differences, since while all castes consider cows as sacred animals, upper castes are mostly vegetarian and lower castes are mostly non-vegetarian. The remaining 19.5 per cent are followers of a wide range of other religions. Muslims are generally non-vegetarians but with a taboo on pork, while Christians are mostly non-vegetarian with no taboo. Sikhs are partially vegetarians, while Buddhists and Jains are mostly vegetarians (Central Intelligence Agency 2011; Promar International 2005).

With reference to other categories of food, India is different from Italy for the usage of particular products. For instance, while in Italy olive oil is typically adopted for cooking, in India, historically, olive oil is appreciated and consumed as a massage oil. Only during the 1990s, due to increased foreign travel and advertising campaigns, did olive oil begin to be used in cooking. The growing emphasis on olive oil is a direct consequence of the increase in income of upper castes, but it is also due to the growing need to adopt the Mediterranean diet, in order to prevent heart disease and obesity (L'olivo news 2008). However, olive oil is considered too expensive and it can also change the traditional flavour of Indian cooked foods. Therefore, the majority of Indians still prefer the olive-pomace oil, both for the lower price and for its lightness and flavour which does not alter the taste of Indian dishes.

Finally, while protection from imports of agricultural products is decreasing, India continues to use trade policy – particularly tariff and non-tariff barriers – to ensure sufficient domestic supply of key food products and also for other particular purposes, like protection from some 'negative' products. For example, wine is one of the most taxed products in India as it is considered a luxury, not a necessity. Moreover, the Indian Constitution discourages the use of wine and the government is willing to protect Indian citizens from negative products through specific measures, such as serving alcohol only at specific outlets and during specific hours, or establishing the age of legal alcohol consumption at 25 years old (JBC International 2011; Sandrey et al. 2008).

3. RESEARCH OBJECTIVES AND METHODOLOGY

Existing management literature does not provide insights over the effective role and behaviour of export consortia in the new global market scenario, which is characterized by increased complexity and uncertainty, affecting mainly smaller size firms. It is not clear whether and how firms are eager to exploit opportunities in newly emerging markets and are interested in aggregating forms through export consortia, which thus could be renewed in terms of mission and organizational configurations. Moreover, such tools could be strengthened if adequately linked to the strategic use of COO. However, management literature on this theme is very limited and some authors call for research on this topic (Bhaskaran and Sukumaran 2007).

This chapter aims to assess the role of COO in facilitating export consortia market penetration efforts in emerging markets. Given the exploratory nature of such research goal this chapter adopts a case study approach through the in-depth analysis of an Italian food export consortium active in the Indian market. The case study methodology has been selected in order to gain new insights into an international business topic (Eisenhardt 1989; Ghauri 2004; Mintzberg 1979).

The consortium analysed – Alpha – has been selected as it is one of the few export consortium cases concerning the food sector active in the Indian market. Alpha consortium was founded in 2007 by the most important Italian organization representing food–farming cooperation, with the aim to promote, enhance, spread and popularize quality food–farming cooperative products in the world. Alpha comprises 15 associate cooperatives, 100 000 producers as partners, has a turnover of 3 billion euros, and represents the six main chains of European agricultural production, which are examples of quality and typically Mediterranean alimentary tradition – from fresh fruits and vegetables as well as their processed offshoots like conserves, juices, peeled, pulped and ready-to-eat packaged products, to dairy products, from wine to olive oils, from cold cuts to the choicest meats are all covered.

This chapter aims to address the following research questions:

- to what extent and how did the Alpha consortium use COO effects in supporting market penetration of associated firms in the food and beverage market in India?

- to what extent did the COO effect facilitate market penetration of Alpha consortium and its members in the food and beverage market in India?

With regards to data collection, Yin (1994) recommends the adoption of different sources, in order to enhance the validity and reliability of findings (Ghanatabadi 2005). Therefore, even if this research process has mainly focused on in-depth interviews, other documents (for example export consortium and firms' websites, annual reports and marketing material) have been used as complementary sources for data collection. In order to understand the COO effect from different perspectives, nine semi-structured interviews have been held with the director of the Alpha consortium, representatives of consulting and services companies involved in promotion activities, and representatives of the consortium member companies.

4. THE EMPIRICAL ANALYSIS

The empirical analysis is structured in two sections. The first examines the set-up process of the consortium and the evolution of the main promotional activities implemented within the Alpha project. The second examines in more depth the specific sectoral patterns among consortium members.

Evolution of Consortium Activities

In 2007 an Italian national association of cooperative companies in the food sector launched a proposal to set up an export consortium in order to receive financial support from the European Union in the area of exports of food and agricultural products in emerging markets (Table 8.2). Various cooperatives joined this project. Then the consortium was structured and judged eligible for financing by the European Union, ensuring a total funding of 1.84 million euros for two years. EU financial support reached a maximum of 50 per cent of the total costs of the project, while 20 per cent was provided by an Italian government agency active in the agricultural sector, and the remaining 30 per cent was given by member cooperatives, which contributed a share in proportion to their size and turnover.

The focus on the Indian market did not derive from a formalized and systematic decision process, in order to analyse the potential of several target markets, but rather from the willingness to take advantage of

Table 8.2   Characteristics of Alpha consortium

Dimensions	Alpha Consortium
Number and characteristics of members	15 associated cooperatives of agricultural enterprises.
General purpose	Born in 2007 to obtain funding from the European Union for a specific project. Main purposes: to promote, enhance and distribute food and beverage products in India.
Organizational structure	Consortium Coordinator, Board of Directors, Technical Committee and two consulting firms.
Project's objectives for Indian market	Consolidation of knowledge, awareness and consumption of quality European food products.
Main targets and activities in Indian market	Three main targets: retailers, importers and professional food operators. Main activities: press dinners, tasting workshops, gala dinners, professional courses, business-to-business corners.
Organizational solutions adopted for the development of Indian market	Programme implementation by two marketing consulting firms, operating in collaboration with a technical committee, composed of one representative from each member company.
Funding for Indian project	50% of total costs of the project derived from European Union funding, 20% provided by the Italian Government, and the remaining 30% given by member companies, in proportion to their size and turnover.

the opportunity offered by the Memorandum of Understanding signed between the Italian Minister of Agriculture and the Indian Minister of Agriculture. The Memorandum represented a key step for establishing close cooperation between the two countries, in order to facilitate access to markets and increase trade relations.

Under the perspective of member companies, involvement in this project was not the result of strategic long-term planning, but rather a contingent opportunity proposed by external actors. Indeed, the project consortium allowed for exploring a new market that companies alone could not easily penetrate.

Alpha was created as a multi-sector and promotional consortium, and to this end it did not foresee the achievement of specific target sales: the main thrust was to initiate an intense dialogue between Indian and Italian culinary cultures, integrate cooking styles and ingredients, provide sustained training to sector professionals and knowledge to opinion-makers and media. Therefore, it aimed at developing a better understanding of Italian food products, by strengthening the reputation of the cooperative's products and brands towards several stakeholders, such as importers, professional food-sector operators, journalists and consumer associations.

With reference to the organizational structure, Alpha was organized into three main bodies:

- a Consortium Coordinator – this role was taken by a manager of the National Association of Agricultural Cooperatives;
- a Board of Directors, constituted by the directors of each member company and responsible for providing general guidelines for the consortium's actions;
- a Technical Committee, composed of export and area managers from each of the associated cooperatives, that defined the action programme.

In addition, the Alpha consortium selected two Italian consulting firms for the implementation of promotional activities in India, previously set out by the board of directors and the technical committee. These external partners involved local services companies in India to provide local support in the planning and implementation of projects and events. A local firm specialized in Italian language and culture was involved as a translation services provider. Over time it has been actively participating in the design of promotional material and then as a partner in event planning and management of contacts with relevant media channels.

During the first phase of activities the focus of the consortium was on setting up relationships with local importers and trading partners. In the first phase institutions were the main target of promotional activities. The main effort was directed towards involving journalists, government authorities, importers and distributors. The main targets were local chefs, buyers for hotel chains, international food chains and single shops.

In the first year Alpha organized three promotional missions to India. In all missions, institutional communication initiatives could not use the Made in Italy brand pervasively in the light of the European profile of the project. Therefore, Italian colours and images were carefully adopted in order to comply with requirements set up by the European Commission financing the project. Notwithstanding this, Alpha has been always perceived as an Italian initiative by Indian counterparts, since it promoted Italian food products. Italian cooking tradition and culture already had a distinctive and specific image in India when Alpha consortium began its activities. Key choices such as the consortium brand name and logo were made to exploit well-known Italian words and colours, taking explicit advantage of the COO.

Alpha started its activities in a phase of opening and change in the Indian cultural and social environment. The first mission was launched in January 2008, when the consortium joined the Italian government delegation on a visit to New Delhi in order to lay the foundation for the establishment and development of strong cooperation between Italy and India. This mission established initial contacts with potential Indian partners, thanks to networking activities developed among associated cooperative firms, technical committee members and Indian industry associations. The first mission created the opportunity to identify three main targets of the promotional programme: retailers, importers and professionals in the food sector (for example restaurant and canteen managers of five-star hotels).

Then Alpha chose to proceed with the organization of specific events for each identified target. In the second mission (May 2008), Alpha carried out all the activities foreseen by the promotional programme in New Delhi and Bombay: press dinners, tasting workshops, gala dinners, professional courses on wine, training in oil and cheese tasting techniques and business-to-business (B2B) corners, namely a sequence of scheduled meetings with some selected Indian companies, F&B dealers, importers and distributors. Alpha bodies assessed the results of the second mission and opted to change the promotional approach partially to take into consideration the requirements by the European Union of pursuing a clear and extensive communication of European denominations of origin.

During the third mission (November 2008), all the promotional activities were carried out in the cities of Mumbai and Bangalore. The main Alpha initiative was related to the participation in Mumbai – World of Food India 2008, an exhibition dedicated to the food industry that provides a strategic platform to explore and invest in the Indian food market. In this case Alpha set up a personalized stand of 125 square metres in which a kitchen was staged for all three days, where an Italian chef pleased the many guests crowding the stand. Visitors could also get more information and promotional material such as gadgets, brochures and the exclusive cookery book made by Alpha. The same format was adopted later in Bangalore.

The diffusion of knowledge about Alpha products was also fostered by two incoming missions to Italy involving Indian delegates from F&B sectors and Indian institutional and government representatives. The main goal was to allow the delegations to visit and enjoy the local environment where Alpha companies' offering is produced. The first incoming mission held in December 2008 focused on olive oil and wine, while the second incoming mission in February 2009 concerned cheese, fruit and vegetables. A conference in Rome in December 2008 was held to present the first year of activity.

During the second phase of the project the major commitment was to get in touch with local consumer targets, attempting to gain valuable market information and diffusing knowledge about Alpha products. Thus the main efforts focused on accessing Indian consumers directly, mainly through in-store promotional activities, and cooking demonstrations for both Indian chefs and families.

In large cities – such as New Delhi, Mumbai and Bangalore – there is a growing segment of potential consumers among foreigners living in India and Indian citizens with international living and travelling experience. There is a growing interest in Italian food and cooking among Indian families, also thanks to the diffusion of Italian restaurants, Italian coffee shops chains and to the high number of TV programmes on international cooking.

Two missions were carried out during the second phase. The fourth overall mission was held in May 2009 and focused on Mumbai. In this period the Alpha consortium decided to conduct more consumer-oriented innovative activities through a communication experiential approach. In detail, the main players from the Mumbai Ho.Re.Ca sector (banquet, buying and F&B managers of five-star hotels) were invited to an Italian style picnic brunch. The chosen location was converted into an Italian-style piazza made pleasant by a live orchestra, where guests were able to taste products and were introduced to the consortium's representative firms, obtaining information on products and certification systems. This event was characterized by an explicit use of COO symbols organized to evoke unequivocal recall to Italian cooking traditions and culture. The events organized in this mission received a positive evaluation by the consortium members, especially from wine, olive oil and cheese cooperatives, which were able to meet and get to know representatives of their potential consumers.

The last mission (from November to December 2009) focused on the cities of Mumbai and New Delhi, where promotional events were organized in a similar vein to previous missions. The most significant event was participation in the International Food & Drink Expo India, an important seasonal fair for food and beverages in New Delhi. Specifically, the consortium participated in the exhibition with a personalized stand of 125 square metres in the international area. Moreover, a stand of smaller dimensions was also set up in the dedicated area World Wine Spirits, where Alpha was gold sponsor of the Sommelier Championship 2009, a competition between sommeliers.

Two more activities were organized in March 2010. However, very few consortium members accepted to participate. Despite intentions to start a new project after the Indian one, the Alpha consortium was dissolved in 2010 because there was no longer a common purpose. Among the initial 15 cooperative firms only a few were still interested in exploring the Indian market further, others voted for a new project, while others opted to leave the consortium.

The results of Alpha's promotional activities have recently become visible. Today olive oil is becoming known as an ingredient for cooking and not as a cosmetic product. Indian consumers have started to buy and use olive oil coming also from Spain and Greece. Alpha is still recognized as a reference point for Italian food products.

Sectoral Patterns

Consortium members display different experiences depending on the type of product and sector. The dairy cooperatives did not face specific trade restrictions on exports to India, despite the presence of 'parmigiano reggiano' cheese produced with animal rennet and not suited to a vegetarian diet. However, Italian producers could not benefit from European quality certifications. In the case of cheese DOC and IGT, European denominations were not locally recognized and it has been complex to promote cheese products in light of the limited knowledge of these products by Indian consumers, who are used to buying a limited number of local fresh cheese products and are aware of well-known international products as Cheddar and Emmental cheese. Consequently, from the beginning the Alpha producers began to organize professional courses to explain the origin and features of the products. At the end of the programme Indian counterparts had a clearer understanding of the differences between 'parmesan cheese' and 'parmigiano reggiano'. Moreover, cheese producers explicitly played the regional origin as a source of tradition, culture and established quality.

For those cooperatives that already had an importer in India the main objective was to increase notoriety in the consumer's mind, and that was achieved thanks to Alpha's programmes. Otherwise, for those cooperatives that had no previous Indian experience, Alpha consortium has been very useful in order to gain knowledge of the local market, and to create contact and network relationships. However, after the end of the project these cooperatives did not manage to exploit any contact for exporting and penetrating into Indian market.

With regard to beef and pork, and specifically cured meat, consortium members had many difficulties due to the fact that the majority of Indian people are vegetarian for religious reasons. Moreover, another factor impacting negatively on the perception of foreign meat was the spread of the A/H1N1 epidemic. The COO was not helpful and could not be fully exploited during the promotional programme. However, the Alpha consortium allowed the associated cooperatives to learn about the Indian market, to establish relationships and to exchange business information with Indian operators, although they did not achieve benefits in terms of export sales.

For wine producers duty and brokerage costs represented a relevant entry barrier that was difficult to overcome, especially for low-range wine manufacturers. Nevertheless, wine manufacturers have been effective in using regional origin while promoting their products. Moreover, they could also use DOC and IGT European denominations to signal quality levels to Indian counterparts, who already were familiar with such type of certifications. In general, Alpha's project helped companies to gather much information about market characteristics and to discover strong interest among Indian operators and consumers, who significantly attended wine tasting events. However, results were different depending on the product's brand awareness. Commercial penetration was facilitated for those cooperative firms with higher brand awareness among Indian counterparts. A wine producer involved its Brand Ambassador for Asia, based in Singapore, who could professionally support the penetration of the local market. Such a process was further supported by its region of origin – Tuscany – a region well known in India. Conversely, wine producers with low brand awareness had more difficulties in penetrating the Indian market, because the events organized by Alpha were mainly focused on high target consumers.

With regards to the fruit and vegetable industry, there are several non-tariff barriers in India, which are accompanied by a rigid law that only allows imports of fruit and vegetables that have received chemical or heat treatments before shipment. Moreover, producers of fruit and vegetables had various problems in communicating the COO, in light of the strong differences in consumption patterns between Italy and India. Nevertheless, thanks to the consortium, fruit and vegetable cooperatives were able to deepen their knowledge of Indian restrictions and to explore the market, although the diversity of the products made their effort more complex, as not all the promoted products could have a penetration in Indian market. At the end of the project most cooperatives did not create any relevant contact with importers and operators.

Finally, olive oil was the product with the greatest difficulties at the beginning, because of its different local use and adoption as a cosmetic product. In the light of this diversity the communication of COO has proven very difficult. One of the two members producing olive oil decided to leave the consortium after the first year of activities, while the other was quite satisfied with the project's results, although it did not achieve substantial benefits in terms of new sales to the Indian market.

5. DISCUSSION OF RESULTS

Regarding the first research question of this chapter (to what extent and how did the Alpha consortium use the COO effect in supporting market penetration of associated firms in the food and beverage market in India?), it could be argued that Alpha consortium adopted a promotional approach largely exploiting the COO brand. This behaviour was in line with the explicit goal of exploring the Indian food market and spreading the food culture of the products of the consortium members. However, the use of COO had to be balanced with the requirement imposed by the European funding to maintain a European dimension of promotional activities, placing great emphasis on diffusing knowledge about the European origin certification system.

Before these activities no specific market research concerning COO had been implemented by the consortium. However, various promotional activities were developed during the programme to link the products' offer to the attributes of the Made-in-Italy brand in the food sector, highlighting the role of tradition and culture. This approach was adopted with regard to the consortium's brand name and logo, content of cooking demonstrations, design of stands in trade fairs and organization of social events. These initiatives were meant mainly to attract institutional actors and potential trading partners within business-to-business interaction patterns. With regard to Indian consumers, Alpha used the COO within cooking demonstrations and the set up of commercial corners in those chain stores involved in promotional and sales activities.

Policies behind the use of COO within Alpha consortium activities were designed and implemented in agreement among the various actors within the consortium and the consulting firm in charge of implementing initiatives in India. Consortium bodies were eager to maintain a balance with the requirements by the funding agencies, while consulting and services companies were mainly focused on proposing and implementing promotional techniques and solutions able to adapt to Indian taste and perceptions and successfully attract Indian operators and consumers.

Regarding the second research question (to what extent did the COO effect facilitate market penetration of Alpha consortium and its members in the food and beverage market in India?), the use of COO has proven beneficial both at the consortium and individual cooperative level, even though in different ways.

The adoption of a COO image allowed Alpha to be perceived as a reference organization for Italian food products. The choice of setting up a multi-sector offer and therefore a wide range of products reinforced the effect of COO in the eye of local trading partners. Still today Alpha is recognized as an 'umbrella' brand for high quality Italian food products and wines. However, heterogeneity also led to some problems in consumers' perceptions, due to the different impact of cultural distance on food products. This situation made the management of promotion and communication activities more difficult. Moreover, cooperatives also had different company dimensions and international experience, affecting the degree of adhesion to consortium initiatives along the evolution of the project.

The use of COO also had positive effects for individual members of the consortium, who were facing – with a few exceptions – a new market to be explored in terms of local taste and preferences and also in terms of contacts with new trading partners. Moreover, the strong linkage between the Alpha brand and the COO helped individual cooperatives to make their own brand name more visible in the Indian market. In fact, higher visibility for companies' brands and products in the local market and in some cases establishment of contacts with Indian importers have been the main results of Alpha's programme from the companies' perspectives. Mixed results, instead, have been registered with regard to actual sales in the Indian market. Even though Alpha's main objective was related to the promotion and diffusion of Italian food culture, over time various member companies became somewhat dissatisfied with sales performance, in the light of their relevant investment in terms of organizational and financial resources.

At the company level, COO has affected three distinct dimensions. First of all, European origin was highlighted with regard to European quality certifications, which in some cases were already known by local operators, while in other cases they had to be communicated actively. Secondly, members exploited the COO image both indirectly through Alpha's promotional activities and directly through specific promotional initiatives undertaken individually. Thirdly, some members – notably wine producers – have been able to successfully exploit the region-of-origin effect, even though this has not been possible for most of the wine cooperatives.

6.   CONCLUDING REMARKS

The case of Alpha has shown that the strategic use of COO could provide advantages in terms of image and market penetration to export consortia, notably in new and complex markets such as India. In the case of

Alpha the use of the COO effect in communication processes was strongly directed at enhancing the COO image of products, even if partially limited by the constraint of European funding that required European level product promotion. Export consortia can actively design and implement marketing and communication activities exploiting COO in foreign markets (Beverland and Lindgren 2002).

However, this approach might face various obstacles. The case study under examination highlights a few critical aspects, providing valuable insights in terms of both scientific knowledge and managerial implications to be taken into consideration for further research. First, the Alpha export consortium shows that COO management is a complex activity in the light of the various dimensions involved: European origin denominations, COO, export consortium branding, member companies' brand names, region of origin. Therefore COO is a dimension to be integrated within a very composite picture (Pharr 2005).

Secondly, complexity might further increase when the consortium has a multi-sector configuration; thus COO might play different roles in the light of the specific sectoral and local conditions, which could require careful adaptation due to economic, cultural or institutional factors.

Thirdly, effective use of COO might be impaired by the organizational configuration of the export consortium. The sharing of objectives and the division of labour among consortium internal actors and among the consortium and external partners, such as consulting and services firms, is likely to have an impact on whether and how COO policies are designed and implemented.

Lastly, Alpha was organized according to a fixed amount of funding and a given duration. Consortium objectives were defined and a strategy was attempted on this basis. This analysis shows that promotional efforts, based on an active use of COO in complex markets, such as those of emerging countries, require a long-term perspective and a significant use of resources, associated with a considerable degree of risk. Some Alpha member companies have been able to conduct a market development programme in the Indian market after the end of the project, enjoying various advantages due to the positive reputation built by the consortium. Therefore, it is necessary to combine synergistically promotion/communication activities with sales developments programmes, going beyond a short-term approach and supporting consortium members to build a stable presence in the foreign market. This implies the need to overcome the limited function of promotion/communication of export consortia and to extend it to all processes of company internationalization.

This research has some limitations. First of all, the analysis is focused on a single case study. Although there are only a few cases of export consortia in the food sector active in the Indian market, a comparative analysis should be conducted in order to better highlight the main influencing factors on their performance, such as heterogeneity in size and level of specialization of associated firms, in number of participants and type of activities conducted by the consortium. Comparative analyses should also be conducted with reference to other sectors and other emerging markets.

REFERENCES

Agrawal, J. and W.A. Kamakura (1999), 'Country of origin: A competitive advantage?', *International Journal of Research in Marketing*, **16** (4), 255–267.

Ahlgren, M., I. Gustafsson and G. Hall (2004), 'Attitudes and beliefs directed towards ready-meal consumption', *Food Service Technology*, **4**, 159–169.

Albaum, G. and E. Duerr (2008), *International Marketing and Export Management*, Harlow, Essex: Financial Times-Prentice Hall.

Ali, J., S. Kapoor and J. Moorthy (2010), 'Buying behaviour of consumers for food products in an emerging economy', *British Food Journal*, **112** (2), 109–124.

Al-Sulaiti, K.I. and M.J. Baker (1998), 'Country of origin effects: a literature review', *Marketing Intelligence & Planning*, **16** (3), 150–199.

Baldoni, G., C. Belliti, L. Miller, P. Papini and S. Bertini (1998), *Small Firm Consortia in Italy: an Instrument for Economic Development*, New York: UNIDO.

Bertoli, G. and P. Bertuzzi (2002), 'I consorzi export nei processi di internazionalizzazione delle imprese minori', in C. Guerini (ed.), *Export Marketing*, Milano: Egea.

Beverland, M. and A. Lindgren (2002), 'Using country of origin in strategy: the importance of context and strategic action', *Brand Management*, **10** (2), 147–167.

Bhaskaran, S. and N. Sukumaran (2007), 'Contextual and methodological issues in COO studies', *Marketing Intelligence & Planning*, **25** (1), 66–81.

Central Intelligence Agency (2011), 'CIA World Factbook – India', https://www.cia.gov/library/publications/the-world-factbook/geos/in.html, accessed 5 December 2011.

Choo, H., J. Chung and D.T. Pysarchik (2004), 'Antecedents to new food product purchasing behavior among innovator groups in India', *European Journal of Marketing*, **38** (5/6), 608–625.

Coviello, N. and H. Munro (1997), 'Network relationships and the internationalisation process of small software firms', *International Business Review*, **6** (4), 361–386.

Depperu, D. (1996), *Economia dei consorzi tra imprese*, Milano: Egea.

Di Gregorio, D., M. Musteen and D. Thomas (2008), 'Offshore outsourcing as a source of international competitiveness for SMEs', *Journal of International Business Studies*, **40**, 969–988.

Dollinger, M. and P. Golden (1992), 'Interorganizational and collective strategies in small firms: environmental effects and performance', *Journal of Management*, **18** (4), 659–716.

Eisenhardt, K.M. (1989), 'Building theories from case study research', *Academy of Management Review*, **14** (4), 532–550.

Ghanatabadi, F. (2005), 'Internationalization of small and medium-sized enterprises in Iran', Ph.D. dissertation, Luleå University of Technology.

Ghauri, P. (2004),'Designing and conducting case studies in international business research', in R. Marchan-Piekkari and C. Welch (eds), *Handbook of Qualitative Research: Methods for International Business*, Cheltenham, UK and Northampton, MA, USA: Edward Elgar.

Ghauri, P., C. Lutz and G. Tesfom (2003), 'Using business networks to solve export marketing problems of small and medium sized manufacturing firms from developing countries', *European Journal of Marketing*, **37** (5/6), 728–752.

Goyal, A. and N. P.Singh (2007), 'Consumer perception about fast food in India: an exploratory study', *British Food Journal*, **109** (2), 182–195.

ISTAT-COEWEB (2012), 'Esportazioni italiane di prodotti alimentari e bevande nel mercato indiano. Classificazione per ATECO 2007', http://www.coeweb. istat.it, accessed 10 January 2012.

JBC International. (2011), 'Comprehensive Study of the Indian Wine Market', Report prepared for the Wine Institute, http://www.indianwineacademy.com/ Comprehensive_Study_IWM_Reference_Section.pdf, accessed 10 June 2012.

Johanson, J. and E. Vahlne (2009), 'The Uppsala internationalization process model revisited: from liability of foreignness to liability of outsidership', *Journal of International Business Studies*, **40** (9), 1411–1431.

Kinra, N. (2006), 'The effect of country-of-origin on foreign brand names in the Indian market', *Marketing Intelligence & Planning*, **24** (1), 15–30.

Lall, S. (1991), 'Marketing barriers facing developing country manufactured exporters: a conceptual note', *Journal of Development Studies*, **27** (4), 137–150.

Lanzara, R., R.Varaldo and P. Zagnoli (1990), 'Public support to export consortia: the Italian case', in F. Seringhaus and P. Rossen (eds), *Government Export Promotion: A Global Perspective*, London, UK: Routledge, pp. 19–41.

Leonidou, L.C. (1995), 'Export stimulation: a non-exporter's perspective', *European Journal of Marketing*, **29** (8), 17–36.

Ling, S., D.T. Pysarchik and H.J. Choo (2004), 'Adopters of new food products in India', *Marketing Intelligence & Planning*, **22** (4), 371–391.

L'olivo news. (2008),'L'India apre all'olio d'oliva', http://www.pieralisi.com/olivo/ pdf/olivo_4_08.pdf, accessed 4 December 2011.

Mahadevan, M. and D. Blair (2009), 'Changes in food habits of south indian hindu brahmin immigrants in State College, PA', *Ecology of Food and Nutrition*, **48**, 404–432.

Mintzberg, E. (1979), 'An emerging strategy of "direct" research', *Administrative Science Quarterly*, **24** (4), 582–589.

Oviatt, B. and P. P.McDougall (1994), 'Toward a Theory of International New Ventures', *Journal of International Business Studies*, **25** (1), 45–64.

Papadopoulos, N., L.A. Heslop and G. Bamossy (1993), *Product Country Images: Impact and Role in International Marketing*, Binghampton, New York: Business Press International.

Paterson, R.A. and A. Jolibert (1995), 'A meta-analysis of country-of-origin effects', *Journal of International Business Studies*, **26** (4), 883–900.

Pharr, J.M. (2005), 'Synthesizing country-of-origin research from the last decade: is the concept still salient in an era of global brands?', *Journal of Marketing Theory & Practice*, **13** (4), 34–45.

Pingali, P. and Y. Khwaja (2004), 'Globalisation of Indian diets and the transformation of food supply systems', ESA Working Paper No. 04–05.

Promar International (2005), 'The market for confectionery products in India', a report prepared for The National Confectioners Association, http://69.17.111.188/site/c4/w116/downloads/India.pdf, accessed 10 June 2012.

Rabellotti, R. (1998), 'Collective effects in Italian and Mexican footwear industrial clusters', *Small Business Economics*, **10**, 243–262.

Ruzzier, M., R.D. Hisrich and B. Antoncic (2006), 'SME internationalization research: past, present, and future', *Journal of Small Business and Enterprise Development*, **13** (4), 476–497.

Sandrey, R., L. Smit, T. Fundira and H. Edinger (2008), 'Non-tariff measures inhibiting South African exports to China and India', Tralac Working Paper.

Stanton Emms & Sia (2010), 'India: Is this Market now Ready for Foreign Food and Drinks? A Reality Check for 2011 to 2016', http://stantonemmsandsia.foodandbeverage.biz/images/Brochure_-_New_India_Research_Report_Stanton_Emms_Sia_11.1.11_.pdf, accessed 10 June 2012.

Tripathi, A. and S. Srivastava (2011), 'Interstate migration and changing food preferences in India', *Ecology of Food and Nutrition*, **50**, 410–428.

UNIDO (2009), 'The strategic management of export consortia: an analysis of the experience of UNIDO in Morocco, Peru, Tunisia and Uruguay', http://www.unido.org/fileadmin/user_media/Publications/Pub_free/Strategic_management_of_export_consortia.pdf, accessed 25 June 2011.

Valdani, E. and G. Bertoli (2010), *Mercati internazionali e marketing*, Milano: Egea.

Welch, L.S. and P. Joynt (1987), 'Grouping for export an effective solution', in P.J. Rosson and S.D. Reid (eds), *Managing Export Entry and Expansion: Concepts and Practice*, New York: Praeger.

Yin, R. (1994), *Case Study Research: Design and Methods*, London: Sage.

Zhou, L., W. Wu and X. Luo (2007), 'Internationalization and the performance of born-global SMEs: the mediating role of social networks', *Journal of International Business Studies*, **38** (4), 673–690.

Index